Advance Praise for *America in Perspective*

"In *America In Perspective,* David Sokol and Adam Brandon powerfully make the case for preserving our constitutional system of government. America's problems are solvable—if we use the means the founders provided to us. *America In Perspective* traces our nation's rich history of doing just that."

—Senator Mike Lee, Utah

"America is unquestionably a force for good in the world. We have a unique ability to heal divisions and overcome our past mistakes. Those who doubt American greatness need only to read *America In Perspective,* which offers an optimistic vision for the future of our great country."

—Bob Woodson, founder,
The Woodson Center

"*America In Perspective* offers a timely defense of the American Dream, which today is under threat like never before. Through a free economy with no unnecessary governmental interference; meritocracy; and equal opportunity, we can beat back these threats."

—Steve Forbes, chairman &
editor-in-chief, Forbes Media

AMERICA IN PERSPECTIVE

Defending The American Dream For The Next Generation

David Sokol & Adam Brandon

Post Hill
PRESS

A POST HILL PRESS BOOK
ISBN: 978-1-63758-813-0
ISBN (eBook): 978-1-63758-711-9

America in Perspective:
Defending the American Dream for the Next Generation
© 2022 by David Sokol and Adam Brandon
All Rights Reserved

Cover design by Maddy O'Connor

Post Hill Press
New York • Nashville
posthillpress.com

Published in the United States of America
1 2 3 4 5 6 7 8 9 10

To Our Founding Fathers

CONTENTS

FOREWORD

by Secretary Ben Carson

People from around the globe are familiar with "the American Dream." Have you ever considered the fact that there are no other countries with a well-known dream? Obviously, there's a reason for that, and it is something that we should be proud of and anxious to perpetuate. Despite the horrible things that many on the progressive left say about America, it remains the desired destination for many immigrants, both legal and illegal. They are undaunted by the inaccurate charges of racism and general evil. If those charges were true, how long do you think it would take people to realize that and to warn their friends and relatives to stay away as well as try to escape themselves?

America as we know it was established by people who cherished liberty. They wanted the right to express themselves without fear and the ability to worship according to their conscience as opposed to by government decree. They wanted to be able to use their own talents to benefit themselves, their families, and their communities without some overarching authority dictating how their earnings were to be distributed. They discovered that by doing the right thing and working hard, they could experience true freedom and contentment.

These early Americans also embraced a system of values that included faith, liberty, community, and respect for life. Those foundational pillars provided the basis for civil interactions that quickly produced a unique and very strong nation. Our desire for liberty produced the Constitution, which is a rare and lasting document that supports "We the People" and constrains the natural tendency of government to dominate the people (see Appendix B). Our ability to work together, even though we came from diverse backgrounds, created a sense of community that provided the strength to overcome the Axis powers during World War II and become a world leader. Unfortunately, a lot of these foundational pillars are being severely challenged in modern-day America. But life is full of challenges, and as this book clearly points out, we are up to the challenge.

Many have sacrificed in order to give us a free country endowed with a lot of economic opportunities for everyone. America is also a place where many parents have undergone enormous sacrifices in their lives in order to provide a better pathway for their children. My mother worked two and three jobs at a time as a single mom to provide my brother and me with the head start we needed to succeed. Even though we came from a poverty-stricken background, my brother became a rocket scientist, and I became a brain surgeon. Those kinds of achievements were made possible not only through my mother's sacrifice but also by the legions of people from all backgrounds who worked tirelessly during the civil rights movement to break down barriers of injustice. We indeed have a lot to be thankful for and a lot to protect.

David Sokol and many other members of the Horatio Alger Society of Distinguished Americans came from backgrounds that would have made success difficult in America and virtually impossible elsewhere. But through this book, he and his coauthor, Adam Brandon, provide a prescient guide to the challenges and opportunities that are available to all in our nation.

By creating an environment that encourages entrepreneurship and innovation as well as equality of opportunity, we have succeeded in establishing a nation from which no one is trying to escape and to which many are attempting to immigrate. It is necessary for Americans to understand how this nation was created and how it can be lost. There are many things going on in today's society that threaten the continuance of a nation that emphasizes life, liberty, and the pursuit of happiness. Through its very fine historical analysis, this book provides that understanding.

We have seen enormous social changes in America, some of which are extremely helpful, but we have also seen the agents of division become much more powerful in our nation. We have seen the attempt to change us from a "can do" nation to a "what can you do for me?" nation. In order to gain political power, there are those who want to change us from a meritocratic society to one focused on dependency. The bottom line is that "We the People" will be the final determinants regarding what kind of nation we have going forward. The things that provided our success in the past will also provide success in the future if we understand and use them. Those things include courage and willpower. We must remember that we cannot be the land of the free if we are not the home of the brave.

Benjamin S. Carson Sr., MD
Founder and Chairman, American Cornerstone Institute
17th Secretary of the United States Department of Housing
and Urban Development Emeritus Professor of Neurosurgery,
Oncology, Plastic Surgery and Pediatrics, Johns Hopkins Medicine

WHY AMERICA'S SUCCESS IS NO ACCIDENT

"You cannot push anyone up a ladder unless
he be willing to climb a little himself."
—*Andrew Carnegie*

I. The Land of Long Shots and Ambition

There are many reasons to celebrate and love America. When faced with challenges and conflict, our system of government allows us to self-correct and self-heal. Moreover, America is home to some of the freest and most prosperous citizens in the world, it boasts outstanding job opportunities that attract immigrants from all over the globe, and it is home to some of the most beautiful natural scenery imaginable. America's best days are still ahead, but only if we continue to embrace the ideas and values that made that all possible.

When faced with challenges and conflict, our system of government allows us to self-correct and self-heal, and world history shows that this is uniquely American. Today, however, essential American values, such as the American Dream and our meritocratic spirit, are being discredited. The story of Sara Blakely, founder of Spanx, is a story that most clearly and convincingly illustrates how the American Dream is still a reality today.

Sara Blakely was born into a middle-class family just outside Tampa, Florida. At the dinner table every night, her father would ask her and her brother about their failures.[1] Her father did this not to scold them but to teach them that failures should be celebrated because there is always something to learn from them.[2]

Nothing about Blakely's early life or upbringing suggested anything about her trajectory in life. She was not born with superhuman athletic abilities like NFL star Patrick Mahomes or a genius-level IQ like Stephen Hawking. By all appearances, she was an ordinary woman.

After graduating college, Blakely worked odd jobs as she tried to figure out her career. In a tryout to play Goofy at Disney World, she was told she was too small, so she started selling fax machines.[3] She worked selling fax machines for seven years and moved up quickly. Part of Blakely's job was meeting with people to build relationships, and the demands of a smart appearance in professional environments often meant she needed to wear pantyhose. On account of the Florida heat, Blakely struggled with the discomfort caused by the seamed foot at the bottom of her pantyhose. So, she decided to cut the feet off and see how they felt.

The modification was not perfect, but it was an improvement. She now had all the benefits of normal pantyhose without some of the usual discomfort. Blakely thought her idea would resonate with other women, so she spent two years and $5,000 of her own money to revise and improve her product—and she did all this at night while she continued with her sales job during the day. She liked her product and met with scores of representatives from hosiery mills in North Carolina. Every representative passed on the idea. Maybe there was no market for her idea after all.

But a few weeks later, she got a call from a man who was curious about her product. As it happened, his three daughters liked her idea and encouraged their father to explore it further. The next iteration of the prototype was developed the following year. Blakely hired an attorney to assist with the patent, purchased the "Spanx" trademark, and finalized her packaging.

Blakely worked tirelessly to market her product, and after meeting with a representative of the Neiman Marcus Group, she managed to get Spanx in stores. The product caught on, and soon, other large chains began to carry it. Shortly thereafter, she sent a few pairs of Spanx to Oprah Winfrey with the dream that the product might make it onto her show.

At this point, Spanx was entering the mainstream. What makes this so amazing is that Blakely was running the business *entirely on her own*. She was taking care of logistics, tracking finances, and even modeling her own products. In 2000, Oprah fulfilled Blakely's dream by advertising Spanx on her show, causing sales to skyrocket. In roughly a decade, the brand was a global success. Blakely had become the youngest, self-made female billionaire in the world.[4]

In the time since, Blakely has leveraged her business success to become an active philanthropist. She runs her own charity, the Sara Blakely Foundation, which helps women pursue their education and learn about entrepreneurship. During the COVID-19 pandemic lockdowns, her foundation donated $5 million to protect women's businesses.[5] On top of that generosity, she has given money to organizations that help girls in Africa gain access to education.[6] Blakely is a great role model for the next generation with her business acumen, hard work, and compassion.

Blakely's story is an inspiring one, and it showcases just how much is possible in America for people with drive and vision. It's unlikely that many predicted she would become a billionaire so early in life. And yet, Blakely became a billionaire over a relatively short amount of time simply because she believed in her idea and persevered through struggles to see it through.

This is not normal—at least outside of the United States. There is a reason why more great products and entrepreneurs originate in the United States than any other country in the world. We are a land of believers, achievers, and excellence. And since our beginnings, America and its people have consistently outperformed and overcome what is expected of them. In the early days of the Revolutionary War, most of the world thought that England would steamroll[7] the ungrateful and arrogant colonists. Not only were the English wrong, but their professional army and generals were also beaten back by militias led by gentlemen and farmers such as George Washington.

What few appreciate is that the Founders gave up their lives as they knew them in pursuit of a dream that most doubted could even be accomplished. Indeed, they took on substantial risk when rational thinking told them to maintain the status quo. Life was pretty great for most of the Founders in the colonies: they were rich, and their property was mostly protected by the law. Still, the Founders wanted something more, and not just for themselves, but for others. They dreamed of a new political system, one with more civic involvement and greater limits on government. And for that dream, they risked everything they had.

Even more amazing, just consider that after defeating the most powerful empire in the world, the nascent American nation transformed the country from a constellation of small, disjointed communities along the Atlantic to a world power and the standard against which all countries measure themselves today. And they did this in only a few generations.

That is amazing, and that is to say nothing of the fact that the American system of constitutional government is a model[8] for other countries, that our companies are among the most prosperous and innovative in the history of the world, and that our society comes closer than any other to providing equality of opportunity for all citizens, irrespective of how long they have lived in the United States.

This fact of American life—that, no matter how long the proverbial odds are, they are never too long—is as true today as it was for the settlers who came to the New World in the early 1600s. There is always hope in America, and that is because the American system and the universal values that underpin it provide everyone with the chance to get ahead, no matter what they look like or where they come from. Opportunity and meritocracy for everyone are at the core of what makes America unique. Times in which we have failed to live up to this promise underlie some of the most shameful moments in American history, but it is America's eternal aspiration to apply these values more fully that should define its future.

Most Americans know the stories of great entrepreneurial Americans like Andrew Carnegie, George Washington Carver, and the Wright Brothers. These are incredible, entrepreneurial Americans whose impact on American life left the country and their fellow citizens better off. These people all realized the American Dream by achieving what they set out to do.

What is unfortunate is that not enough Americans know that these kinds of stories are ongoing and common even today. In fact, there is a growing narrative that our best days are behind us. This is false. The American Dream is alive, but only if we embrace it.

The American model of working hard, utilizing one's talents, and getting ahead can and does work for all Americans. The American Dream and the promise of the American system of government provide a path to get ahead for all Americans—no matter what they look like or where they were born.

To see the truth of this fact, it is necessary to compare America with another similar state, one with a related past, albeit without the unique culture and institutions. The history of Argentina provides a sharp contrast that reminds us of how special America really is and what could have easily been its fate.

II. The Best of All Worlds

If one had to identify or list the factors that contributed most to American success over the last century—especially its consistently robust economic growth and stable political situation—it is likely that some ordering of technological innovations, our heritage (or the practices and institutions we inherited), and our values would occupy the top spots.

What makes this scenario interesting and important is that many other countries were influenced by similar factors over the last hundred years—some even share our values and demographics. And yet, even the most similar countries experienced vastly different economic and political situations.

Consider the case of Argentina: its recent history was shaped by these same factors and trends, and like the United States, it was molded by the same European legacies, and it was just as isolated from the political vicissitudes and chaos of the Old World.[9] Based on these factors, Argentina was positioned to succeed like the United States. And for a while, it did.

If some of these forces alone were enough to produce American-style excellence, then one would expect to see Argentina in the Group of Seven (G7), a political forum of the world's largest economies, and as a major force in the Western Hemisphere. After all, it compares nicely to the United States in so many ways.

But strangely, Argentina falls far behind the United States in every metric. Indeed, its economy now tracks more closely with poorer European countries.[10] Why is that? What is it that has held Argentina back? Or, put differently, why was Argentina unable to capitalize on the factors and trends that propelled the United States to new heights in the twentieth century? To answer these questions, it is necessary to look back on Argentina at the turn of the twentieth century.

It is difficult to assess Argentina's history in the eighteenth and nineteenth centuries and not see a multitude of parallels to the United States during that same time. Both were originally constituted as colonies of European imperial powers; each country was forged out of an uprising against a major European empire; and both countries overcame regional political divisions and civil wars to become unified modern states under the protection of constitutionally chartered federal governments.[11]

One important difference during this era, which became relevant later on in the twentieth century, is that Argentina lacked a democratic tradition of the American variety. Specifically, Argentina was ruled for long periods of time by dictators and other nonconsensual regimes, while Americans, going back to their days as English subjects, enjoyed a more democratic government.

For instance, the figure of the *caudillo*, or the strongman, in particular, became a recurring one in Argentina's history. Typically, this person would emerge during times of protracted unrest to put an end to political divisions for a time, often violently.[12] Unlike the United States, which had the political traditions and civic practices necessary to endure and overcome intense political trials, Argentina did not have those safeguards. There were attempts to adopt constitutions and other mediating institutions in Argentina, but they did not last because they lacked firm checks and balances.[13] The basic American idea that big changes should be determined by consensus, not one vote or one election, did not factor into the equation in Argentina. Consequently, Argentina struggled to navigate political and social crises, and ultimately reverted to authoritarianism when compromise and dialogue proved difficult.

Still, despite the periodic upheavals and chaos, Argentina pursued pro-growth policies from 1880 through the early 1900s.[14] It became one of the largest exporters in the world. These trends led to substantial immigration from Europe and a nationwide movement towards industrialization. During this era, Argentina developed and modernized at an amazing pace. Most importantly, it mirrored America's laissez-faire, pro-immigration policies and trajectory over the same period.[15]

Consider a few statistics. First, Argentina became a top-ten economy over the course of only three decades.[16] It surpassed numerous European countries and was on track to become a top-five economy in the world. Second, its population exploded over the same period, and like the United States, most of its immigrants came from Europe. Third, literacy, gross domestic production, and per capita income all rose to dizzying heights, thanks in part to Argentina's emphasis on education.[17] Again, it outpaced most European countries and appeared poised to soar even higher.

By the 1910s, it looked as though Argentina would eclipse most of Europe in virtually every economic metric. It was a rapidly developing country with the resources, infrastructure, and capital necessary to transition to industrialization; its fortuitous and relatively secure geographic position meant it had little reason to fear involvement in destructive foreign conflicts.

In short, Argentina possessed numerous advantages compared to European states. Yet, in only three decades, it would be on the same lethargic economic path as the countries of Europe—and this is despite the fact it was not devastated by involvement in the world wars.[18]

What happened to Argentina was a mix of bad policy and social instability. On the one hand, its economic growth was hampered by the Great Depression, which seriously reduced foreign investment.[19] To make matters worse, the government foolishly tried to move the economy toward communism.[20] Thankfully, this did not translate into manmade famines or vicious political repressions. But the legacy of this shift was that it encouraged the state to interfere with and micromanage the economy. This strategy did more harm than good in Argentina.

Argentina's political situation also completely broke down. Military uprisings became more common and the elected officials more radical. Juan Peron, in particular, used his cult of personality to nationalize huge segments of Argentina's economy and repress dissidents, all in the name of social justice and service to the Argentine nation. Civil society and the economy were irreparably damaged.

Peron's influence on politics radicalized society, which, in turn, weakened civic institutions and slowed economic growth. Argentina was no longer on track to be a leader in the region, let alone the world. It fell into a cyclical malaise in which the economy slowed down, Peron and other radicals took turns holding power, and the military asserted itself.[21] Extremist ideologies vied for political supremacy, and terrorism became the preferred method for "solving" political disputes in Argentina from roughly the 1930s on.[22] Inflation became endemic, which destroyed the stability of the country's currency, and Argentina floundered.

In every sense, Argentina failed when compared to where it ought to be today. America benefited from many of the same factors that Argentina did, and it suffered from many of the same problems that vexed the Latin American country, from economic decline to political radicalism and challenges from a non-homogenous culture.

Like Argentina, America had low points that created intense conflict, sometimes incredibly violent conflict, across the country. From slavery to the Civil War, the issues during Reconstruction, the Depression, and many others—the challenges were numerous. But unlike Argentina, America has always faced these challenges head-on, and, in the spirit of self-healing, America has become better *because of* those failures. When problems confront Americans, they work together to fix them.

America can overcome its problems, and we believe world history has shown that this is only possible because of a unique blend of values, institutions, and norms that constitute the American system. In short, our Founders were self-reflective and self-critical, and the regime they built works because it operates on those principles. And it is for this very reason—that our system works and improves our lives—that we believe America needs to be preserved and defended.

III. Why We Wrote This Book

In the world today, too many people do not understand how unique the American story truly is or how it got to its position today. Right now, more people and institutions than at any point in our lifetimes are defaming this country and talking about it in the meanest, most uncharitable, and most misleading ways imaginable. From accusations that the country was founded to preserve slavery[23] to insisting that every single difference between different groups of people is attributable to racial malice within the law and society writ large, America is being abused nonstop.

This raises the question: Is America awful? Is everything so rotten here that we deserve every bit of criticism we receive and more? Absolutely not. We wrote this book because we want to remind everyone that this country is special and worth defending.

We also want to give a voice to those who still believe in this country, to those who think that while there are problems with America that need to be solved, we can solve them together, and that this perspective deserves more serious attention. After all, we are a country made up of only a fraction of the world's population, and yet, we have built a disproportionate amount of wealth, founded the most successful and innovative companies in the history of the world, and improved the lives of millions both domestically and globally by lifting them from poverty. We want the larger American story to be known because it is overall an extremely positive one that everyone should be proud of, even if we're not proud of *every* moment.

We are a self-healing country, and that is *not* the norm. As the case of Argentina should make clear, it is easy for political disputes to ruin countries, and it is hard to bridge partisan divides. This must be kept in perspective because what we have accomplished is amazing. Multiracial empires are not the norm; their record is pretty bad historically, i.e., the Austro-Hungarian and Ottoman Empires. America is not perfect, but it does have a workable solution to these problems that has succeeded time and time again: our constitutional process of electing representatives to work on the behalf of citizens to make and enforce laws. Importantly, our institutions do *not* make radical changes unless there is consensus across the country. It is only through these institutions that we have remedied past failures, and we should be mindful of these achievements and those who made them possible. This means that the history of America should *not* be judged by uncharitable and unrelated modern standards.

The Founders were smart, but we are not here to argue they were all-knowing and perfect. They had a mixed record on slavery, and some had other moral failings that are well documented. In part, this book is about how our Founders set up a transformational system of government that has changed the lives of millions of people for the better despite their other failings. Part of our unique American story is about self-healing, and while the Founders left behind a series of serious problems, future generations have worked tirelessly to fix them by building consensus and working together.

Our constitutional government works well for the most part, and that is because, when it was designed, the Founders knew clearly what they did not want it to be. Specifically, they did not want a European model of concentrated[24] power or a model from antiquity where either a mob or an elite clique ruled.[25] They gave us a limited government with the power to fulfill essential functions without the tendencies to trample individual rights. They also gave us the power to amend the Constitution when future generations wanted to put issues beyond the reach of democratic majorities. Importantly, amending the Constitution requires a consensus of Americans, which ensures major changes occur not just when a simple majority agrees but when most Americans do as well.

What this means is that the American style of government is a mix of the best elements taken from various types of government. For instance, the Founders incorporated democratic[26] elements without creating a direct democracy and did the same with other models, including mixing autocratic[27] aspects into the office of the executive to provide for decisive independence in times of crisis, among other things. Our system is a unique attempt to blend the best features of governing models that history has to offer, and it was designed with the combined historical knowledge of some of the greatest political theorists in history.[28]

Seeing the American system as a hodgepodge of good ideas from the brightest thinkers at the time is a nice starting point. We think it is also helpful to understand that in comparison to other countries, our system works well and is still the best of many bad options. To appreciate this unique blend of political systems, just consider that in America, we do not need coups to select new leaders, we do not need to overhaul our system from scratch to solve problems, and we do not rely on repression to show why certain ideas are bad. The American government allows us to correct our past errors and charter a path into the future. People ought to understand this fact. The challenges we currently face should not be an indictment of our capacity to address them within our current framework.

This point cannot be overstated: America has previously corrected itself without bloodshed, repressions, and other radical, extralegal means, and it will continue to do so in the future. In world history, events like the French Revolution, the Bolshevik Uprising, and a number of other armed coups have been the standard response to political problems. What was originally seen as a crazy and radical idea given to us by our Founders in a constitutional system of government has actually solved the worst problems that have confronted America. And as a result, our system not only still exists but has also been replicated by a whole host of other countries.

There are many other reasons why our constitutional structure endures, and they all relate in some way to our meritocratic ethos. In America, a person can and should get ahead with talent and hard work. In our view, this defines our country and separates it from other regimes and states. The American Dream is the realization of this promise by citizens, which we define as the unrestrained use of individual talents to pursue a particular goal. This idea of meritocracy, or "the best will succeed," also characterizes our politics. Not only was our system built around that idea, but that ethos also continues today as bad laws are publicly debated and then rejected by voters, good ideas are replicated, and society progresses. The same holds true for politicians (at least most of the time).

Risk-taking, trial and error, and failure are important aspects of our system. And ultimately, America enjoys
its favorable position in the world today because we give
ideas and individuals an equal chance to prove their worth.
Returning to the story of Spanx, Blakely's achievements are
not simply due to where she was born, her degree, or who she
knew. Instead, she became the success story she is today by
using her natural talents and persevering after a few failures
to create a product that is enjoyed by millions. Put simply, she
is a billionaire icon because of what she can do. Blakely was
not interfered with or held back by law, and she did something incredible with her life.

Crucially, Blakely's success is not a one-off story. People
all around the United States, of all different backgrounds,
get ahead by using their talents, believing in themselves, and
enduring through struggles. For instance, the same is true of
Peyton Manning, who used his natural strengths and hard
work to become one of the most beloved and successful athletes in American history. Countless other Americans have
done the same and made our country special.

As a reminder, this is *not* how other countries work. In
China, a mix of a specific kind of raw intelligence, one's ethnic background, moral ambiguity, and party loyalty determine a person's fate and if they will move up in the world or
remain in place.[29] Meritocracy is uncommon, and America is
amazing because it understands that fact and rewards individual ability accordingly. Our Founders recognized that we
are different, unique people. Our skills, interests, desires, and
energy levels vary widely.

America is a land of opportunity because it gives people the chance to experiment, to take risks, and to bet on their gifts. That is an amazing thing, and it is a big reason why the United States has the greatest, most successful, and impactful entrepreneurs on the planet.

Equal opportunity, or the ability for everyone to give their dreams a shot, is in America's DNA, and it is inseparably tied to the idea of meritocracy. America needs to give everyone an equal shot—both because it is the right thing to do from a moral perspective and because the alternative approach of elites picking winners and losers has always failed.

To be clear, everything that we have said is uniquely part of the American experience. Meritocracy, equal opportunity, personal freedom, and the chance to capitalize on one's gifts—these are virtues that everyone can hopefully get behind. Unfortunately, these institutions, values, and practices are at risk today because the spectrum that for so long defined and constrained our politics has moved sharply over the last few years.

The recent fixations with "equity,"[30] unending "social engineering," and large-scale "redistributionism" are incompatible with our system. For some, these terms may sound nice, but when they are applied to the real world, as they were in China and Eastern Europe last century, they look very ugly in practice. If programs based on these ideas are implemented, we would stand to lose our Constitution, America's free speech culture would wither, and civil society would suffer.[31] This would be nothing short of a revolution,[32] and it would permanently change how we elect our representatives or select our Supreme Court justices and thus engage in politics.

These views, which amount to uncompromising partisan cronyism, are incompatible with our constitutional, meritocratic system. To solve our problems, we must embrace our founding principles and universal values, not abandon them. We must strengthen and retain our government's checks and balances because they are the tools that prevent America from becoming an authoritarian state. We want all Americans to understand the roots of American success because it is those fundamentals that make our personal American Dream possible.

If America should succumb to these forces and abandon its tradition, it is unclear whether the current system of government, which has survived for many generations, can ever be restored. And to those who propose to abandon or dismantle our current system of government simply to expedite their own ideological worldview, we implore them to take on the difficult task of persuading their fellow Americans to build a new consensus among them, regardless of where those beliefs may lie on the political spectrum.

After all, our history has shown, regardless of what struggles we face, if this process is embraced, we will endure and progress into the future.

CHAPTER 1

OUR PERSONAL AMERICAN DREAMS

*"My parents shared not only an
improbable love, they shared an abiding faith
in the possibilities of this nation."*
—Barack Obama

I. American Dreams

The American Dream is a shared, aspirational belief that people can come from anywhere to America, no matter who they are, what they believe, or what family they were born into, and if they work hard, believe in themselves, and persevere through challenges, they can achieve a higher level of success and prosperity than what they were born into. This is a *uniquely* American idea, and our system of meritocracy further underscores it. This system is under attack today, but it must be maintained at all costs for the American Dream to endure as well.

But the American Dream is achieved with, in most cases, a substantial increase of freedom that only financial security can provide. For most of human history, as political philosopher Thomas Hobbes described in his classic book *Leviathan*, life was "nasty, brutish, and short." Basic needs such as food and shelter consumed much of the daily activities for most of the world's population. Only a few well-connected elites, such as kings and queens, could live a prosperous and comfortable life. The American Dream is the hope that *any* person can live the life that they want to live, rather than one of just basic needs. It comes with the freedom to raise a family, to start a business, to develop new skills, to speak your mind without fear, or to find fulfillment through one of the millions of other life paths that Americans are free to pursue.

Some believe that instead of a system of free enterprise and meritocracy, the government should step in to help Americans realize their own individual versions of the American Dream. The *uniqueness* of our American system recognizes that there is a role for government. It exists to defend life, liberty, and property, among other rights. It does *not* exist, however, to pick winners and losers in our economy, favoring the well-connected few over the aspiring many.

The American Dream, while often lamented in recent times as useless or even dangerous, is still a powerful and widely shared value among Americans. Its definition, though, is evolving. In fact, we were surprised to find in recent polling that, for many Americans, better financial prospects are not necessarily essential aspects of the American Dream.[33] We also learned that Americans are still mostly optimistic about their prospects for realizing the American ideal—at least at the individual level.[34]

Much like the definition we believe in, for millions of Americans, though, the American Dream still hinges on one's ability to pursue their dreams and follow their goals, no matter where they are born or what they look like.

While these new understandings show an evolution, the core principle is the same: to be an American and to realize one's abilities and to pursue their goals, which, in turn, requires the ability to do what one wishes with their life, to choose their own path. And that ability rests on a person's individual freedom to live their life as they please. But that system can only work in a country that values and appreciates meritocracy. Without meritocracy, there is no reason to believe, to work hard, or to persevere.

The freedom that the American Dream provides hinges on financial autonomy and access to opportunity. We believe personal freedom, which most Americans define as the core basis of the American Dream, is inextricable from economic freedom.

No government, however well-intentioned, has succeeded in achieving this in the past, nor will it likely ever in the future. In fact, one of the explicit goals of some of the worst governments in recent history, such as Nazi Germany and militarist Japan, was to build communities that were explicitly monocultural (in opposition to multicultural societies like America) and exclusionary. While some might fault America for previously embracing these ideas, in the spirit of self-healing, the majority of Americans have largely grown to believe that these ideas were fervently wrong and have fought tirelessly to ensure they were abolished. Americans, contrary to many current depictions, are largely tolerant of each other so long as they don't encroach upon each other's freedom, and those who actively engage in bigotry are widely excluded from civil society.

The reader must understand that we've chosen to examine America because, for all her imperfections, her aspirational nature is exceptional and unique. America did what extremists a century ago thought to be impossible: created a mostly harmonious and successful community for all people, regardless of their race or religion, contributed to the betterment of the country, and supported the ongoing process of self-healing. Therefore, we've chosen to share our own stories, which underscore what has led us to defend the American Dream.

II. Unassuming Beginnings: David's Story

In some parts of America, there is a belief that someone's success is owed to something or someone else, that their individual efforts did not get them to where they are today. This idea was captured in President Obama's remark years ago that "you didn't build that," but it is hardly a novel view these days.[35]

What surprises many who know me and my beliefs is that I actually agree with this view: I think that we succeed in life because of others, specifically those who teach us and shape our moral and personal character. But, unlike President Obama, I do not see the impact of those influences as perverse or problematic. This is because, in my own life, I owe so much of my success to my family, upbringing, and work experiences.

I grew up in a big family as one of five children in Omaha, Nebraska. My ancestors came to the United States in the early 1900s from Europe with the hope of establishing a new life, something they believed to be impossible in Europe at that time. My grandfather worked as a laborer in the timber industry in Europe and did the same in the United States.

My grandfather died in a mill accident when my father was a senior in high school, and he left a permanent mark on him by emphasizing the importance of self-worth and the desire to build on the work of the older generations to raise the standard of living of the next generation. In a lot of respects, I hit the proverbial lottery with my family: I had two loving parents who supported me and took an active role in my upbringing and four siblings who pushed me but whom I could also count on. My parents, both of whom were conservative Democrats, stressed responsibility and the importance of committing to a goal and seeing it through. My grandfather's optimistic, entrepreneurial spirit lived on in our family. I wish I could have met him.

Some of the virtues my parents emphasized, which I will always remember, include my father's advice to do the right thing, even when nobody's watching. This simple moral precept is central to how I live my life and do business. Another recommendation my parents made was to take risks, because it is through experiences—especially bad experiences—that we develop good judgment and a realistic outlook.

Economically, my family was in the middle class, but by today's standards would be considered poor. At the same time, our financial situation was far from secure. I learned this early on when my mother was diagnosed with breast cancer.

My entire family worked together to help with the costs of treatment, and I took a job as a paperboy. This was my first experience with real work, and it taught me a valuable lesson: my abilities could be rewarded if I applied them diligently.

The other valuable takeaway from this experience was that we all need some help from time to time. My father believed that asking for help was natural and integral to solving problems. At the same time, he was also clear that a person should only ask for help if they truly need it; otherwise, they are taking advantage of others. This is true of business and of the government. People who need assistance should request it, but only if it is to address a sincere need, and if their goal is to help pick themselves back up. One of my hopes is that we can collectively do more to live by that idea.

I also found a sense of purpose and self-respect in my work, and I liked that feeling. Today, I believe that work is essential to the development of a healthy pride, self-respect, and sense of purpose.

As I got a little older, I became passionate about sports. In seventh grade, I played baseball, basketball, and football. Soon, I dreamed of playing football in college and perhaps professionally. I was a fair athlete through high school, so my dreams did not seem too fantastical at the time. I was fortunate to play football for the University of Nebraska at Omaha, which at the time was a Division II program.

However, I received a heavy dose of reality in the form of playing against kids who had the size and skill to play at the next level. Effort is a big part of football, and I worked as hard as anybody. Sadly, height and weight matter a lot too, and I did not have the athletic ability for the next level, so to speak.

Yet I still had an intense desire to achieve and a deep competitiveness, so I turned my attention to a place where I could get ahead with my abilities: the classroom. At that point in my life, I was admittedly an average student; I did not do well in elementary school, I did okay in high school, and I was a pretty good student in college.

As a kid, I was not especially passionate about my classes. My effort was particularly lacking during that time. I refocused myself and fully committed to learning, and developed an interest in engineering, discovering, in the process, that I had a talent for it. This became my focus in college, and I ultimately graduated with a degree in civil engineering. But college was only possible for me through hard work, and I believe it is a key part of my personal story.

The most influential job of my life might also be one of the least remarkable if seen alongside my later roles. During high school and college, I worked at a local grocery store owned by a wonderful man named Abe Baker. I started at the bottom of the proverbial totem pole: I was the bagger, packaging the foods as the cashier rang our customers up. Eventually, after a few years of experience, I was the manager of the night shift.

This was a chance event that changed the course of my life. Mr. Baker imparted early business principles to me; working at his grocery store also exposed me to the power of meritocracy. He rewarded the best, hardest working people, and everyone—the workers, customers, and so on—was better off for it. Meritocracy defined the culture of Mr. Baker's grocery store.

Mr. Baker's son, Bob, later helped me land my first job after college. The role was with the architectural engineering firm Henningson, Durham and Richardson, Inc. (HDR), and a big reason I was hired was because of Bob Baker.

Specifically, Bob Baker recommended me to Mr. Durham; he spoke highly of my work ethic and character and promised Mr. Durham that I would help his team and his bottom line. This recommendation helped me immensely and proved a point my parents taught me years earlier: a person's reputation matters enormously and should never be taken for granted. Because I worked hard for Bob Baker and always tried to do the right thing, he went out of his way to help me. In other words, meritocracy played a large part in Bob Baker's recommendation of me. I was greatly touched by his generosity, and I share his view that personal reputation is everything—in business and in life.

Mr. Baker opened a door for me—it was my job to take full advantage of the opportunity. The principle of meritocracy taught me that if I believed in myself, worked hard, and persevered through tough times, I could succeed in this new opportunity.

At HDR, I was given a huge amount of independence while also working under Mr. Durham. My time there was a mix of an apprenticeship and an MBA program. I never learned so much so quickly.

And it was through my work at HDR that I was given an incredible opportunity for a young man: I was asked to build a business from nothing by the Ogden Corporation, an industrial conglomerate. Pay did not matter that much to me, but the experience did, and I knew this was as rare an opportunity as any. My new company, Ogden Projects, Inc., caught fire and expanded rapidly; our employees ballooned from a few dozen to over a thousand. At the age of twenty-seven, I was the CEO of Ogden Projects, Inc., and only six years later, it was a billion-dollar company on the New York Stock Exchange.

My career path eventually moved me away from Ogden Projects, Inc., but I am forever grateful for my experiences as a young CEO. Looking back, I think the most universal and valuable lesson I learned from my early career in business is that taking care of everyone is mutually beneficial. Rewarding workers motivates and attracts more talent, which improves the work product; finding the best suppliers ensures the highest quality outputs; and this, in turn, guarantees that customers' needs are better met, which translates into profits for the company.

To be sure, my company was built and thrived on meritocracy. Our hiring practices were not focused on race, religion, who was in your family, or where you came from but instead were focused on work ethic, skills, and character. In turn, our employees responded because they knew what mattered at our company—believing in yourself, working hard, and persevering through tough times. Employees who did these things were very successful, and I am immensely proud of the work we accomplished. It may seem simple when written succinctly, but my experience taught me that many business leaders, in the name of improving margins, forget these lessons during both good and difficult times.

I also applied these lessons to my work building MidAmerican Energy, and I am extremely proud not only of what we accomplished but also of how we accomplished it. Not only did the business do a great job of providing customers with an affordable and effective product, but we were also able to use our profits to innovate and promote green technologies and renewable energy. In my view, this is free enterprise at its best: helping consumers and producers and generating revenue to promote social goods through employment, environmental advances, and rewarding investors. The government did *not* mandate we use our revenue to promote the social good, we made that decision on our own, and the market rewarded us for it. In 2000, I sold 80 percent of MidAmerican Energy to Berkshire Hathaway. To this day, its over $100 billion in assets are run according to the same basic principles by my business partner and closest friend, Greg Abel.

I came away with a deep sense of optimism that we can solve the greatest challenges of our times through a *uniquely* American system that values meritocracy and the creativity and ambition of individuals, not through the edicts of politicians in Washington or abroad.

An added benefit of my success in business is that it has allowed me to take care of those I love.

My sister, to use one example, is a wonderful woman who was tragically diagnosed with multiple sclerosis years ago. This is an awful, degenerative disease, and the prospects are often not good. I am fortunate that I can help my sister, and it is my hope that American society will provide a means to help those whose families are unable to assist themselves. This is one of the many proper and necessary roles for a limited system of government. That I have the capacity to take care of my sister, and that our society generates the resources and technologies that can do the same for other people, is one of the great achievements of our free-enterprise system.

This experience with my sister is one of the reasons why I have spent time over the past decade attempting to fully understand America's welfare system and its successes and failures. As a nation, we have expended many hundreds of billions of dollars on a welfare system that, data show, in many ways has harmed those it tried to help. Today, we have far too many citizens who are third-generation welfare recipients. What was intended to be a "helping hand" has in far too many cases become a lifestyle. This is harmful to both those who live a life of dependency and society at large.

As a wealthy nation, we can and should provide a safety net to the truly physically or mentally disabled. We can and should *also* provide a helping hand to those citizens who have fallen on hard times. But we must also expect that citizens who are able to work to get their lives back on track of their own volition when provided the opportunity will do so.

Today, far too many welfare dollars are going to this second category. As such, the first category, those who are truly disabled, receive too little of what is optimally beneficial for society. It is compassionate to help those who cannot help themselves. It is destructive to destroy people's self-esteem through never-ending welfare benefits. As it is said, "give a man a fish, and he eats for a day; teach a man to fish, and he eats for a lifetime."

One of the most important lessons I learned in business and in private life is that relationships are essential and that the best relationships are founded on good principles. America is built around the same idea: that the relationship between citizen and government is important and does best when our foundational principles of meritocracy, equality, freedom, self-determination, and mutual respect are adhered to.

III. My Immigrant Family's Experiences: Adam's Story

I believe in America, in the American Dream, and that both are worth defending at all costs. What a person sees and experiences in their life shapes the way they decide to live. My experiences have taught me that the best way to truly know things about the world is to see and do things for yourself while also talking with those who came before you. The story of my family not only shapes the way I live but also underscores my view that America must be defended at all costs.

My family's story is not an uncommon one: I am the descendant of Czech immigrants who came to the United States to find a better life. Europe did not offer them a path forward, so they left the Old World and ultimately settled in the Midwest, specifically Cleveland, Ohio.

They worked hard and sacrificed so that their children—and their children's children—could get access to better opportunities, an education, and, in turn, better-paying jobs. They lived their lives in accordance with the simple principle that hard work pays off. They lived their lives with the goal of achieving the American Dream. I'm grateful to be taught these lessons, learned over generations, from my parents, who learned them from their parents.

When I think about the American Dream, it is families committing to the goal of social and economic improvement for themselves with the understanding that, over time, it will multiply for their descendants. At the heart of this approach is the recognition that one must believe in themselves, work hard to achieve their goal, and persevere when they believe all hope is lost. Our system of meritocracy rewards this behavior.

At the same time, something that I think people lose sight of today is that while huge individual sacrifices are often necessary components of the American Dream, the entire enterprise is more cooperative than it seems. America is a land of opportunity, and with the right policies in place, it always will be. But getting ahead is, to some extent, a group effort. That is a truth I learned from my family.

Not only did my grandparents rely on their families, but they also counted on their local communities and institutions. Whether it was a neighbor down the street, their church community, or others in their professional union, they could always rely on someone to assist them when they were in a bind. And my parents were the same way. They helped neighbors and friends when they needed assistance, returning the favor whenever they could.

This is not an unrepresentative anecdote either. Looking back at American history shows that this is the norm—or it *was* the norm when we had a more vibrant civil society.

In perhaps the most famous survey of early American life, Alexander de Tocqueville's *Democracy in America* (1835) details how small communities and self-reliance were at the core of social and civic life.[36] People worked and worshiped together, and these bonds not only made their friendships deeper but also created a shared set of values in which people could trust and work with each other on common goals.

Perhaps the best aspect of this kind of communal living-working situation is it exposes people to true diversity. That is true of the America de Tocqueville saw, and it is true of the America I grew up in. As a kid in the Cleveland suburbs, I interacted on a daily basis with folks of a wide variety of political beliefs, races, classes, and personal experiences. I had friends all over the place, and I quickly gained a perspective on how fortunate I was to have my community. It taught me the importance of tolerance and empathy.

One of the main reasons I even had these formative experiences is because my father successfully earned an education and was able to rise above the situation he was born into. Specifically, he did what no Brandon had done before him— he went to college. Nowadays, a lot of people get an education, but my dad was the first in his family. On top of that, he worked and supported his family while in school. While it was extremely hard, he persevered with the goal in mind to provide a better life for his family.

What makes this all the more impressive is that my dad's living situation as a kid was not at all ideal. Growing up in a poor Czech neighborhood in Cleveland was tough. People had an edge, and fighting was frequent, both at home and on the street. There were distractions all around him, and any one of them could have derailed his life. But my dad was focused and driven, and he had a goal: to get out of the city and to do something with himself.

And Dad did just that. He went to college, married my mom, and worked multiple jobs to put himself through dental school. On top of that, my dad struggled in school; it was not a pleasant experience for him, in no small part because he spent the nights working at Cleveland Ball Bearing, where he polished landing gears, and days learning. He even took a step that most wouldn't today: he changed our name from Busta to Brandon during dental school in order to more easily integrate his family into America. But in the end, he succeeded in becoming a professional and starting a family. I learned from him the importance of believing in yourself, working hard, and persevering through tough times. These lessons, passed down to me by my parents, helped guide me in my early life.

After graduating from college myself, I worked a number of different jobs. Just because I didn't know my ultimate goal at the time, it didn't mean my bills would go away. I think this was a hugely positive experience because it gave me perspective and enhanced my general skills. I met more people who were different from me—especially when I worked as a teacher—and saw new sides to our country.

During this time, I enrolled in a graduate program in Washington, DC, and simultaneously worked as an American history teacher in a local school to support myself. I reviewed the books we would use for the class in the lead-up to school, and they were far worse than I could have ever imagined. They were too dry and overly ideological. I resolved to change the curriculum.

During these revisions, I remembered how boring high school classes could be. I made a promise to myself that I would engage with my students and keep things interesting. And the best way to do that was, in my view, to give them as varied and open an inspection of their country's past as possible. My students read writers from across the ideological spectrum; I made sure to keep them busy and stimulated intellectually; and no chapter of American history was ignored—even the ugly and sad moments.

My students read everyone from Howard Zinn to Milton Friedman. We explored every perspective and debated the tension between security and liberty. It was an awesome experience, and I loved the opportunity to talk about our country with young people.

My time as an instructor provided clarity: for the first time, I was able to align my intellectual interests, my study of history, government, and economics, with my passion for talking with people about our country. Now that I understood this and better grasped the reasons why the United States is so special, I realized that I wanted to get more involved in America's civic culture. Sharing this message would be necessary to make sure that America's values and opportunities remain open to all.

Later on, when I attended graduate school abroad, I was more organized and prepared to learn, and I attribute that to my work experiences after college.

Not only did I enter graduate school with a better idea of why I wanted to learn and what I wanted to do, but I also brought with me a greater understanding of our country and its people. Most importantly, I had a more fully formed idea of what made the United States special and the uniqueness of its system of opportunity and advancement.

For example, when I studied in Poland, I saw so many people who were like my fellow citizens back in the states: they were hard-working, eager to learn, smart, and community-minded. Despite being equally capable people, the two countries were markedly different in terms of what they offered people with these qualities.

The big difference in Poland was that the opportunities we enjoy in America are not nearly as numerous or accessible. Entrepreneurs have fewer opportunities to test out their ideas. I gained immense gratitude for the fortune of being born an American. Equality of opportunity is also a *uniquely* American idea that sets us apart from anywhere else.

This point is crucial for understanding America. Our country has other attractive features—good social services and benefits, to name a few—but the defining features of the United States are its wealth of opportunities and its hands-off political culture.

Our argument is *not* that America is perfect or beyond reproach; our argument is that compared to the other systems around the world, America is the best. Because of our system of self-healing, so many of America's problems have been overcome by Americans of all backgrounds coming and working together. While there is no doubt that divisions do still exist and grow at times, those divisions are resolved mostly peacefully through the democratic process. And if our system does need to be radically changed, our Constitution allows us to build a consensus to meet that moment.

Unfortunately, it seems that a significant portion of the country no longer sees things in this glass-half-full way. Recent polling indicates that too many citizens have adopted a very negative view of the United States.[37] For them, America's problems are worse than its accomplishments, and the only way to fix them is to abandon our current system entirely. Sadly, these citizens fail to understand how America has confronted its previous challenges head-on and has always come out better as a result.

They are a minority, but their views are amplified by opinion-forming institutions, from media corporations to institutions of higher learning. These views have become particularly pervasive among younger Americans. We must work hard to not allow this group to fundamentally transform America. The things that make America truly *unique* cannot be found in any other country. Once America is gone, its unique, responsive, and largely resilient system of government will fade and be ultimately replaced by increased government control of daily lives by a well-connected elite.

These negative beliefs about America have not always been the norm. My family is mostly composed of political moderates, and my uncles, who were more committed to the Democrats as blue-collar union members, are among the most patriotic Americans I have ever met. They fought for their country in World War II and had a deep and sincere sense of patriotism. They were not ignorant, and they understood things could be better. But they were not idealists or endless critics in the way that so many are today.

Moreover, their views—that the country was something to take pride in, that it did so much for them that they owed it service, and that they were blessed to live as American citizens—were in the mainstream and the majority. Back then, the only people with truly harsh opinions about the United States were limited to a few ornery professors and media critics, and large swaths of the country rightly saw them as people who deserved limited consideration. Pride in your country was not confused as an acceptance of all of its mistakes.

What is worrisome is that many in the media, government, and academia like to pretend that the shift in public opinion they have helped to usher in (and opinion *has* sadly changed) is natural, that it has existed over time. It amuses me to see some of the most anti-American critics of the day try to couch their animosity in some supposed tradition when no such legacy exists. They want to legitimize their views while also avoiding ownership of them.

A cursory glance at the remarks of politicians of the mid-twentieth century shows how far off this argument is. Perhaps the most well-known and ubiquitous quote from a president that people from my generation know is President Kennedy's famous quip to Americans during his inaugural address: "Ask not what your country can do for you, but what you can do for your country."

Kennedy's exhortation was a call to action for Americans, young Americans in particular. The idea of serving one's country implies loyalty and an obligation to personally work to make life better for your fellow citizens.

Kennedy, like most Americans in the 1950s and 1960s, obviously thought that the United States was largely good and worth defending, and that latent idea underpins the speech. Today, his call to service is a reminder of how far out of balance things are today and how far many have drifted ideologically.

Just because America can do better does *not* mean our entire system must be thrown out. I believe in the American Dream in part because I saw my parents base their lives on it. My father was able to work at night and go to school during the day because that opportunity was afforded to him here.

While working to change careers is extremely hard, my father believed in himself, worked hard, and persevered so he could provide a better life for his family. The American system that gave him that opportunity is worth fighting for, and I will always defend it.

IV: The Purpose of This Book

We do not think one needs to be an especially close reader of what is written above to understand that we love America. Our country is special, and we are fortunate to have grown up here. We want our kids, fellow citizens, and future Americans to enjoy the same benefits that we did, chief among them access to a good education, protection from crime and violence, and ample opportunities for meaningful work.

It is our love for and gratitude to this country that led us to FreedomWorks, a network of grassroots activists who fight for limited government and free enterprise, and it is that same passion that drives us to write this book and share a warning with our fellow citizens. Most FreedomWorks activists understand that our unique system is potentially one generation away from extinction, and that many will ignore or fail to understand these threats properly and, even further, be unable to advance solutions to address them substantively. Right now, our country is headed in the wrong direction, and it will take a movement of passionate, concerned citizens to get it back on the right track.

We look around today and find an economy that is moving in the wrong direction; we see virtually every institution in our country declining in public trust and in general effectiveness, from the military to our schools; and we observe a closing window of time available to us to arrest and reverse these trends.

Our unique combination of institutions, norms, and traditions provides us with something that few other regimes in human history have enjoyed, namely the ability to correct and heal ourselves. In fact, self-healing is a *uniquely* American idea that most do not appreciate. With our Constitution, we can fix the mistakes of our predecessors without throwing out all the good we inherited from them. In other words, we do not need a revolution to correct an error. In other countries, this success is exceptionally rare.

Thanks to the *unique* constitutional system we have in America, we believe our system is the best to address the challenges of the future, and it can improve. But improvement does not mean throwing out our system. Improvement means working together through democratic majorities, reaching a consensus, and facing our problems head-on in the spirit of self-healing.

In America, power is divided, and the rights of minorities, the smallest of which is the individual, are protected. In the political sphere, citizens can advocate for causes, and if their ideas are good and persuasive, they can change the law and, in turn, the country through their representatives. Participation is key, and our system is built to reward the engaged and committed.

America has had serious problems in the past where democratic solutions were impossible. But these exceptions can be counted on one hand. In almost all cases, the tools the Founders left us have presented us with solutions to the vast majority of our problems. Contrary to what many assert today, the system has worked in the past and continues to work today.

In fact, in 2022, our biggest challenges are not *within* our governmental system but outside of it. Specifically, it is the threat by some on the furthest left of the ideological spectrum to destroy our constitutional system—its hard rules and soft norms—that we must take seriously and counter accordingly. We cannot compromise on the American system. While it has been repeated before and will be repeated throughout the book, once our system is gone, it is gone forever. There is no other country in the world that has what we have for so long.

Put simply, these "progressives" want to "fundamentally transform" the Constitution and the norms built up around it because they see them as an impenetrable obstacle to their extreme and largely unpopular political goals. To be clear, they do not like the division of power between the state and federal government, the independence of the Supreme Court, the Senate filibuster, which forces consensus, the genuine equality of opportunity, America's meritocratic ethos, or its governmental structure. They also fail to recognize the hope that our system of meritocracy puts in every American.

In short, this movement wants to fundamentally change our country because they do not like it as it currently exists. While change is sometimes required to advance, that doesn't mean we should reject our culture and institutions. They purportedly want to change America because they love it. But if we truly love America, then we should all work to defend and improve it and not abandon its unique system of government.

People need to understand why the "progressive" critique is factually wrong and politically dangerous. While our system provides for a large amount of individual liberty, its best element is its conception of and process for securing justice. Some problems are solved legally through deliberative, representative bodies, and others are fixed socially through civil society. When things really break down, they can be changed and amended over time as needed. Our system allows for change, but consensus is needed before it can be accomplished. "Progressives" think that idea is radical only because they *cannot* build the consensus needed for their changes.

Self-healing and meritocracy are *uniquely* American ideas that define our country. But these beliefs could be easily lost without a thoughtful defense by all Americans who share these values. While our system can be improved, it should not and cannot be fundamentally changed or altered. Once our system is gone, millions of hardworking people all across the world will have few places to turn. Our hope for this book is that it will analyze the history of America, explore why our past allowed for us to be successful, and put forth a few ideas on how to improve this country while recognizing how we learned from our past.

CHAPTER 2

1776

*"The basis of our political systems is the right of the
people to make and to alter their Constitutions of
Government. But the Constitution which at any time
exists, till changed by an explicit and authentic act of
the whole people, is sacredly obligatory upon all."*
—George Washington

I. How Did America Get Here?

We arrived at the America we know today because of our
past. Our country cannot be one that places a special emphasis on self-healing if there is nothing to heal from. And to
truly appreciate this, we must understand the key historical
moments that got us to today.

Moreover, the American Dream, our unique shared belief
that anyone can come from anywhere and achieve a better
life, was no accident. It took generations upon generations
to build a country that could allow the American Dream to
thrive. It is through these generations that we have advanced,

prospered, and adapted as the largest superpower in the history of the world. To be sure, these generations of citizens have helped us heal when we needed it the most.

Of course, self-healing and the American Dream underscored by meritocracy were possible because, as a nation, we have built a consensus on major issue after major issue about how our country should be run. Some of the earliest and most consequential developments in our country occurred at the beginning. There was a consensus to write the Declaration of Independence (see Appendix A) and go to war with Britain. After winning the war, there was a consensus that the Articles of Confederation did not work, and a new government was needed under the Constitution. At no point was any colony forced to join the Articles of Confederation or the Constitution. They chose to only because there was a consensus that doing so was in their own best interest.

Today, we see the bashing and obfuscating of American history in many of our important institutions, such as the media and academia. Although, in popular culture, it is easy to engage in this relentless deception, it is on us to understand the pivotal moments that shaped who America is today. We believe that to understand the United States today, it is necessary to look back several centuries, even before its ultimate founding, to understand America's fundamentals as these core features shaped its trajectory in the nineteenth century and beyond.

II. A Land of Plenty and the People Who Populated It

America's story begins well before the Founding, in part because the norms and habits that contributed to its economic growth in later decades have their genesis in the pre-American colonies and their people.

Starting in the early 1600s, European powers established permanent colonies in the New World.[38] Over the next century and a half, give or take, these small communities developed dynamic economies and unique cultures, both of which multiplied their success and their civic freedom. When looking at the pre-American period, one must understand who these people were and that they brought with them their institutions and practices from their own respective heritage.

Those who immigrated to the American colonies from Europe were largely industrious people. Many were seeking improved financial prospects or attempting to escape religious persecution. The differences in background determined their actions in America, e.g., some Europeans came to establish political communities in line with their theological views, while others sought to make money off ventures outside of England.

At a base level, they came to North America for a better way of life. Of course, not all immigrants to America were voluntary, as was the case of slaves who were brought here without their consent. But for those who did come freely, a better way of life was a shared goal for many immigrants, even if the specific details of what they wanted to do were different. For them, they did not have a place in the Old World, and this was their new beginning.

Crucially, these immigrants brought their unique cultures, tendencies, and norms with them. Over time, they built their own institutions, which reflected those sociopolitical and religious predispositions, practices, and beliefs. These cultural legacies matter a great deal and represent another piece of the metaphorical puzzle in explaining how and why America developed such strong communities.

But what were these specific norms and beliefs?

First, an idea of charity (understood as service to others) and communal living influenced the behavior of immigrants in the American colonies, i.e., colonists established roles and universal guidelines to live by and divided their work to survive.[39]

Second, the family played a critical role in these communities, in large part because the first immigrants to arrive eventually brought their wives and children with them—something that did not happen everywhere in the New World.[40] People within families owed each other certain things through these norms, like children learning to respect their parents and help with chores at home.

When these norms and beliefs were taken together and applied to the natural resources that North America offered, the colonists were able to focus their time and energy on their own business, the fruits of which included substantial economic development and the literal growth of their communities. One measure of this is the expansion of the British American colonies over the course of the eighteenth century: in 1700, the number was about a quarter of a million; by 1770, the colonists numbered over 2.1 million.[41]

In summary, the colonists succeeded because they had resources, an excellent work ethic and social norms, and clear standards regarding their behavior and the expectations of them within their communities. But the other reason that the colonists thrived, particularly on the economic front, was due to what they did *not* have: an onerous and expansive regulatory system to deal with.

This period was largely laissez-faire in that there were few to no burdens on business and no barriers to entry. What regulations did exist were limited and fixed on specific, consumer-minded goals, such as ensuring that products meet basic standards.[42] The American colonies were *the* place for entrepreneurs to test their ideas in the market—something that was not possible in the Old World, where feudal legacies arrested social mobility and economic opportunity.

The comparative results of these practices are striking: the average colonist in the American colonies was over four times as wealthy as the average Englishman living in Britain.[43] A big reason for this was the fact that taxation in the colonies was one-twentieth what it was back in the Old World.[44] In America, citizens had more opportunities and greater economic freedom because laws were not designed to tax wealth or discourage entrepreneurship.

The laws that did exist in the American colonies were rooted in English customs and artifacts, the most influential of which was the common law, or the law created from precedent (the decisions made by courts).

The great thing about the common law is that it was understood by the regular person. It was *not* a system of complex legal rules that's sole purpose was to put up barriers between those with power and those without it. The virtue of this system, beyond its familiarity, is that it was built upon basic precepts that were intelligible to colonists.

Property rights were also essential and generally protected. The common law pertained to all kinds of disputes, and the rules that extended from it were commonsensical and obvious. For instance, there was a property right in a person's reputation, and people were allowed to sue when it was damaged. This applied in cases of defamation, where the truth mattered, and where a person's reputation—perhaps their most valuable "property" of all—was protected by law in cases where it was unjustly damaged.

The larger point of this discussion is that the colonists in America enjoyed a relatively open economic sphere with a larger social sphere that influenced the behavior of individuals and the law. The colonists thus enjoyed a peaceful civic society in which people could focus on business rather than worry about politics and moral disputes.

To be sure, colonists needed to do certain things to survive, such as gather resources and contribute to certain communal projects. But from a commercial perspective, they were able to trade goods and cultivate and sell so-called cash crops. This was a special kind of economic freedom that did not exist in that form anywhere else in the world at that time, and it made a real difference in terms of the wealth and growth of the North American colonies.

III. The English Legacy

In 1776, thirteen colonies in America declared their independence from the English Crown. This historic decision happened because the colonies built a consensus that this was the right move. The genesis of the colonies' collective decision to break with Great Britain was a dispute over representation in the political process. Specifically, the colonists felt that they had no meaningful voice in Parliament on the issue of taxation (which became prominent after the French and Indian War), and thus no ability to challenge what they believed to be an unfair tax regime imposed from afar.[45]

Their central issue with King George III (but in reality, Parliament) was their exclusion from the governing process. Up until this point, involvement in the political process defined colonists' experience as English citizens in the North American colonies, and now it had been taken away from them.

Colonists also believed they were being denied their due rights as Englishmen. In other words, they believed that Parliament and the king were out of line by excluding them from decision-making processes. In fact, it was the colonists who were acting normally and in sync with their political traditions by protesting this development, at least as they saw it.[46]

The decision to declare independence from Britain was earth-shattering, and even more so when one considers how different the colonies were. The colonies were completely independent of one another, and the uniqueness of their respective backgrounds contributed to the formation of distinct cultures and institutions. For decades, these independent jurisdictions operated autonomously—at least insofar as they possessed and followed their own political and social systems and engaged in regional economic practices, e.g., Southern states like South Carolina were more agrarian and one-dimensional, other states more democratic and religious, like Rhode Island.

The point of the discussion to this point is two-fold. First, it demonstrates that, prior to the issuing of the Declaration of Independence, most colonists saw themselves as English citizens living abroad and ruling themselves. What this means is that the decision to break with Great Britain was internally significant as the colonies came together to pursue a larger common interest: their economic health and, as they saw it, their integrity as English citizens. This decision required great consensus. It would not be enough for a few colonies to band together; it would take the strength of each one. These colonies were largely independent of each other, and their coming together to unite represents one of the greatest political unifications in history, similar to that of Germany or Italy in the nineteenth century.

Second, the issue of taxes was a microcosm of a larger phenomenon, namely that the colonies had, over decades, established their own political practices and economic preferences. They wanted to continue to live as *independent* English citizens without sacrificing their independence. As noted above, they remained loyal to the English government and saw themselves as citizens, e.g., they accepted many of its obligations and restrictions, many colonists identified as English subjects, and so on.

But what the early Americans would not ultimately concede were their rights. Indeed, it was their concern that they were transforming into something less than citizens that spurred their protests.[47]

The colonists crucially shared an identity as English citizens, even if they had regional loyalties or identities based on their location. Because they saw themselves as English citizens, the colonists enjoyed an appreciation for the customs and institutions discussed earlier, from limited government to civic participation and a conception of individual rights over which the government could not tread.

But the colonists also liked the space to experiment and do their own thing, so to speak. In the end, they could not tolerate threats by London to limit their liberty in economic and political affairs, particularly when they had no means to participate in the decision-making process. Importantly, the colonists did not reject their Englishness and heritage. Rather, they wanted to preserve it and build on it in ways advantageous to their own interests and needs.

If these ideas sound familiar, it is because these points all (in one way or another) made their way into the foundational documents of the United States government. The Declaration of Independence articulates an idea of inherent rights as well as the idea of consent-based rule. We owe a great deal to our English influences, and in a way, the Declaration of Independence is an homage to our shared political history and beliefs.

The Declaration of Independence also represents our country's first attempt at a major consensus. A seismic shift like declaring independence from Britain was consented to by all thirteen colonies. While this might seem obvious today, that same need for consensus in making radical changes also reflects our current political system. As we will see in later chapters, it is reflected in the Senate's filibuster rule as well as in amending the Constitution.

The upshot is that the Declaration of Independence is a conservative and very English document rooted in over one thousand years of historical tradition from post-Roman Britain and the Magna Carta. In short, the colonists saw the English government as reneging on its promises to its citizens (i.e., them) by excluding them from a political process through which they retained connections to the home country.

Political autonomy and economic independence mattered a great deal to the colonists because they defined their approach to government. Unsurprisingly, London's interference in both was sufficiently outrageous that these disparate colonies forged an alliance to defend their practices when negotiations broke down.

This point is essential because it gets to the core of what makes the colonists' efforts against Great Britain so important: they rebelled primarily to protect their property and their involvement in the political procedures that impacted their lives—two features that they felt defined their status as English.

The reason that the colonists rose up, and the reason they fought as long as they did, is simple and obvious: they had a *lot* to lose should the English succeed. That was because, by the mid-1700s, the colonies were governing themselves effectively and largely independently after experimenting with different approaches to government.[48] Plus, the colonists and their ancestors built real wealth in the New World, and they did not want to turn it over. The colonists felt they knew how best to spend their own money, and they did not want a distant government making those decisions for them.

In sum, the colonists could be generally ascribed the belief that their way of doing things was superior to the "new" (read illegal and radical) methods of the English, including the exclusion of the colonists in the political process. They were closer to their problems, they understood their needs and challenges better, and most importantly, they did not want to surrender the old, workable English traditions. To fight for their rights against Great Britain, the colonists built a consensus that their way of life was good and worth dying for. That is why we have the America we know today.

IV. The Anglo Divide

Perhaps the event that had the largest transformational effect on both the Founders' and the colonists' way of thinking was the Enlightenment. Where the Magna Carta and common law were products of English practices and history, the Declaration of Independence and Constitution arose primarily out of the political theories of Enlightenment thinkers and the experiences of the colonists.[49]

The Enlightenment was neither a single event nor a harmonious ideology. Rather, there were multiple enlightenments, and each emphasized different values and types of knowledge. On top of that, individual enlightenments were hardly monolithic.

To use one example, consider Great Britain. In the Anglosphere, there were two enlightenments, one English and the other Scottish. Some thinkers in these movements advocated for the supremacy of reason, while others stressed that instinct, feelings, and the irrational were valid and essential aspects of the human experience.

Broadly speaking, it was the Scottish Enlightenment that shaped the views of the Founding Fathers and, in turn, influenced the country's two foundational texts. The Founders were strong believers in the social contract theory expounded by liberals like Thomas Hobbes and John Locke of the English Enlightenment. However, the philosopher Adam Smith of the Scottish Enlightenment had an even larger impact.

Smith is perhaps best known for his early articulation of capitalist principles in *The Wealth of Nations* (1776).[50] In it, Smith outlines core ideas that later became the basis for much of modern economics, including the "invisible hand" of the market and the division of labor. Important as this book was, it was Smith's earlier text, *The Theory of Moral Sentiments* (*Sentiments*) (1759), that likely had the larger impact on the creation of American political institutions.

In *Sentiments*, Smith sets out to provide an account of how and why humans make moral judgments since, at birth, they are blank slates in the moral sense.[51] Ultimately, Smith concludes that human relationships are natural and essential and that they form the foundation of our moral systems by teaching us sympathy via human interaction.[52] It is through these interactions and judgments that we come to understand the value of abiding by a moral, sympathy-based code.[53]

Taken together, Smith's two great works had a tremendous influence on American practices in the social and economic spheres: the former promoted fair treatment of others, while the latter explained why self-interest in one's finances and business life would ultimately benefit a greater number of people. These lessons appear in both the Constitution and Declaration of Independence and are reflected in the pro-trade, pro-entrepreneurial economic behavior of the early Americans.

One reason that the Founding Fathers were so support-
ive of Smith's views is that they studied history and learned
from their experiences. They knew growth was not the rule,
e.g., from 0 BC to 1820 AD, economic growth in the Western
world averaged a pitiful 0.11 percent per year[54]; the corollary
was that their experience in America was the exception and
deserved protection. The great drivers of economic growth
in America were entrepreneurship and private property. This
system was so important to the Founders that private property is explicitly protected in the Constitution.[55]

The benefit of this system is that when the creation of
wealth and the promotion of moral principles are combined,
it creates a situation where individuals contribute to and lift
up their fellow people. That, combined with the shared belief
in promoting the common good of the American public,
encouraged (and continues to drive today) charitable giving
to the most vulnerable.

In other words, Smith's insights, when applied, create a
maximally beneficial situation in which everyone does better
when the economy is allowed to flourish without excessive
government intervention. Smith's ideas promote economic
growth through a market-oriented economy, which allows all
people to specialize, cultivate their skills, and benefit from the
products of their labor through exchange with others. This
economic model easily demonstrates why America embraced
the concept of the American Dream and was an attractive
destination for any immigrant who wanted to take a bet on
themselves.

The Constitution is built around Smith's ideas but was also
written to protect liberties, including property rights. At the

same time, it was set up to be durable. The Founders did this because they understood the power of ephemeral urges and the self-destructive nature of democracy. Building a workable and durable system is hard; tearing one down is easy.

Consequently, the Founders set up a process to amend the Constitution that requires great consensus.[56] If the country truly comes together to agree on an issue, there is a way to take it completely out of the democratic process. For all other issues, citizens are free to debate their ideas, vote for politicians who support their ideas, and advocate for them to be enacted into law. The consensus needed for amending the Constitution promotes further discussion and deliberation that, in theory, ensures that (most) bad ideas do not make it through. This way, there would be no tyranny of the majority over the minority, an idea articulated best by the British philosopher John Stuart Mill.

By erecting guardrails around the revolution's signature artifact, the Constitution, the Founders ensured that their effort would not go to waste or be commandeered by demagogues, which sadly is exactly what happened in France with Robespierre and the Jacobins.[57] It is through the Constitution that the American Revolution and its values live on and reach future generations.

V. The Founders' Long View of America

Just as there were competing views of the Enlightenment, so too were there disagreements about the trajectory of the young American nation. Should the country expand? What role (if any) ought the US to take in the hemisphere? What role should the federal government play in relation to the states?

One question that especially divided the Founders was what the future of the society and economy would look like. One of the best-known disagreements concerned the Jefferson-Hamilton dispute: the former conceived of America as a land best ruled by virtuous and independent farmers, while the latter wanted a more industrial society in which power was more urban than rural.

For Jefferson, the independence necessary to sustain oneself would cultivate the republican virtues that would sustain the nation and its spirit.[58] Eventually, the political ideology of Jeffersonian democracy would support candidates and policies to empower yeoman farmers, namely anti-industrialization programs through the vehicle of the Democratic-Republican Party.[59]

In opposition to the Democratic-Republican Party was the Federalist Party,[60] organized by Alexander Hamilton. This political organization, the first of its kind in the US, stood for those very positions and values that Jefferson rejected, including banking, industrialization, infrastructure, and modernization.

What is notable about this disagreement is that as far apart as Hamilton and Jefferson were on central political questions—the role of the government (state and federal) in everyday life, whether there would be a central banking system, America's role in the world, and so on—there was agreement on one issue that would prove disastrously contentious, but which they assumed would be reduced to a relic in the future: slavery. While there was large division on the issue of slavery in the early US, many of the Founders opposed it, including those who paradoxically owned slaves themselves.[61] In fact, in the Constitution, the Founders left the issue of slavery, like almost every other issue, to the states. As a result, some states, like Pennsylvania, Massachusetts, New Hampshire, Connecticut, and Rhode Island, banned slavery very early on.[62] Importantly, both Jefferson and Hamilton saw slavery as degenerative to all parties and as an immoral mistake.[63] Too few know that the first abolitionist convention was held in Philadelphia in the 1770s.[64]

Unfortunately, what some Founders believed about slavery, that it would die out on its own, did not come to pass. Instead, it would take years of activism followed by bloody fighting and literal sacrifice to end slavery and realize the American promise to protect the liberty and independence of its people. But while that fighting and sacrifice were horrific, it resulted in America's first moment of self-healing. Importantly, the Union fought for what was right, namely that the Declaration of Independence's central promise that all men are created equal be extended to everyone.

CHAPTER 3

CIVIL WAR

*"It is rather for us, the living, we here be dedicated
to the great task remaining before us that, from these
honored dead we take increased devotion to that cause
for which they here, gave the last full measure of devotion
that we here highly resolve these dead shall not have
died in vain; that the nation, shall have a new birth
of freedom, and that government of the people, by the
people, for the people, shall not perish from the earth."
—Abraham Lincoln*

I. The Causes and Crises

The Civil War is one of the most important eras in American history, both because it was so tied to the country's past and because it set a better course for its future by finally making good on the Constitution's original promises. Certainly, the Civil War began the resolution of the most significant mistake made by our Founders. They allowed states to make their own decision on the issue of slavery because they thought that's how it would end. And in some states, that was how it did end. But unfortunately, the Founders could not ban slavery in the Constitution because that Constitution would have never been ratified. They did not make this calculated decision lightly.

The issue of slavery and the Civil War is debatably the most extreme example of self-healing America has gone through. After the Constitution failed to live up to the Declaration of Independence's promise that all men are created equal, hundreds of thousands of men, both Black and White, died fighting to achieve this fundamental promise.

In short, the outcome of the Civil War was the ultimate resolution to the problem of the Founding, i.e., the contradiction between its principles (liberty, equality, and economic opportunity) and the reality of American society in the South (slavery, despotism, and theft). It is a horrific tragedy that it took years of war and tremendous bloodshed, but the silver lining—namely the end of slavery and the realization of America's promise for more of its people—deserves to be appreciated.

The Civil War was about slavery. And yet, contrary to how it is talked about today, the Civil War was also a complex conflict over many disputes and disagreements, many of them long-standing. It was also the first and most dramatic step in our country's journey to healing itself.

Some Americans in the South fought for the Confederacy out of a sense of regional loyalty and pride, while others fought to preserve slavery. The importance of regional loyalty and pride flowed from the fact that the states were unique political communities. During this time, it was more common for people to identify as a citizen of a state rather than a citizen of the US.

During this time, the federal government in Washington was tiny and the means of travel more limited, meaning that the average citizen did not have any immediate connections to his or her identity as an American citizen. It was rare for Americans to travel to the District of Columbia not only because travel was limited, but also because the federal government was of little importance and Americans were more concerned with what was going on in their state. This means one's place of birth meant more, and people were loyal to their local institutions and governments rather than the federal government.

This regionalism does not excuse what these people did, which was to engage in a vicious war of secession against their country. Nonetheless, this nuance ought to be understood and appreciated because it provides necessary context for grasping the reasons that some Americans with no ties to slavery—*the* issue that divided the North and South—took the side of the Confederacy in the conflict.

The second-largest group that supported the Confederacy was the plantation class that profited from slavery and wanted to protect the institution because it made their lifestyle sustainable. This group was extremely wealthy and politically powerful. Slavery was at the core of their economic model, and they wanted to do everything possible to protect and promote it.

In our view, this politically connected class is responsible, in large part, for the outbreak of the war because it wanted to expand slavery—even when some of the Founders were explicitly opposed.[65] As will be explained below, it was this class that instigated many of the crises in the decades before war broke out in 1861, and which was so protective of its own status that it wished to remake the US as a nation based on slavery.

Others—the smallest group—supported the Confederacy out of a sincere belief that the Constitution had been violated in a fundamental way. For this contingent, the Constitution was a limited agreement between states that chartered a federal power but not a national power.[66] In other words, they believed there was no power with sovereign authority *over* states; instead, the Constitution set up a federal government with the power to address only disagreements *between* states.

Under this theory, the federal government had no power to limit slavery in the states because it was powerless to interfere unless there was a dispute between states. For those who subscribed to this theory, the right to exit the Constitution's agreement is obvious and legitimate, and so was the right to veto federal laws. In a way, this group embraced a view of government in the vein of the anti-federalists,[67] although they drew most of their inspiration from John C. Calhoun, a politician from South Carolina who articulated a similar nullification theory found in the Constitution decades earlier.[68]

While this discourse on the particular groups that supported the Confederacy provides reasons as to why people took sides, it says little as to the specific events that pushed people to secede. This is a big gap that must be filled in.

First, though the issue of slavery was always contentious, it was widely assumed to be a declining institution by the Founders.[69] While some of the Founding Fathers owned slaves, many of them recognized the many obvious problems with slavery, perhaps the most obvious of which was that it was antithetical to the principles of the regime they built. The lofty language of the Constitution and the Declaration of Independence sounds a bit absurd when one realizes that slavery was practiced in so many states.

Slavery, tragically, was integral to the economic model of the South, and for the young American nation to survive, it needed the assistance of those slave states, hence the compromise on slavery during the Founding Era. Sadly, the Founders had no choice but to do with slavery what they did with every other issue—give it to the states.

Second, the issue of slavery became more protracted and divisive due to technological advancements. Specifically, the introduction of the cotton gin made the cultivation and sale of cotton—a notoriously difficult crop to raise—easier and thus more lucrative.[70] This, in turn, meant that slavery would be more valuable than ever. The tragedy here is that an institution that most assumed would collapse under its own weight as an economic model was revived via the introduction of this new tool of efficiency.

This had the ugly secondary effect of giving the plantation class in the South a reason to affirmatively support slavery. It went from an institutional practice to an economic necessity for the Southern ruling class in a generation. Moreover, the continuation of slavery was a lazy, inefficient gambit by these Southern elites to avoid the harder process of industrializing and opening up their region to competition—competition that could change the political economy to their disadvantage. In that way, the South's economy represented the opposite of what is so good about America today. The South promoted and, consequently, relied on a culture that was based entirely on cronyism, *not* merit.

Third, a series of political developments, many of them related to the rapid expansion of the US and its territories, shook the balance of slave states and free states.[71] These contentious and occasionally violent disputes raised the proverbial temperature on the broader political situation in America, and they further separated what was quickly becoming an acutely bifurcated cultural situation between North and South. In the North, abolitionists eventually took over political parties and institutions, resulting in the creation of the Grand Old Party (GOP), or the Republican Party. Increasingly, the conflict in America was transitioning from an imperfect but tenable disagreement into a more straightforward conflict over whether the US should abolish or spread slavery.

Perhaps the worst Supreme Court decision of all time only heightened tensions further. In *Dred Scott v. Sandford* (1856), the court incorrectly held that under the Constitution, Blacks could not become citizens of the US.[72] It also held that the Missouri Compromise was unconstitutional because Congress exceeded its power by depriving slave owners of their right of property in slaves under the Fifth Amendment's due process clause.[73] While we think this case was egregiously wrong, the important point here is that, like most other issues, the original Constitution gave the issue of slavery to the states to decide. The Supreme Court then took that issue away from the people who had reached a consensus over what to do about it. *Dred Scott* only moved the nation closer to the Civil War.

Finally, the election of Abraham Lincoln sparked Southern secession. Lincoln was a Republican who did not hide his affiliations with the abolitionist movement; he campaigned on the supremacy of the Declaration of Independence and its assertion that "all men are created equal."[74] Lincoln made clear that he believed, as many Founders did, that slavery's course was towards "ultimate extinction." Moreover, Lincoln believed that *Dred Scott* was wrongly decided and that the fundamental promise of the Declaration of Independence included all men, not some.[75] Lincoln's positions were anathema to the elite plantation class, and it responded to his election in 1860 by following through on its threat to secede from the Union.

II. Civil War: Importance and Aftermath

Americans, some in the Union and others in the Confederacy, fought across the country over the future of the United States. Both sides, in most cases, believed that they were defending and furthering the will of their ancestors and that they were in the right. Confederates thought that, in seceding, they were invoking the same right to revolution that the Founding Fathers did when they declared independence from Britain. And they thought that their defense of states' rights to continue the institution of slavery was in the American tradition.[76] On the other side, those in the Union fought to maintain the Constitution and end slavery in the US for good.

The horror and scale of loss caused by the Civil War cannot be overstated. Over 750,000 Americans died in the Civil War, and thousands more were wounded and maimed. This number represents roughly 2.5 percent of the population at that time.[77] In today's terms, this 2.5 percent would equate to over eight million citizens.

To say that the war was anything other than a tragedy would be a massive understatement. And this does not even touch on the scale of the destruction: infrastructure across the US was destroyed, and battles were fought in nineteen different states. The carnage was pervasive, and virtually every American was impacted by the conflict in some way.

After over four years of fighting, the Union defeated the South and settled several key political questions, including whether states have a right to exit the Constitution (no), whether Black Americans should be citizens (yes), and whether slavery should be abolished in the US (yes). A large part of the final question was famously answered by Abraham Lincoln when he issued the Emancipation Proclamation, a legal command that freed enslaved people in the South.

In issuing that command, Lincoln affirmed the heretofore unfulfilled guarantee of America's two founding documents—that of the possibility of citizenship for *all* people, no matter where they were from or what they looked like—and, in doing so, brought the American way of life into harmony with the intentions of the Founders. Put simply, in ending slavery, Lincoln and the Union universalized the American regime and its principles, which were designed to be universal in the first place.

Luckily for Americans, this watershed moment is widely known since it is crystallized in Lincoln's famous Gettysburg Address (see Appendix C). Lincoln's iconic remarks serve as a reminder that our country has not one birthday but two, which reflects the protracted nature of our founding: our original birthday in 1776 and our second birthday on July 4th, 1863, the day after the Battle of Gettysburg, which was the high-water mark of the Confederacy. We think it is essential to keep this fact in mind when talking about the Civil War because it underscores a crucial point, namely that the American story is not contradictory and that our origins are not tainted. The massive death and destruction of the Civil War was the first step America took toward self-healing. As will be examined later in this book, it should be encouraging to today's Americans that we have a system of government that allows us to address our challenges without a civil war.

Modern attempts to relitigate the past and transform the meaning of the Civil War, Declaration of Independence, and the evil of slavery are divisive and counterproductive. The politicization of history and the belief that race exclusively defines the prospect of access to the American Dream will weigh heavy on our meritocracy and freedoms. We all agree that children should be taught the important parts of our nation's history, even those that failed to live up to our ideals. After all, a key piece of healing is learning the lessons of the past.

Instead of tearing each other down by focusing on the most negative parts of this period, we believe there is one story that perfectly exemplifies America's culture of self-healing. Robert Smalls was born in 1839 into slavery. Before the Civil War, Smalls's owner Henry McKee allowed him to work in and around Charleston Harbor. There, he met Hannah Jones, an enslaved hotel maid. He married Jones, had two children with her, and saved for years to buy her freedom.

However, her owner refused, asking for $800 while Smalls only had $100. From that point, it was Smalls's dream of living a free life with his wife and kids.

During the Civil War, Smalls was assigned to a Confederate military cargo ship, the *Planter*, located in Charleston Harbor. Eventually, he gained the trust and confidence of the Black crew members and White officers because he was such a good captain. With his belief in freedom for his family fully in mind, Smalls came up with a plan to escape. One night, when the officers departed the ship to sleep ashore, Smalls and the crew piloted the ship out of the harbor. Before leaving South Carolina, Smalls stopped to pick up his wife and children, along with four other women, three men, and another child.

Smalls piloted the *Planter* to Union shores and then surrendered it and its cargo to the Union Navy. Immediately, Smalls was received as a hero. Congress awarded him half the value of the *Planter*. Moreover, he also met with President Lincoln and persuaded him to allow Blacks to fight in the Union Army. As a result, Secretary of War Edwin Stanton commissioned five thousand former slaves to fight for the Union. In fact, Smalls became the pilot and later captain of the USS *Crusader*, a Union ship. Smalls was the first Black man to be promoted to captain in the history of the United States military.

After the Civil War, he returned to his native land of Beaufort, South Carolina, and bought his former master's home. Smalls then ran for and won several different political races. In 1868, he was elected to the South Carolina House of Representatives and later to the South Carolina Senate. Then, in 1874, he was elected to the US House of Representatives.

He fought hard against the disenfranchisement of Blacks across the South.

The story of Robert Smalls should be widely taught and celebrated. In his life, he saw slavery, emancipation, the right of Black men to vote, and the ability of Black men to serve in high-ranking positions in the military and government. Moreover, Smalls was one of the main reasons the Union allowed Blacks to fight in their ranks. Smalls is nothing short of a hero, and he is a perfect illustration of the country learning from its mistakes and correcting course to do what is right.[78] He would later go on to found the South Carolina Republican Party.

Tragically, Lincoln did not live to see the full effects of Union victory as John Wilkes Booth assassinated him days after Robert E. Lee surrendered at Appomattox Court House. Booth murdered Lincoln because he did not want to see Blacks granted US citizenship or the right to vote, which Lincoln promised days before.[79] In other words, Lincoln was murdered because after winning the Civil War, he wanted America to heal in the only way possible, which was to extend citizenship and the right to vote to Blacks across the country. Before the Civil War, free Blacks in a few states, such as Pennsylvania, New York, and New Jersey, possessed the right to vote in state-level races at various points in history.[80] Lincoln would not live to see the ratification of the Fourteenth Amendment[81] that overturned *Dred Scott* and granted citizenship to Blacks or the ratification of the Fifteenth Amendment[82] that granted the right to vote to Blacks.

These constitutional amendments that extended funda-mental rights to Blacks were not radical attempts to remake

American society, as some assert.[83] Rather, they were adjustments meant so Black Americans could partake in the promise of the Declaration of Independence: that all men are created equal. Though this was possible only through the blood and suffering of civil war, the goal was right and just.

The transition away from slavery and towards the rebuilding of the American nation was a period defined by the principle of creative destruction: what was old and inefficient was uprooted to make room for something better. This story played out across the United States and especially in the South, where the old slavery-based economy no longer existed. Unsurprisingly, this set off massive migratory movements, particularly of Black Americans to Northern states.

All of these changes were shaped in some ways by the larger trend in the American economy toward higher levels of industrialization, the consequences of which would transform the country in the following decades.

Something that we think is worth repeating about the Civil War period is that some aspects of the South's resistance to the abolition of slavery arose from the anxiety of the Southern plantation class about what *its* future would be in a new competitive economy and egalitarian society. To be sure, some in the South fought the war to preserve slavery. But some drivers of the conflict were a clear cohort that did well under the prevailing economic system and did not want to risk losing out. Their worry was that if the South moved on from slavery, they may be eclipsed by new wealth and new people. In this regard, wealthy slave owners were no different than the feudal lords of Europe who waged war for their own personal enrichment, cementing their social status by no merit of their contributions to society.

Another sad but important lesson from the Civil War is that the political process is often one of the greatest impediments to market forces and the positive changes they so often usher in. While not perfect, a rule we largely subscribe to is this: those most opposed to creative destruction are often those defending the least defensible institutions and policies. Rent-seeking, or the use of power by individuals to extract wealth without earning it, is almost always about one group of people doing everything possible to shield itself from change—even when doing so hurts others (and often the majority too). When the American system of meritocracy is at its best, the principle of creative destruction flourishes, and rent-seeking is minimized. Those who believe in themselves, work hard, and persevere cannot reach their full potential with impediments put in place by people at the top who are afraid of new ideas.

Fortunately, the Constitution provides our government with a safe means of embracing creative destruction in the political sphere without the drawbacks of a process predicated on fleeting popular sentiments. For popular sentiments to be enacted into law or taken away from the democratic process by a constitutional amendment, consensus is needed. The Founders mixed the need to build consensus, republican principles, and democratic practices to obtain the greatest benefits from each without the threats. America is at its best when it embraces creative destruction. The constitutional amendments that resulted from the Civil War and Reconstruction emphasize this point.

III. The Work Is Never Done: The Reconstruction Period and Beyond

A fact that is both great and tragic in American civic life is that the struggle toward a better future is unending. That is especially true in America because of our culture of self-healing with respect to the aftermath of the Civil War, both in the case of reconstruction and of the country more broadly. Lincoln led the country through the Civil War, defeated the Confederacy, ended slavery, and was assassinated for it. Thankfully, he put forth a plan to physically and politically rebuild the almost shattered country even though he did not live long enough to see it through.

While the Reconstruction Amendments, the Thirteenth, Fourteenth, and Fifteenth Amendments were a start, a new problem developed in the South. Specifically, elites began to push back on the efforts of Reconstruction as a means to renege on America's commitments to the civil rights of Black Americans.[84]

In a similar regard, the Founders created a system of government designed to promote individual liberty and opportunity. But the Founding was *not* enough on its own so long as the injustice of slavery was tolerated on American soil. The US thus did a great thing in ending slavery and taking the first step toward embracing a culture of self-healing. Still, a new problem emerged: the Jim Crow laws. Federal legislation alone could not remedy the culture that had previously supported a society that had repeatedly and systematically violated the rights of men through slavery.

Jim Crow laws sprung up around the South and created a split legal system: there would be rules for White people, and there would be rules for Black people. And in all cases, those rules were meant to empower the same elite class of Southerners whose fixation with and commitment to slavery had brought about the Civil War. In other words, through Jim Crow, the South sought to nullify the Reconstruction Amendments, put Blacks in the position they were in before the Civil War, and preserve the power and influence of the ruling class.

Sadly, the Jim Crow phenomenon gained steam in the nineteenth century and was not finally resolved until the latter half of the 1900s, almost seventy years later. This is a deep embarrassment to the country, and one that everyone should acknowledge. At the same time, we should embrace the fact that America arose from the turmoil of the Civil War in better shape than before. After all, the Union persevered, slavery was ended, and Blacks finally began to be afforded the fundamental promises made in the Declaration of Independence. To be sure, these events also demonstrate America's unique culture of self-healing. We must recognize that the Civil War and Reconstruction were necessary to repair the damage done by slavery.

The United States' shared cultural aspiration of working towards a better future is a recurring phenomenon in our history, and we should be proud of it, both because it shows that our past is bigger than its failings and because it highlights our capacity for growth and self-reflection. On top of that, this kind of self-correction is rare. In our view, the later story of the Confederate General Robert E. Lee is striking proof of these ideas.

Many Americans know how he was a renowned general who was originally tapped to lead the Union Army but could not fight against his native Virginia. What is less known about Lee is the work he did *after* the Civil War concluded.

After the Civil War concluded, Lee was stripped of his citizenship. But he could not leave Virginia. Resolved to stay, he originally believed that he would spend the remainder of his life as a farmer.

But his life took a very different turn when Washington College in Lexington, Virginia, asked him about joining the school as its president. Lee came aboard and quickly righted the university's financial situation; his name brought hundreds of new students into the school, and its future moved in a better trajectory. He also famously told the trustees of the university that, "it is the duty of every citizen, in the present condition of the Country, to do all in his power to aid in the restoration of peace and harmony."[85] Lee was determined to do something right with this new opportunity.

This position gave Lee a chance to help the country at large. In his role as an educator, Lee pushed his students to grow into American citizens, which was an acute contrast with how he himself had been raised, i.e., to see himself as a Virginian first. There is a famous anecdote concerning Lee during this time in his life, and it involved a bereft and angry widow of a Confederate soldier. The woman wrote to Lee about her bitterness and resentment toward the North. To this, Lee responded that she should "dismiss from [her] mind all sectional feeling, and bring [your children] up to be Americans."[86]

Lee's life after the Civil War perfectly captures the redemptive nature of American history, and it showcases how our civil institutions make this kind of correction possible. Something to take away from this is that while this kind of reform is possible, it is ultimately a choice. Lee decided of his own volition to do this, and he did so because he understood that the war was over, the side he led lost, and everyone needed to move on for the better as Americans, not Virginians.

This is also a wonderful example of how our country provides second chances and is stronger for granting them. Lee could have lived out his days bitter and isolated. In fact, he could have just as easily aligned himself with the wealthy Southern class (of which he was a member) or done what his former comrade, Nathan Bedford Forrest, did when he founded the Ku Klux Klan.[87]

Lee did not do this, and it is for this reason we believe that the end of his story is more complex than simply judging him as good or evil. This is not to say Lee redeemed himself for his actions—far from it. But like America, he aspired to be better and engaged in self-healing, which must not be forgotten. In the end, America's ability to engage in self-healing is the reason America is here today. And it is a big reason why so many people want to come here and become permanent members of our civic community.

Still, there are some who look too negatively on this aspect of American life and history. For these critics, it is an indictment of our country that we have these struggles rather than a point of celebration that we have these problems and can work to overcome them.

In our view, this is the dividing line in politics today: is America bigger than its problems, even and especially the problems that it works to fix? And contrary to what some critics suggest, we want everyone to know all aspects of American history, because it is only then that they will fully appreciate the totality of what we and our ancestors have accomplished.

The American story is an inspiring one, and it is not over, just as the struggle for the Constitutional rights of Black Americans did not end with the North's victory in the Civil War. In the following chapter, we will discuss the developments and problems posed by segregation, as well as some of the disruptive forces that further transformed American life.

CHAPTER 4

INDUSTRIALIZATION, MODERNIZATION, AND WAR 1850S–1940S

"The only thing necessary for the triumph of evil is for good men to do nothing."
—*Edmund Burke*

I. The Original Tech Boom

In the early decades of the nineteenth century, there were significant changes to the world's economy that reached down into the lives of all populations, rich and poor alike. Technology was changing at a rapid clip; people were moving from rural areas to cities for work; and new business opportunities and industries were developing. More people than ever were engaged in commerce, and that generated tremendous capital, which, in turn, spurred investment in infrastructure and other development projects.

In many ways, it was the beginning of a Golden Age for the American Dream. Anyone who had the determination and vision to succeed had more opportunities than ever before. And as time passed, those opportunities continued to expand and become more accessible to all Americans.

The engine behind these changes was technological innovation, and it would revolutionize how people lived and worked in only a few decades.

Much of the force behind this movement had its roots in the thinking of the prior century, which by the early 1800s had become ascendant. Specifically, the Enlightenment era, with its varied emphasis on rationalism, empiricism, and rigorous analysis of previously held beliefs, influenced people across Europe and North America to rethink core aspects of the world around them as well as man's potential to shape human existence.[88]

In practical terms, this situation translated into heightened levels of interest in education, innovation, and technology.[89] It is no surprise that there were so many life-changing breakthroughs in the sciences and medicine during this age. On top of that, inventors were actively engaged with rethinking technology, and they kept these new methodologies in mind.

Unsurprisingly, their contributions arrived quickly and made an impact. A few of these innovations include the electrical battery, the steam locomotive, and the sewing machine. Taken together, these developments are part of the larger period known as industrialization. Technology ultimately drove social and political changes, and wealth accumulated like never before.

In this chapter, we will focus on these changes in the American context, as they transformed the economy, politics, and civil society. While most of these changes were net positives, there were some drawbacks, and we will address these in the second half of the chapter.

II. Why We Grew

There is a famous saying about how Rome was not built in a day. This is true, and it captures the reality that, most of the time, a civilization takes decades (if not centuries) to mature and build out its infrastructure and hegemony. But to emphasize a point, this is true *most* of the time. There are exceptions, and America is an example.

While it was not built in a day, America as it exists today— i.e., as a major industrialized power—was to a large extent built in the second half of the nineteenth century and in the first decades of the twentieth century. It was during this time when the fundamentals of the modern American economy were established.

In our view, there are three principal reasons for this uniquely American boom, all of which were touched on earlier in the book and have their genesis in the pre-American period.

First, America had a favorable situation when it came to resources. There was lots of land, relatively favorable topography for travel, and low barriers (proverbial and real) to travel so that almost everyone could participate in the economy in a new state or territory with little geographic difficulty. As the western half of North America opened after the Civil War, this factor came into play again in a big way.

Second, the New World and later America attracted immigrants who dreamed of better lives and wanted to work to manifest their goals. To put things in perspective, the population in the US increased from forty million in 1870 to ninety-nine million by 1914.[90] This was a major boon for economic growth. While in the colonial period, these immigrants were predominantly European, in the nineteenth century and beyond, the makeup of the immigrants evolved. Still, their desire to come and work did not. America's workforce also grew in another significant way internally during this time: millions of Black Americans were now free citizens who could begin to participate fully in the workforce.

Third, America's shared culture promoted social continuity and stability and led to a relatively tranquil political situation. Notable features included honesty, fair play, and shared moral values.

The added virtue of this stable political situation (aside from the fact that politics was not as existential and violent as it was elsewhere in the world) was that people could focus on their own lives. On top of that, Washington, DC, was not micromanaging people's affairs, and civil society was robust. People were more concerned about their own affairs, and improving their own financial well-being became the primary focus for millions of Americans. Calvin Coolidge's observation in 1925 that "the chief business of the American people is business" rings especially true of this era.

But another factor that matters a great deal to the American story during the period from 1865 to 1900, and that deserves special consideration, is that in this era, entre-preneurs and market forces were empowered. To be precise, these forces were empowered because there were very few barriers to market entry and very little regulation once individuals and businesses entered the market.

In practical terms, this meant that the government did not impose constraints on contracts, did not mandate terms, did not require costly inspections, and generally allowed people to make their own decisions concerning their employment.[91] How the government regulates the market matters, as there are certain cases where regulations can create a necessary public good for monopolistic markets, such as utilities. Regulations, when done properly, are the messages that workers and entrepreneurs receive from the government about if and how they can go about starting their businesses and earning a living. The message from the government in the 1860s onward was clear: go out and pursue your interests—we will not stop you. Regulations during this period were few, clear, and easy to understand.

The government's message in this period was heard by Americans and immigrants interested in coming to America loud and clear. From 1860 to 1890, the US Patent Office issued five hundred thousand patents. But while this might not sound like a large number over thirty years, this was actually more than ten times as many issued in the previous seventy years and far more than any other country during this time.[92] Between 1865 and 1914, inventions like a new basic material in steel, a new basic fuel in oil, a new power source through electricity, a new transportation vehicle in the motorcar, a new communication device in the telephone, and the internal combustion engine were all created. In terms of producing steel, the US went from producing a yearly total of 380,000 tons in 1870 to 28.4 million by 1913.[93] And while the US only produced a yearly total of 26 million barrels of oil in 1880, it was producing a yearly total of 442 million by 1920.[94] All of this was possible because the government's message to the economy was that innovation is a good thing.

Consider what this looked like in America during this time. A person could be born and raised in Georgia, where he could master a particular craft. If he wanted to travel out past the Mississippi, he could do so and continue to use his talents to practice his profession. There was no government exam he needed to pass to work and no forms to fill out. In short, people who wanted to work could, and they got to keep more of the proceeds of their labor. This created a positive feedback loop that incentivized individuals to work hard and achieve more.

We think that in America today we have gotten away from that simple idea. Incentives matter, and not all companies and people can negotiate them in the same ways. All too often, smaller firms and more limited people opt not to take risks, and that works to the advantage of the larger firms that can absorb the higher costs. In the end, people and industry suffer as competition and innovation decline. Barriers to entry, when created predominately by the government, exist to serve the political elite and prevent competition or new ideas from those who want to provide a better service or product. This is another factor of what made America so dynamic during this period: there were very few barriers to entry, allowing competition and ideas to flourish.

A serious virtue of the incentive structure of the second half of the 1800s is that the relatively lax stance of the state vis-à-vis the costs it put on business encouraged risk-taking: an invaluable incentive that is often found in the stories of the greatest business ventures and scientific breakthroughs. In the nineteenth century, America encouraged risk-taking by rewarding the winners. The American people of that time and their offspring benefited from improvements in their health and well-being. Life expectancy in 1860 was just 39.4 years, rising quickly to 54.1 years in 1915.[95]

Take the example of Hetty Green, who in many ways exemplified the spirit of the times. While today she is known as the Witch of Wall Street, she was born in 1834 and raised as a strict Quaker in a powerful business family. Growing up, her family encouraged her to develop an interest in finance. As part of her education, she was required to read the financial pages in the newspaper to her father and grandfather, both of whom were successful whaling agents. At age eight, she opened her first bank account, and at age ten, she was sent to a strict Quaker boarding school in Massachusetts.[96] After boarding school, she served as the family's bookkeeper and accountant.[97]

Even though she was raised with the importance of finance in mind, Green needed to find her own way into the industry. During the 1860s and through the 1920s, women played almost no meaningful role in the financial services or investment field and certainly no role on Wall Street. That industry was exclusively for wealthy men. Women, on the other hand, were expected to stay at home and raise the family. For the most part, they had no role outside the home.

While Green was fortunate to inherit money from members of her family, albeit in strange circumstances, she took that money and made smart investment decisions. It was because of these decisions that she ultimately earned the respect she deserved, despite being a woman in this field. She prioritized value investing and refused to buy stocks on the margin.[98] She also invested in railroads and government bonds and always had a large amount of liquid assets on hand in case she needed to make a loan.[99] It is estimated that she died with $100,000,000 in her estate.[100]

Green's story is too often discounted because she was born into money. But that misses the larger point. Green succeeded based on hard work and talent in an industry that was run by and featured only men—and she did so because her talent for investing could not be suppressed or stolen by the men who dominated that industry at the time. In our system of meritocracy, there can be no place for industries that toss work ethic and smart ideas aside solely to appease those at the top. As stated earlier, industries erect barriers to protect those at the top and prevent new people and ideas from finding success. However, our system of meritocracy embraces new ideas and competition, and it allows people to succeed who believe in themselves, work hard, and persevere even when all the odds are against them. Green had these characteristics, which is why she was able to succeed.

When this favorable business climate was combined with a glut of natural resources, a stable political situation, and a stream of immigrants ready to work, the combination produced astounding levels of growth across the US. Immigrants fled Europe for the US, looking for a new beginning at an incredibly high rate. In the 1880s, 5.3 million people moved to the US from Europe, an increase of 10.5 percent from the beginning of the decade.[101]

What is more, the development of infrastructure, especially railroads, and innovations in transportation meant that people could easily move around the country to put their talents to use. In every way, the second half of the nineteenth century was an advantageous environment for workers and businesses. In fact, the annual rate of productivity growth from 1800 to 1890 was just 1.4 percent on average, but that rate grew from 1889 to 1899 to an average of more than 2 percent.[102]

While we think there are many great aspects to this period, there were also downsides. To be precise, there were two big issues. First, businesses did not always abide by best practices with workers; some people were selfish and did not provide safe work environments, while others did not treat their employees fairly, either because they wanted to cut costs or because they simply did not care about them.

Second, some large businesses, once they successfully cornered their respective markets, engaged in abusive behavior toward consumers. These companies degenerated into monopolies and set arbitrary prices, which boxed out competitors and hurt consumers. This is because, by keeping competitors out, they limited innovation and negated one of the virtues of competitive markets, namely that they force businesses to adapt and take risks. This was an anti-market stance, it was incompatible with the risk-taking ethos of American business and life, and it went against everything inherent to an effective meritocracy.

Both of these problems were bad, albeit for different reasons. Thankfully, they were resolved through a mix of changes in civil society and politics. Laws regulating monopolies and worker health and safety both sprang up in the later years of the nineteenth century and ensured that bad business practices would be checked when and where the market could not do so itself.[103]

The upshot is that America enjoyed robust economic growth and its attendant beneficial social effects for decades. The country grew richer, and opportunities for social advancement became more accessible to a greater number of people.

Thanks in large part to the industrialization of America, men like John D. Rockefeller and Andrew Carnegie built enormous fortunes as they produced essential goods for the country.[104] And in keeping with the spirit of charity that defined early American life, these men also gave back, and their donations helped establish medical research institutes and public libraries. The market was working incredibly well in the US during this time.

Still, we would be remiss not to mention one of the defining features of this age: change. Industrialization was a radical, at times uncomfortable, and at all times fast-moving process. People who started off poor could quickly reverse their fortunes, and vice versa. The glut of opportunity available to many Americans at this time meant that the proverbial "rags to riches" cliche was a very real and relatively common part of life in the country.

To reiterate, this was *not* the norm within the developed nations of Europe. The influences of the aristocracy and their institutions constrained opportunity in the Old World, and they put a ceiling on social advancement. Industrialization in America, while problematic in some ways, did not suffer from this setback; that is a big reason why the country did so well during the final decades of the nineteenth century and the early years of the 1900s: it had a better system, and it showed.

III. Industrialization's Critic: Marx, Communism, and the World Wars

The history of industrialization is largely a positive story. Ordinary people prospered, the standard of living rose, and the early societies to industrialize advanced at a tremendous rate by virtually every metric.[105]

Make no mistake, early industrialization was at times brutal, even as it brought on a rapid decline in poverty. Again, as we mentioned, some of these included ugly and unfair conditions for workers and anti-competitive behavior. But there was another downside to this period, one that changed the course of the following century and had more far-ranging and disastrous outcomes than any poorly managed steel mill.

Unfortunately, instead of looking at the industrialization period as a positive, one person in particular looked at it solely through a critical lens. And even worse, many people agreed with his assessment across the industrialized world and took political action accordingly, both in the 1800s and in the 1900s, when Europe was more modernized and less sound politically.

That person was Karl Marx, and the collection of his writings forms the intellectual underpinnings of a critique of capitalism that, if taken seriously, is incompatible with free markets, individual choice, and an open society.[106]

According to Marx, virtually all aspects of capitalism are bad because, as a system, it structured the economy in such a way that exploited workers insofar as they did not receive the total benefit for their labor. What is notable about this critique is that workers were free to work as they pleased, but to Marx, this freedom was illusory. In the end, capitalism was no different than slavery or feudalism, at least as Marx saw it.

All of the defining features of a market economy are a cause for concern under a Marxist interpretation because of the inequality inherent in a free society. As Marx saw it, the nature of the capitalist enterprise was contradictory and exploitative, so it needed to, and would, be replaced.[107] Marxism is *not* based on meritocracy, skill, talent, or hard work. It is the opposite of what our American system represents and celebrates.

Marx was convinced that the capitalist system would be replaced because history is dialectic, an evolving process moving towards the future by way of the resolution of conflicts in the present and by way of changes in the ways goods are produced.[108] Each advance of industrialization in the economy would lead to capitalism, but the failures of capitalism would make way for communism. Markets will ultimately fail, and they will be replaced along the road to communism, an idyllic world that Marx said very little about and for which he supplied no political roadmap.

What is strange about Marx and the ideology he left to those who believe in his theories is that it said very little about policy and left much up to the imagination of its adherents. Instead, it created a new moral framework to analyze politics. The soil where Marxism took hold was not without its problems. For instance, some people had to leave behind their families to move to urban areas for work, some factories were unsafe and workers were seriously injured, and absolute gains were not felt immediately throughout society. General discontent was funneled into ideological fervor.

As a result, political movements that espoused Marxist principles arose across Europe in the 1800s; by the early 1900s, these organizations had real teeth. The strategy of these extreme groups was to appeal to people by speaking to them not as individuals, but as members of a class, the pro-letariat. Together, they could improve their collective stand-ing. And the suggested method to achieve their shared ends? Violent revolution.

In the early 1900s, especially in the lead-up to and in the period directly following World War I, when socialism and political chaos were rising to a uniquely high degree, Marxism was ascendant and omnipresent, particularly in Germany and Russia. Virtually every country that participated in the war had a burgeoning socialist party, which was predominantly influenced by Marxism, and there was a belief by the radi-cals that they were on the cusp of taking over the "decadent" Western states. Moderates were mortified and unsure of how to handle these groups.

These efforts at regime change did not always succeed, but in one famous case, revolutionary socialists *did* over-throw a government: the tsarist regime in Russia. The success of the *Bolsheviks* in 1917 marked a turning point in history that would lead to a century of conflict and oppression.[109]

For the first time, the communists were in charge of a major country (albeit one that was not exactly fully industrialized), and they quickly went to work butchering dissenters, repressing Russian national history and traditions, instituting aggressive discriminatory policies, crippling the economy, and initiating a series of horrific man-made famines that claimed the lives of millions. Marx would have been shocked to see Russia take the mantle as the leading communist country of the time as it skipped what he believed was the necessary capitalist period.

The other aspect of communist rule in Russia is that its leader set up organizations and channels with socialists abroad to try and foment uprisings in other European countries.[110] The Comintern, in particular, was a tool that they used to further this goal, and while it had mixed success (there was never an internationalist socialist revolt across Europe, as Vladimir Lenin thought there would be), it put conservatives and liberals in Western Europe on alert that, if they were not vigilant, they could have a socialist revolution in their country to contend with.[111]

While one legacy of the communists was the tremendous loss of human life that they were *directly* responsible for, they have another even darker achievement: engendering a massive, bloody response to their terrible programs. Specifically, the communist threat to European culture and freedom was one of the primary factors in the rise of Nazism in Germany in the 1930s, an equally unhinged and violent movement.[112]

This secondary effect of the communist movement deserves special attention.

The Nazis offered another ideology in fascism: they were not communists because they believed in nationalism and the importance of German history, but they were also not capitalists, who they saw as responsible for the rise of communism in the first place. The defining characteristic of the Nazi regime was corporatism, or the organization of the economy by the country. The government would pick all winners, and the market would be a slave to the whims of the party.

It should be said that Germany was in a bizarre place politically after World War I. The old political system—something of a mixed regime with monarchical and republican elements—was thrown out, and disorder ensued. A series of revolutions, some successful and others failures, occurred in the following years. This period of the Weimar Republic was a scary time, and ordinary citizens looked east to Russia and wondered if a *Bolshevik*-style government was on its way with the next upheaval.

The Nazi Party was determined to prevent this, and over several years, they engaged in escalating levels of violence to repress the communist, moderate, and conservative parties. By the early 1930s, the party and its leader, Adolf Hitler, had secured power and were busy militarizing the state and harassing their perceived enemies.

To distill the Nazi ideology, one must understand that they were radicals who hated communism and blamed Jews for its rise. And though there were some Jewish communists in Germany, there were also many Muslim, Christian, and atheist communists as well. Neither race nor religion dictates political views, or much else for that matter. Once the common framework in Germany dissipated, politics became existential, and this kind of dangerous thinking took hold.

Nonetheless, Hitler's fixation with the supposed Jewish responsibility for Marxism and the policies of the *Bolsheviks* was one of the reasons for his decision to commit horrific crimes against the Jews, as well as others who opposed him. This rage led to massacres, pogroms, and eventually the Holocaust, or the industrialized attempt at the extermination of an entire group of people because of who they were or what they believed.

This is the condensed story of the ideological conflicts that led to World War II. Hitler decided that he needed to build a non-capitalist, non-Marxist future for Germany. And when he acted on that urge, he threw the industrialized world into another vicious, worldwide conflict that, in the end, claimed over one hundred million lives.

We do not think it is too extreme to say that this was perhaps the worst point in human history, both due to the ugliness of the ideologies responsible for the conflict and because of the staggering loss of life. World War II was, put simply, an international war that was the result of a dangerous, disintegrating worldview that brought out the worst of humanity.

Ultimately, the Allied powers triumphed, but at a tremendous cost: France, England, and the USSR (which fought with the allies after Hitler violated the Molotov–Ribbentrop Pact) were bled white. On the Axis side, every state was wiped out. Only the US left World War II with an assuredly promising future ahead.

It should be added that there is another prominent example of the ruin of Marxism from this era, and it serves as a powerful counterargument to the claim that socialism simply went off the rails because of the particular factors at play in Russia. The case of China shows that, wherever it is tried, socialism, Marxism, communism—whatever flag these policies fly under—will lead to the same awful outcomes. And if we fixate on creating specific material outcomes, we will be well on our way to another calamitous mistake.

Without getting too far down in the weeds on communism in China, it can summarily be said that, following the communist victory in their civil war, the Chinese Marxists, led by Mao Zedong, got their chance to build a socialist state.[113] The results were a series of man-made disasters on a mind-numbing scale, which included the death of millions.

Over the course of only a few years, Mao and his allies had forcibly restructured the Chinese economy and, in turn, its agricultural system. This directly led to a series of famines that killed millions.[114] At the same time, the communists executed a plan to reshape Chinese culture, which set off a series of enormous political repressions, forced deportations, and violent conflicts between classes.[115]

The Chinese communists ruined China, trashed its economy, and killed millions of people. In other words, they did the exact same thing that the Bolsheviks did in Russia. While it is true that China is a significant global power today, and though it remains a communist state, it has survived only because it has embraced many market principles while remaining true to its autocratic history, or market totalitarianism.

For now, the main takeaway is that the communist exper-iment failed massively during this period of history, and the socialist ideology is largely responsible for some of the biggest wars and largest atrocities in recent human history.

IV. The World After War

World War II was a terrible time in human history, and in our view, it is irredeemable. The loss of human life, the destruc-tion of so many countries, the loss of irreplaceable history, art, and architecture—all of it is as sad as the destruction was pointless.

If there is one silver lining, it is that the US did not lose as much as the other participants in the war, and it enjoyed a rise to hegemony after the war. But one should not think this came without its own costs. As will be discussed in the fol-lowing chapter, America went through its own struggles and political transformations in the decade leading up to its entry into World War II.

Some things in society progressed, such as women gain-ing the right to vote, while others were damaging and a sign of things to come in the future, such as the massive expan-sion of government during the war effort. The most import-ant aspect of all these changes, though, was the fundamental transformation of the way in which Americans conducted politics. Specifically, in the 1930s, the Constitution sustained a challenge from which it never recovered. We turn next to domestic American history, from 1930 through 1990.

CHAPTER 5

THE RISE OF BIG GOVERNMENT

*"In a composite nation like ours, as before the law,
there should be no rich, no poor, no high, no low,
no white, no black, but common country, common
citizenship, equal rights and a common destiny."*
—Frederick Douglass

I. Economic and Constitutional Backsliding: 1929–1945

As the previous chapter should make clear, the period from roughly 1910 to 1945 was a profoundly unstable, bizarre, and disturbing time in pretty much every European state, much of East Asia, and Eurasia. But North America and Australia were also touched by the conflict.

Obviously, the European and Asian states got the worst of it, so to speak, when World War II ended, while the US remained relatively undamaged. America was in a relatively great position after the world wars, was not involved in any ethnic cleansings, and avoided communist and fascist revolutions. Plus, it was American intervention in both world wars that saved Europe from being consumed by those dangerous ideologies. This was all possible because the fundamentals of America worked; namely there was a consensus that we were playing the right role on the world stage, and this consensus insulated the US from threats while also providing it with the capabilities to win these wars.

At the same time, we said very little about what went on politically in the US during this period. In this chapter, we fill in that gap because it is an essential piece of modern American history; we will also focus on the transformations in American life from the 1930s up to the tech boom of the 1990s. These moments were revolutionary and created the America we live in today.

The place to start in America is in the 1930s for this discussion. It was at this time that the economic explosion from about 1860 onward slowed down and eventually reversed itself by some measures. The defining event of this period was the Great Depression, a massive period of stagnation and pain for millions of Americans and for people around the world.

The Great Depression was instigated by the crash of the stock market (though many still disagree about whether this was *the* cause), and its fall was felt throughout the US and the world. Many people who bought stocks did so on loans, which generated leverage, so when the stocks went down, their losses were magnified many times over. For example, a 5 percent drop in price could result in a 25 percent loss on a particular investment, and with additional leverage, many times more.

Over roughly the next decade, markets were sluggish, unemployment was high, and consumer optimism was abysmal. By some measures, America's GDP fell 15 percent, a figure that is almost unimaginable given that the crash of 2008 and 2009, awful as it was, reduced America's GDP by a puny 1 percent in comparison.[116]

As deflation (the reduction in the value of goods and services) took hold, people grew more pessimistic, and consumption slowed down. This, in turn, hurt domestic companies, which prompted the US to adopt harsher anti-trade measures to boost domestic manufacturers. All this accomplished in practice was to limit global trade, which did not work because trade is a key aspect of the American market system. Everyone was made worse off.

The Great Depression was fundamentally different from other economic crises to this point because of the interconnectedness of American industry and financial activity. To try to illustrate this, consider that because people lost money on their investments, they opted not to invest their money elsewhere, which, in turn, impacted their consumer behavior. These secondary and tertiary effects touched all aspects of the American market, from the automobile industry to agriculture. Without the demand for goods, the need for workers fell. Consequently, unemployment ballooned in urban areas. The Great Depression, therefore, is an example of economic weakness in one segment of the economy infecting others and, in the process, creating a negative feedback loop that drives economic activity down broadly as that contagion spreads.

The cumulative effect of these trends was a total slowdown in almost every American industry.[117] People felt this and were unnerved when these trends did not reverse themselves over time; when the country plunged deeper into economic distress, it looked as though the entire American enterprise was vulnerable in a way it had not been since perhaps the Civil War.

The acute economic decline of the late 1920s through the early 1930s created a unique political situation. President Herbert Hoover and the Republicans in Congress, which implemented many of the same anti-market programs of the Roosevelt administration that succeeded it, were blamed for the recession and voted out of office in 1932.

Hoover's challenger, Franklin Roosevelt, won in a decisive landslide. The Democratic governor of New York, Roosevelt campaigned on, and won with, a promise: to end the recession.[118] To achieve this goal, Roosevelt said America would need the government to act—and in a big way. There was a role for government in Roosevelt's platform that was unlike anything that came before it. After his record-breaking tenure, Washington would become a part of the average citizen's life.

This message was well received by voters, and Roosevelt was propelled to the White House with sizable majorities in Congress. Over the first years of his administration, Congress would pass a constellation of bills that together would constitute the first New Deal (the Second New Deal would pass later on).[119] While controversial in their scope and dubious in their effectiveness at dealing with the economic problem, these laws, as well as Roosevelt's executive orders, were popular, and he won more seats for his movement in 1934.[120]

Taken together, the New Deal put the government on the side of labor, provided subsidies to various industries, legalized or sanctioned *some* cartels, transformed the relationship between industry and the state, and regulated banks, among other things.[121] These laws had a profound impact on American political institutions and norms, and they worked to enhance the power of the White House and the importance of the presidency, as well as the expectations for presidents. In other words, Roosevelt radically altered the political structure and trajectory of the US.

Roosevelt's personality and ambitions were larger than the Constitution, as evidenced by his critiques of it and disregard for the practices built around it. At a time in Europe when dictatorship, demagogic promises, and the cult of personality were on the rise, it looked as though America might get its own taste of authoritarianism in the form of a charismatic and ideologically strident president who would dismiss the rule of law for political expediency.

For some, these fears were substantiated when Roosevelt infamously tried to pack the Supreme Court. He wanted to add more of his own justices to the bench because the current court had ruled against him in a series of high-profile cases involving the New Deal.[122] In short, many of the New Deal proposals were flagrant violations of the Constitution, but Roosevelt did not care. To him, the Constitution was an impediment, and he sought to evade the rules rather than build the required consensus to alter the Constitution.

As we have written in previous chapters, consensus is needed for major and transformational changes in America. It was that consensus that led the colonies to sign the Declaration

of Independence, adopt and ratify our Constitution, and ratify the Reconstruction Amendments ending slavery. Instead
of going to the American people and proposing a constitutional amendment that would require great consensus,
Roosevelt tried to achieve the same thing in a much more
nefarious way. By changing the composition of the court,
Roosevelt could change how it interpreted the Constitution.
In short, Roosevelt rejected the American way of consensus.
His agenda was more important than the protections afforded
by the Constitution.

Roosevelt tried to alter the court's composition with the
Judicial Procedures Reform Bill of 1937, a law that would
grant him the power to add judges (up to six total) for every
judge on the court over the age of seventy.[123] This was as
poorly concealed a power grab as any in American history.

This move was also an obvious and deliberate threat to the
Constitution and the American political system. Roosevelt's
plan was really about whether one man could dictate the laws
of the country in direct contrast to the American tradition of
building a consensus for fundamental and transformational
changes. This period also marked a significant moment in
another troubling and growing trend in American government—namely, the expanding reach and influence of the
executive branch over the legislative and judicial branches.

Ultimately, Roosevelt was rebuked by the media and his
own party for the gambit, and the bill failed.[124] That said,
Roosevelt's plan did *not* fail. Specifically, though the bill
failed, Roosevelt nonetheless succeeded in intimidating the
Supreme Court, which reversed itself and consistently ruled
in his favor shortly thereafter. The so-called "switch in time

that saved nine" delivered to Roosevelt the de facto victory that the formal political process denied him.[125]

In the following years, the Supreme Court weakened property rights and rewrote the Constitution to expand government power in a way it never had before, which was very favorable to Roosevelt's political goals. Perhaps the most egregious such case was *Wickard v. Filburn.*[126] Under a New Deal law that limited how much wheat farmers could grow, Filburn grew wheat on his own property in excess of that amount.[127] Filburn argued the law was unconstitutional because he grew the extra wheat for his own consumption, and that the commerce clause, which empowers Congress to regulate commerce "among the several states,"[128] did not reach his wholly local, intrastate activity.[129] In a 9–0 decision, with a court composed of six justices FDR appointed, the court held the commerce clause *did* empower Congress to regulate Filburn growing wheat for his own personal consumption.[130]

The effects of *Wickard* cannot be underscored enough. To that point, the court had consistently held that wholly local, intrastate activities were outside the scope of Congress's authority under the commerce clause. It makes sense as to why. The clause empowers Congress to regulate commerce among the several states, i.e., things that go across state lines, *not* within the several states, and certainly *not* products grown for one's personal consumption with no broader economic impact. In short, under *Wickard*, the commerce clause allowed Congress to essentially regulate anything. In fact, it would take more than fifty years for the court to hold that an act of Congress fell outside the scope of the commerce clause in *United States v. Lopez* (1995).[131]

Roosevelt succeeded in remaking the American regime in his own image. When Roosevelt left this world and the presidency, the executive branch was bigger, the protections of the Constitution smaller, and the property rights of all Americans substantially weaker. Those changes remain in place, and so do the problems they created, some of which we will touch on later in the book.

The great irony of all this is despite how hard Roosevelt pushed to legalize his counterproductive economic schemes, the economy never recovered because of them, and, if anything, the New Deal may have delayed the economic recovery.[132]

Amazingly, Roosevelt's close friend and adviser, Treasury Secretary Henry Morgenthau, admitted as much to Congress in 1939 when he said: "we have tried spending money...after eight years of this Administration we have just as much unemployment as when we started...and [now] an enormous debt to boot."[133] There is a simple lesson here: expanding government spending rarely solves the country's problems and, if anything, can send the wrong messages to businesses, employers, and the unemployed, ultimately leading to a delayed recovery and prolonging the negative effects of a weak economy.

Roosevelt's most praiseworthy accomplishment was his role in guiding the United States through World War II. But perhaps his greatest domestic achievement, depending on your perspective, is effecting a legal and political revolution in the country that remains with us today. His lasting domestic legacy, outside of restructuring the Constitution, is the two-fold tendency of government—first, to promise to fix problems it cannot easily solve, and second, to expand its influence and scope. The state has not stopped growing since the 1930s. This, too, is Roosevelt's legacy, and no American president to date has been able to transcend it.

II. Rising Tides: The Post-War Economy and Civil Rights Movement

If the 1930s and early 1940s were defined by economic stagnation that was exacerbated by President Roosevelt's New Deal programs, then the 1940s through the mid-1960s were defined by the acceleration of growth, opportunity, and civic equality. America underwent profound change in this period, much of it good and well-intentioned, albeit some of it has not aged well.

To begin this period, the American economy finally awoke from its long slumber in the last years of World War II. The wartime economy faded, and private industry began to grow rapidly.

The period of economic expansion following the end of World War II has been called the Golden Age of Capitalism in America. Many industries started out in the 1940s and 1950s, while established ones reached new heights. Agriculture and travel are two great examples of industries that grew exponentially in this period, and the establishment of the Interstate Highway System contributed to both.[134]

But two especially large factors are largely responsible for the consistent growth that the country enjoyed from the 1940s into the 1970s.

First, thousands of veterans returned from Europe and Asia and received assistance (in the form of attractive government loans, to use one example) as they pursued their education, homeownership, and other ends. The G.I. Bill that passed in 1944 helped hundreds of thousands of American soldiers to pursue their dreams in post-war America.[135]

At the same time, during the war, thousands of women entered the workforce, largely to fill in for the men who left to fight in Europe.[136] Women entering the workforce because the men went to fight in World War II was a major turning point for American women and their ability to pursue their own American Dream. Up to that point in America's history, women were generally homemakers and mothers, and not employed. But as we have described in this book previously, the American system is one built on meritocracy. There is nothing meritocratic about excluding someone from the workplace because of their gender or society's view of how someone should live their life.

Employers also learned that women could play an important and crucial role because they performed so well during World War II. In that regard, the post-World War II period also embraced self-healing. Employers could have fired all the women in their workforce, concluded that World War II was a one-off, and returned to the general belief that women belong in the home. But they didn't. Employers kept women in their workforce and hired more women to fill other important roles with the full understanding of how they could create value for their companies and customers. In that way, through self-healing, our system came one step closer to embracing a system more built on meritocracy and not stereotypical roles that far too often exclude well-qualified individuals from important positions.

The incentive structure in America also shifted during this time. Taxes returned to more normal levels (they had been raised during the war as part of the nationwide effort) and were later reduced further by President Kennedy.[137]

In addition, the influence of labor unions, which were productive at first in remedying the challenges of early industrialization, finally began to taper off in the 1950s. That meant businesses could focus more on profits than on internal contractual disputes. The Taft-Hartley Act was instrumental in reversing the reflexively pro-labor position of the government.[138]

Finally, the availability of relatively low-cost housing meant that people could afford to start families again, something that was far more difficult during the nadir of the Great Depression.

These developments generated an economic situation where people could more easily follow their dreams and take risks. People began to start businesses again, neighborhood developments sprung up, and young people—many of them back from war—got married and went to work. For the first time in decades, America was back on track.

The economic trends of this period were, in a way, a manifestation of the American tendency to self-correct and heal. A lot of untenable and drastic policies were implemented during the Great Depression and in the war that followed. The return to relative international peace and economic stability of the 1950s refocused America on domestic growth.

But America healed in more than one way during this period. Specifically, the country finally took real steps to end the Jim Crow system that had existed for far too long in the South.

While it is wonderful that the US was able to end this immoral system of unequal treatment due to nothing other than a person's race, it is tragic that the ultimate promise of equality for all Americans and one of the most difficult times in our history, the Civil War, took decades to come to full fruition.

Thankfully, civil society, state governments, and private organizations picked up the pace. Politics is always downstream from culture, which is to say that the collective private beliefs and values of citizens, and their shifts, will eventually manifest themselves in the law in a democratic republic like the United States. Prior to the passage of the federal Civil Rights Act of 1964, private businesses like the National Football League were hesitant to push back on the norm of segregation. But in the 1940s, after the war ended, Black sportswriters pushed private organizations, like the Los Angeles Coliseum Commission, to offer the Coliseum to segregated and non-segregated teams.

At the time, the Los Angeles Coliseum Commission could not lease the famous stadium to a segregated team because it was funded with public money, and there was no alternative for Black players. Thankfully, the pressure worked. The Rams—a popular NFL team that wanted access to the stadium—integrated when they gave two talented Black players spots on their team.[139] The activists and the institutions got what they wanted in a timely manner, while the government was paralyzed by ideological division.

While this was not a perfect fix, this anecdote demonstrates that the civil rights movement was successful in several different ways before the period of the time most Americans generally understand as the civil rights era. Regrettably, there was a limit to the power of this approach. While some states and businesses took the side of the Black activists, there were many Southern states that refused any attempts at integration.

It was only through relentless public pressure mixed with peaceful demonstrations—on buses, at lunch counters, the March on Washington, and so on—that pushed the movement into the mainstream, which, in turn, made it impossible for Congress to ignore.[140] It's key here to note that government was a follower, not a leader, in the effort to extend equal rights to all Americans—activists were critical to changing public perceptions and ultimately forced government to act.

In the middle of the 1960s, these efforts culminated in the passage of a series of civil rights laws that outlawed intentional discrimination and disparate treatment of people based upon their race, color, sex, religion, or national origin. These laws applied to the public and private spheres. These statutes created a situation where the equality of opportunity was fully protected by law and led to an American system that more fully embraced meritocracy, no matter who you were.[141]

Unfortunately, as the achievements of the Civil War were darkened by the assassination of President Lincoln, so too were the victories of the civil rights movement rendered bittersweet following the murder of Dr. Martin Luther King, Jr.

King is one of the founders of modern America. He advocated for racial harmony and equal treatment on the one hand and more radical redistribution on the other.[142] Today, he is beloved across the political spectrum.

In our current incredibly polarized country, it is important to remember the entirety of Dr. King's legacy because he is an American icon, someone whose legacy we can all rally around and support, even if he wasn't perfect.

Like many heroes America has to offer, King was a great and complicated man—like Jefferson, Hamilton, and Lincoln—whose highs are deserving of praise and whose lows should never discount the totality of his contributions. We should all remember his call to judge people on their character, not their complexion or ethnic background.

The story of the civil rights movement is an American one and a reminder of our self-healing culture. We are a self-critical society that always strives to do our best, even if it takes time to get there. In some cases, our effort to correct past errors creates new problems, e.g., consider the earlier discussion on the compromise on slavery during the formation of the agreement between the states.

While the legacy of the civil rights movement is great in that it overturned the Jim Crow South, the full story is a bit difficult because of what followed. Specifically, there have been numerous misinterpretations of these well-intentioned laws in the decades since; a litany of tortured legal decisions based on these laws have undermined America's democratic ethos and constricted civil society. These new interpretations have harmed what we believe was the primary goal of the civil rights movement, namely that your race should not determine your success or failure in America.

To be clear, these laws worked well to end legal discrimination. It is the expansive misinterpretation of them by courts that changed the legislation Congress actually passed into something that was *not* passed. At their best, the laws transformed American behavior and institutions to an extremely high degree, which, in turn, has contributed to the diversification of our communities, institutions, and organizations. And polling bears that out.[143]

Too often, civil rights laws are misinterpreted from the actual text of the legislation and have been badly abused in the decades since the original bills were written.[144] Indeed, the selective enforcement of these laws is one of the biggest problems in America, both because of the manifest unfairness and because it engenders racial distrust and resentment.

Consider the text of the Civil Rights Act of 1964. The bill's central command could not be clearer: discrimination on the basis of race, color, sex, religion, or national origin is illegal. Race means race, discrimination means discrimination, and so on—this is all straightforward. And yet, decades on, courts, executive orders, and other laws mandate disparate treatment on the basis of group membership in virtually every major institution in America, from higher education to employment.

For example, in *Regents of the University of California v. Bakke* (1978), the Supreme Court interpreted the Civil Rights Act's central command of nondiscrimination to allow colleges and universities to use race as a "plus factor" when comparing applicants.[145] While we disagree with the court's interpretation of the statute, the interpretation also reduces the importance of meritocracy in the admissions process. This is not only fundamentally unfair to those who are denied on this basis, but it also belittles the accomplishments of those whom ostensibly the law is meant to benefit.

Ultimately, this is the fault of the political process, which has failed to address this new manifestation of inequality. In many ways, this interpretation of the law has become a new form of discrimination that decays our meritocratic system.

While we healed in some ways during the 1960s, we are not yet fully inoculated against mistakes, and we never will be. There is always more work to do to make a better America. That is why our culture of self-healing is worth embracing.

III. 1970s–1990s

In the first years of the 1970s, racial strife increased as the hope of the civil rights movement subsided. Elsewhere, the Watergate saga dragged on, and the mood on politics soured. Though the Vietnam War wrapped up, much of the country was still upset about the intervention. And let us not forget that the Cold War still loomed.

But perhaps the most traumatic event was the recession of 1973. This was the first serious slowdown since the Great Depression. What was unique about this recession was that it was exacerbated by stagflation. What made stagflation novel is that there was both high inflation as well as high unemployment—an issue that frustrated everyday people and vexed policymakers.[146] Once a country enters a period of stagflation, policy remedies become either sparse or economically painful.

This economic decline was made possible by a confluence of factors, chief among them being President Nixon's attempt to arrest the rising inflation of the early 1970s.

It wasn't until Federal Reserve Chairman Paul Volcker took office in 1979, when the inflation rate was over 9 percent annually, that the inflation problem was truly addressed by raising interest rates. This was a painful period of economic history for Americans as the correction, while necessary to stabilize the economy, initially slowed economic growth. Interest rates on thirty-year mortgages, for example, peaked over 16 percent in 1980, which drove down home purchasing demand and ultimately sale prices. For many Americans who had benefited from the growth and prosperity of the post-World War II economy, a fall in housing prices correlated with a significant loss of wealth for many new middle-class families.

But in the 1980s, with inflation finally under wraps, things turned around. Economic trends progressed, and President Reagan's low-tax economic program incentivized the same entrepreneurial, risk-taking behaviors that historically always led to growth—and often big booms at that.[147] What is interesting is that the ideas that generated so much wealth in the 1980s were actually from the 1960s and 1970s. The big change in the 1980s was that there was finally capital to finance these ideas, and they exploded in the 1980s and into the 1990s.

Once again, the government was encouraging private action. Taxes were lower, regulations were less burdensome, and people were optimistic, much like President Reagan. And there were a lot of reasons to be optimistic: inflation fell precipitously, and GDP rose by 33 percent.[148]

In the course of only a few years, the capital it freed up would come back to enrich the country and the nation in the form of the tech sector expansion of the 1990s. But this was only possible because Reagan's successors, Bush I and Clinton, largely stuck with his pro-growth program.

Thousands of new companies formed, and many offered new services and products to consumers related to the nascent internet economy. The cumulative effect of this investment was the rise of San Francisco and nearby Silicon Valley as the tech capital of the US and the world. What made this rise especially interesting is that, while most countries have only one major economic center (England has London, France has Paris, and so on), the US now possesses at least *two* massive economic zones: one in New York for finance and one in California for tech. It could be argued that the United States today even has *multiple* global economic centers, such as Houston for energy, Chicago for commodities, and Los Angeles for entertainment.

There is a reason that the high-tech economy of the '90s took root in America: our country—not Germany, England, or China—offered the ideal economic environment for starting a business. Part of being an American entrepreneur is a willingness to put oneself out there, so to speak, and in the 1980s–1990s, the government made that possible again by getting out of the way. Moreover, the money generated by deregulation went back into the economy and made all manner of individual projects and ventures possible. Some failed, while others supplanted former industry leaders. This period generated enormous wealth for some and a higher standard of living for most.

A weird paradox of this situation is that, as wealth, growth, and the standard of living all increased, discontent grew as well. Indeed, one of the most common criticisms one observes from this period—in film, literature, and eventually politics—is that the so-called "1 percent" saw all the benefits of "Reaganomics."

Too often, these policies are described as "trickle down," a phrase that has begun to lose descriptive value as its meaning becomes distorted through its continued derisive use. Wealth does not trickle down in the sense that accumulated wealth is distributed to the rest of the country. A more accurate description recognizes that in a true meritocracy, when an individual contributes a product or service that is preferred to what was available in the past and consequently is rewarded with a tremendous amount of wealth, then their wealth accumulation is of little to no harm to a society broadly that values and wants to encourage this individual's ambition.

Individuals who purchased the goods or services of this entrepreneur, freely and without coercion, did so because it was the best option available to them. And as an added benefit, these entrepreneurs who accumulate wealth are afforded the opportunity to invest that money, which creates a virtuous cycle of economic growth. Through their accumulated wealth, the needed capital to test the next innovative product or service is generated, which, if successful, will restart the virtuous cycle of private investment. Individuals in this system ultimately get rich from solving the problems of other people.

For critics of the approach adopted during this time, the best example is found in health care: prices went up, and many people were boxed out of treatment due to costs. To be sure, the costs of health care did go up over the second half of the twentieth century.[149] But let us not forget that the standard of living, the life expectancy of Americans, and the quality of health care all increased as well—three figures that are of great importance that deserve attention in any serious discussion on the topic.[150] While lifesaving treatments may have been costly, their discovery can be attributed to a dynamic society that promotes innovation. Today, we are curing cancers that, decades ago, we couldn't even diagnose.

Better health care is not guaranteed any more than social improvement is. That the US has been the engine of improvement on this score matters. Furthermore, the proof of American excellence in care is borne out by the fact that wealthy people from other developed countries—including Canada and the UK—come here for care.

Are there opportunities for policies to streamline health care services and practices in America? Of course. But is the overall trend a good one that we should be happy about? Yes. And we owe it to our pro-market approach because it is uniquely responsible for our present situation.

What frustrates us so much is that critics cannot look at the half-full side of the glass; they fixate on the empty side and obsess over what is not there. This kind of thinking is unfortunately ascendant, and it applies to far more issues than just health care. We will talk about this all-or-nothing approach to policy and the danger of not reflecting on why we have what we have now.

We are optimistic (hopefully that has come through so far), but we are not overly idyllic. Like the Civil Rights Act and women in the workplace, America needed to learn from its mistakes to correct and self-heal. Thankfully, that self-healing brought us closer to a system of true meritocracy, where the most important thing is how hard an individual works and whether they are willing to persevere through tough times. That is the system we want America to be known for, and that is why we are optimistic. When America has been wrong, we have learned why and tried to correct course as best we can.

Modern America, the topic we will discuss in the next chapter, is not without its issues. We understand this, which is why, in the following chapter, we will discuss the recent pivot away from the policies, norms, and practices that made us so wealthy and successful over the last four decades, give or take.

We turn next to the present state of American society, economy, and government.

CHAPTER 6

MODERN AMERICA

*"A people that values its privileges above
its principles soon loses both."*
—Dwight Eisenhower

I. An Early Warning

At the end of his tenure in office, President Eisenhower was one of the most popular and praised men in America. After being well admired for his great work as a general in World War II, as president, he presided over an extremely stable and prosperous time in America. During his tenure, race relations finally progressed after the decision in *Brown v. Board of Education*[151] (1954) and his use of the 101st Airborne to enforce the ruling in Little Rock, Arkansas.[152] Eisenhower has become a presidential standard against which others are measured.

Everything was looking up in America, and optimism was everywhere, even as the albatross of the Cold War loomed over the nation. When, in January 1961, Eisenhower delivered his last speech to the nation, one would have likely guessed that it would hit an uplifting tone based on any number of great things that happened under his leadership.

Instead, Eisenhower did what he so often did: he spoke honestly and bluntly and made an attempt to steer the country in the right direction. He decided to focus on the future of the country, which he did not believe to be as optimistic as some might assume.

Looking back, his memorable farewell was a prophetic warning: Americans needed to be vigilant in guarding their institutions and protecting the country's financial position from special interests that would selfishly and recklessly undermine the common good—in no small part by spending the nation into poverty.

Today, what many best remember about Eisenhower's speech is his line about the perils of the "military-industrial complex"—a very real problem in American life today.[153]

The general idea expressed in that phrase—of special interests expanding the state through their rent-seeking behaviors in and around government via the justification of false needs and foolish initiatives—applies to far more than just the military. Indeed, it exists across the public sector; increasingly, it is also a problem in the private sector due to the HR-ization of business and the rise of the diversity, equity, and inclusion (DEI) scheme.[154] This is a vital and salient point that captures one of the biggest issues facing the country. And it is an anathema to our unique American system of meritocracy.

Elsewhere in his speech, Eisenhower also cautioned against scientism (that a scientific approach is in all cases best) dominating public policy, as well as the difficulties that would arise from government funding shaping and controlling scientific inquiry. Politics should not rule science, nor should science solely determine politics. The "unwarranted influence" he decried applies just as much to those trying to make a buck off the state as it does to those ideologues who want to commandeer it to further their insular goals.[155] The inherent problem of scientism rests in the fact that it can create a technocracy that becomes isolated from the majority of citizens. This isolation can eventually breed distrust and resentment between the two groups, and when you lose trust, you ultimately lose legitimacy in the system of government.

In short, Eisenhower felt that, if left unchecked, the trends he observed in and around government would alter America for the worse by promoting bad policies that would enrich the few, ignore the needs of the country, and encourage self-destructive behaviors in America's governmental institutions. If all those things were to happen, the American system described in previous chapters would likely be lost forever. America can only offer a free, prosperous, market-based economy built on meritocracy to its citizens and the world if the American people decide that it's a tradition worth protecting.

If these trends developed and became ascendant, according to Eisenhower, then something essential about our country and the way we govern it would be lost, and we might devolve to something less than a people who rule themselves. The threat of corruption was, as Eisenhower saw it, pervasive, real, and if fully realized, fatal. It threatened our American way of life at its core.

The speech was a grave and prescient warning about the impending threat of a vast, self-sustaining, and rapacious state that threatened American government and civic life. Over sixty years later, the potential risks Eisenhower sketched out have taken on very real forms.

The signature problem facing modern America is the continued degradation of our institutions in government, in the private sector, and in civil society. The state's reach is growing every year, and its corruption is flowing outward into everything that it touches. Eisenhower's fear of a crooked incentive structure is a reality today.

II. The Ubiquitous State and the Problems It Creates

In the last century, America changed in profound ways. Some of these changes were good and reflected our culture of self-healing and learning from our mistakes for the better— for example, ending Jim Crow and segregation, passing the Civil Rights Act, and women entering the workforce during World War II. All these things also moved America closer to a truly meritocratic system.

Some of the changes over the last fifty years were more in the middle or mixed, so to speak. The country's move away from isolationism was good in the 1940s when it took on the Axis powers and won World War II. In other cases, its imperial stance vis-à-vis the world *after* World War II was more negative, both in terms of costs and outcomes, such as during the Vietnam War.

And lastly, there were some changes that were downright bad. The fixation on regulation and the manufacturing of equal outcomes hurt the economy, infringed on individual rights, and ultimately strained national unity.

In this chapter, we discuss several of the major problems facing America today and why they must be resolved. The central issue, and the one from which almost all of these derivative problems flow, comes from the last century: it is the fact that the federal government exerts undue, unconstitutional, and unhelpful influence on the rest of the country and the economy in virtually every regard imaginable.

Today, the federal government is involved in the economy in a way that it never was intended to be, thanks to FDR's New Deal programs, which expanded government in a way never seen in America. For instance, it has a role in granting permits for businesses, it sets terms on contracts between employers and employees,[156] and its pervasive threat to issue penalties over interpersonal issues in workplaces necessitates firms to hire costly and counterproductive HR managers,[157] as well as a collection of other people. In many ways, these HR employees are now in-house government agents, divorced from their valid and original purpose to improve employee interpersonal relationships and eliminate harassment and abuse of employees.

Taken together, these factors promote the wrong incentives. Put bluntly, the American government today sends negative messages to firms, namely that if they want to do business, they must do right by Washington, which means they must be ready to pay up[158] and sacrifice any semblance of a free-speech culture, among other things.[159] As we have said previously, barriers implemented by government or business serve only to protect those at the top, and they make the system less meritocratic. Those barriers are fundamentally un-American.

How did this happen? Where and when did we go wrong? To answer these questions, it is necessary to look back to the 1930s, a point we covered in the previous chapter but did not expound on fully.

As noted earlier, FDR permanently changed the size and scope of the federal government and expanded the Constitution to limits that were wholly unforeseen by those who ratified it. With the constitutional revolution of the 1930s, and its acceleration in the following decades, the state has grown *every* year under *every* administration since Roosevelt took office.

In fact, contrary to what a person might hear about Presidents Trump and Reagan, no president in the last one hundred years, Republican or Democrat, has been able to arrest the spread of the state. This happens because Congress increases the federal budget every year, often creates new spending or social programs, and the executive branch grows as a result to implement these policies.

In other words, once the executive branch receives its funding from Congress, it is shockingly free from most oversight. And often, the executive branch is stopped only because of successful lawsuits brought by private parties or states, *not* because Congress steps up and does its constitutionally assigned job. When Congress throws the towel in on meaningful oversight or reform, our entire system of government fails. Once Congress appropriates money, it has a duty to ensure the executive is spending it properly and implementing regulations to enforce laws correctly. Any lesser role relegates Congress's entire reason for existence into being a permanent bank for the executive.

While one might think no one wins in this situation, members of Congress do. They claim that the executive is acting illegally or unconstitutionally and that if they get elected, they will put an end to the overreach. But in reality, they have no interest in fixing any of these problems once they are elected because they can continue to run on this same platform over and over again, rinse and repeat. The "next election" then becomes "the most important election of our lives" to reelect the same members of Congress who spent the trillions of dollars that got us into the mess.

It's no wonder that Americans have so little faith in Congress. From 2010 to 2020, on average, over 75 percent of Americans disapproved of the job their representatives performed in Washington.[160]

Passing off responsibility is great for elected officials, who can avoid difficult campaign issues, but horrible for the American people who get a less responsive, more powerful federal government. Indeed, a big problem with the executive is that these regulatory agencies are *not* democratically accountable and are unrepresentative of the people.

On top of that, these agencies govern themselves with little to no oversight from Congress. This becomes especially problematic in the age of *Chevron* deference, a legal doctrine that instructs courts reviewing an executive branch regulation to give deference to an agency's interpretation of a law Congress has told it to implement. In other words, courts defer to an agency's understanding of a law, making it very difficult, if not impossible, for someone challenging agency action to win in court. *Chevron* puts a heavy thumb on the scale in favor of a growing and all-powerful executive branch.

We want to be absolutely clear that these developments are bad, even if only for the fact that they bring us far away from an effective understanding of the Constitution. The Founders intended for Congress to do its job, yet it avoids that obligation every chance it gets. All the while, the government grows larger and bureaucrats bolder. This growth has not been cheap, it is doubtfully legal, and it has touched every aspect of American society. And it has come at the expense of serious economic growth for millions of Americans working to live better lives.

The rise of what some have called the "deep state" or the administrative state—a permanent, ideological, and self-interested collection of like-minded regulators and policy-pushers—has created a federal government that has more utopian and less compromising goals. It is also more partisan[161] and less committed to respecting civil liberties.[162] Maybe the clearest explanation of why this is bad and needs to change is the case of the defense budget.

The government throws more money at defense contractors each year (with few exceptions) and gets a questionable return to show for it in the advancement of American security.[163] Because military spending is high, it creates a cottage industry for defense contractors in and around DC. Government officials, especially those in the military, pass through a revolving door between these firms and positions in the military.[164] Despite more money than ever, the quality of the military's products has not improved over the years. Consider the example of Navy combat littoral ships. In 2022, plans were announced to scrap nine such vessels, even though some are less than three years old.[165],[166]

As private citizens, they lobby for more military funding, and they (and their friends) support candidates who promote their rent-seeking. As public servants, they justify more spending on foreign projects, often by exaggerating foreign threats,[167] which instigates resentment against America.[168] This is untenable and dangerous for the country—and, in this case, literally so as more intervention abroad raises the risks against the US at home while promoting rash actions abroad.

This must stop. But beyond that, this anecdote demonstrates a simple fact that all politicians must keep in mind if these bad practices are to be reversed. Specifically, they must know that incentives matter and that people and institutions will respond to them accordingly. When people see that the state rewards certain behaviors, they get in compliance to get in on the grift. Consequently, we understand why defense contractors behave in this manner, and we believe it should be the objective of our leaders to create a system of incentives that better achieves the end goal of a stronger and more efficient national defense.

While we discuss the national defense as an instigator of rent-seeking behavior by American business, in the decades since Eisenhower's warning, it has pervaded all manner of industries, such as health care, housing, transportation, banking, finance, and many more.

The cost of doing business is higher due to all the requirements the federal government puts on firms, big and small alike. Often, the bigger firms can adjust to these costs while the little guy gets boxed out. There is nothing meritocratic about a system where the government enforces costly barriers to entry and pushes competitive businesses out of the market.

And this is only half the issue. On the other side, the federal government, via its redistribution programs (i.e., welfare), signals to people that they can be dependent on the state without giving any thought to self-development, future employment, or personal betterment.[169] While we agree government should supply a safety net for those who absolutely need it, it is another matter altogether when that safety net goes into perpetuity, with no requirement that the recipient look for work or engage in self-development programs. The programs should look to give a hand up instead of a handout.

Consider two contrasting outlooks in the United Kingdom and the United States. In the 1990s, the Social Exclusion Unit (SEU) published a report that identified a problem in English life, namely that there was a burgeoning subcategory of people who were not in school, were not working, and were not developing themselves to work.[170] These NEETs (Not in Education, Employment, or Training) posed a serious problem, and the government took steps to prevent this growing trend.

Skip ahead to America today. Here, we are doing the opposite: we are incentivizing more NEETs through subsidies. The clearest case of this is in the foolish extension of unemployment benefits—a subsidy that pays more than many companies can afford to match, let alone surpass.[171]

Ultimately, incentives against work are just as dangerous as the anti-business climate fostered by the administrative state's vast regulatory regime. We need to start sending the right messages again to ensure our system remains meritocratic and one that values talent, hard work, and perseverance through tough times.

III. American Excellence: Charity and Achievement

While many believe only the government can help those in need, they forget that America remains an extremely charitable and community-conscious country. Americans give more to charity than people from other countries, both domestic and foreign.[172] As a percentage of charitable giving, America dwarfs other states.[173]

If the assumption behind the creation of these enormous redistributionist schemes was that too many people care too little and people fall through the cracks, that idea was misguided and wrong. Americans care about their neighbors and fellow citizens, and they take steps to help them.

Similarly, for all the consternation about poverty in America—a cause that ostensibly drives much of the talk about expanding the state's reach even further—the actual record in the US is something in which Americans should take pride.

To understand how impressive the US is on this front, look at China, a country against which America is increasingly compared. China is constantly adjusting its poverty line and fudging its numbers to seem competitive when it comes to fighting poverty.[174] Playing with the numbers is the only way that socialists can try to keep up with the US. An honest assessment of the facts shows America far outpaces China on this score.[175]

The biggest threat to America—by the permanent bureaucracy and by the political process—is the attempt to undo our meritocratic system. Our meritocratic system is central to how Americans work and govern themselves. Trial and error, the risk of starting a business, getting promoted at work—all of these things are shaped by the simple, deeply American principle that one's abilities and commitment to them ought to dictate whether that person succeeds or fails.

At the heart of our American system is the idea that good, effective people should and will be promoted and that people who embody the opposite of those virtues will not. In a nutshell, this is a meritocracy. It is an economic system based on merit and hard work, not on race, religion, sex, or who you know.

Unfortunately, there are some who dislike this system because it can lead to disparate outcomes, i.e., some people do better than others in some respects or under certain conditions.

And if there are gaps across groups that are especially bad, the state must intervene to readjust. However, inequality is inherent to human nature—we're all born with different natural abilities—and those gaps for some in a few cases are often offset by advantages in other situations.

Before responding to this argument, we would like to add that we are highly skeptical of this claim. There are often other motives at work, and we assume this is the case here. It is likely that these people simply do not want a situation in which people could more easily pass them up and disrupt their position in society, the market, and so on. While we sympathize with the fact that everyone has a different set of skills, it would be wrong to base an entire system on fair outcomes for everyone rather than rewarding those who believe in themselves, work hard, and persevere.

Inequality is everywhere. Some people are not born as smart as others, while others are born taller and more athletic. This is a random aspect of life that cannot be controlled. Rather than focus on the downsides, the focus should be on the half-full side of the glass. We all have gifts and unique talents that we can profit from and take pride in.

But this truth—that differences are natural and acceptable (if not good)—is not enough for the detractors. Natural, observable differences are not the result of different natures and nurtures. Instead, many people today assert that the *real* culprit for such disparities is actually America itself, which suggests that these disparities would not exist elsewhere.

Specifically, critics assert that America is so sick, so terminally ill with a disease of inequality, that when certain people *on average* outperform others in a few narrow situations, this is proof of an intended, manufactured gap.[176] The implication here is of that phantom known as systemic oppression. Systemic oppression has existed in America—look no further than Jim Crow—but our institutions have continued to evolve through self-healing and perform the work of weeding out systemic oppression where it still exists to come to a system that is more closely based on meritocracy.

America has engaged in self-healing on race discrimination time and time again. It outlawed racial discrimination almost sixty years ago and instituted affirmative action programs over fifty years ago. Moreover, to take the systematic oppression argument to its logical conclusion, one also must believe it is creating a system for East Asians and South Asians to outpace everyone, Whites included.

Opponents of America's meritocracy purport to believe this conspiracy. Who knows if this is true? What is *certainly* true is that they want to replace our meritocratic system with a system where they and their friends pick the winners and losers in education, business, and life. In other words, they want to destroy our meritocratic system and tear down what has helped America prosper.

Just think, if we gave up on our meritocracy, what would that look like? To think about this, we will reflect on what would have happened to America if this principle never existed in the first place. To see the danger in this approach, imagine a world without Amazon.

Jeff Bezos's company, Amazon, is one of the all-time great American success stories. The venture, which began as a small online bookstore, has transformed into an enormous titan of the market. Amazon now sells everything from groceries to movies, as well as an electronic virtual assistant to help people with everything from cooking to playing music. In the process, Bezos has become one of the richest people on Earth.

This is an incredible story, and there is a reason it happened in America. In fact, we would go as far as to say that there is a reason that this story and others like it *mostly* happen here, and that is because of America's pro-meritocratic culture.

Bezos was not born with a silver spoon in his hand. He did not enter the world with connections in Washington or wealthy friends in San Francisco or New York. So, in a world without meritocracy, where would Bezos be? We do not know for certain, but it is within the realm of possibility that he would not be revolutionizing the way we purchase things.

These innovations Bezos brought on are not without their negative consequences, though. Hundreds of small booksellers at first, and later larger ones, were pushed out of the market as consumers began to prefer Amazon's services. As Amazon applied its business model to other opportunities for growth, it began taking on other markets, such as the grocery market, with its purchase of Whole Foods. But the business sectors that Amazon entered into did not go down without a fight and, in many cases, found a new home for their ventures. Small retailers, who could list their products on Amazon, were given new opportunities to build a business in a way that consumers tended to prefer and that was not available to them in the past.

And this brings up, in the most dramatic of terms, what the options are: either we have a meritocracy that celebrates excellence, tolerates disparities, and sees the critical value in failure, or we embrace the mediocrity that is equity, where we pretend to not see the failure around us but where some of us can feel good about hitting the "right" metrics on performance. There is neither justice nor improvement on this path.

IV. The Zero-Sum Delusion

To close this chapter, we want to say one last word about the recent anti-meritocracy ethos in American public life.

Too often, the discussion focuses exclusively on the challenges facing Black Americans and intergenerational poverty. To be sure, this is a group that struggles when compared to middle- and upper-income Whites and Asians. There are reasons for that, largely driven by historical failures in public policy. Nonetheless, we believe that those comparisons, of Blacks to Asians or to Whites, cannot be fairly made given the many unique issues—in substance and in scale—that these people face in their daily lives, e.g., failing and unresponsive schools that create educational apartheid, unequal treatment in the criminal justice system, or severely mismanaged local governments in predominantly low-income Black jurisdictions.

In fact, it was President Obama who provided a tough but fair assessment of one factor that leads to the genesis of some of these issues when he said:

> "Of all the rocks upon which we build our lives, we are reminded today that family is the most important. And we are called to recognize and honor how critical every father is to that foundation…But if we are honest with ourselves, we'll admit that what too many fathers are is missing—missing from too many lives and too many homes…You and I know how true this is in the African-American community. We know that more than half of all black children live in single-parent households, a number that has doubled— doubled—since we were children…And the foundations of our community are weaker because of it."[177]

President Obama made a sound point, which is that, in a number of regards, the poor Black demographic has specific challenges. The intention of this discussion is that it's easy to assign blame on large systemic causes when factors that create difficulties for all Americans are particularly prevalent in low-income Black homes.

There also exists a legacy from the unspeakable horrors of the middle passage, the trade route that brought slaves from Africa to America, where families were broken up and auctioned as property into slavery. Of the estimated 12.5 million slaves who were subjected to the middle passage, nearly one in every six people died during their transportation across the Atlantic.[178] It's hard to put all this collective trauma into words, and all Americans should understand and not hide from this history.

The question for Americans today is how they can move forward and realize the potential of their founding ideals that all people are created equal and endowed with certain natural rights. For America to maximize its potential, it must overcome the legacy created by the past.

But we can only understand, not rewrite, the past and remember the lessons created by the suffering and failures of previous generations. One of those lessons is that Americans must embrace their meritocracy, as it functions best when equal opportunity is a shared value. Public policy, therefore, should empower people to break the cycle of intergenerational poverty and avoid creating a dependence on government programs as a long-term solution to the failures of the past.

We also believe that there is a more constructive and fair way to look at the success of meritocracy in America, and that is to review the historic record of immigrants.

From the late nineteenth century on, America became much more diverse. People from all over the world came to the US and quickly built wealth and got ahead in the country. America welcomed new people and gave them access to the same path that native-born Americans enjoyed. These people came because of the American way of meritocracy, and they were rewarded for their hard work.

This is not normal. In other countries, like India, for example, the caste system dictates social hierarchies and limits a person's ability to climb the social ladder because of who their parents are and where they are born.[179] This observation is not to condemn just India—it is one of many countries with such a system. Rather, it is meant to highlight how unique the case of the US is.

Today, the old American royalty is decayed and, to a large extent, nonexistent. People of all races and genders can, in most cases, reach the pinnacle of success in their profession if they believe in themselves, work hard, and persevere. No doubt the challenges are greater for some than others, but the fact remains that it is still possible, which cannot be said of most countries.

This is meritocracy in practice: a fair and open-ended process in which anyone with a good idea or a skill, and the urge to refine and implement it, can succeed. A person's identity cannot matter in this system—but you can be sure that it will be factored in within the system that critics want to implement.

The alternative to meritocracy—of picking winners by their race, political views, ethnicity, sex, creating quotas—is unattractive, ineffective, and retrograde. It will make America poorer, a worse place to live, and less appealing to immigrants and entrepreneurs alike. It will devalue hard work and destroy the incredible economy America has worked so hard to build and has lifted millions out of poverty.

And this is the virtue of a meritocracy: it allows people to succeed, and the fruits of their success touch everyone in the country. Whether it is the introduction of new technology, such as the internet or smartphones, the lowering of the costs of essential goods (e.g., refrigerators and laundry machines), or a better, more effective way to deliver products, this system does great things for everyone. As such, we should be at least critical of those who want to change it and who say that it works only for the few.

As always, there are and have been some problems with our meritocratic market system. In the past, anticompetitive and racist laws limited its potential and excluded people. But we have overcome those issues largely through self-healing, and today, our system is much more meritocratic, and access to it is legally protected across races, ages, and backgrounds. Where we might continue to fail, our system retains a culture of self-healing, and history has shown that the American people are up to the challenge.

With our meritocratic ethos, America is capable of great things. Right now, there are some impediments, including the equity fixation and a host of bad policies built around it. But these issues can be fixed if we work to fix them.

And this is the great thing about our country: it's built around excellent ideas and can be renewed. So long as we understand why that is and which institutions and practices make us great, we will be fine—even in the face of what looks today like a bad situation.

In the next chapter, we discuss some of the reasons for optimism, namely why it is that warts and all, America remains such an attractive destination for immigrants the world over.

CHAPTER 7

WHY IMMIGRANTS COME TO AMERICA

"America is still the land of opportunity more than any other place, for sure. There is definitely no other country where I could have done this—immigrant or not."
—Elon Musk

I. Immigration and Excellence:
We Do Best the Right Way

America is the land of opportunity, and it's because of America's system of meritocracy. One of the many reasons we know this is the large number of immigrants who made dangerous trips or heartbreaking journeys where they must leave their families to come here. When they get here, they are rewarded for believing in themselves, working hard, and persevering through incredibly difficult circumstances. In other words, America is the best place on earth for someone with nothing to achieve more success than they ever dreamed of. That is why America is a preferred destination for many immigrants.

Immigrants' attitudes are a useful tool by which to measure and compare countries—both those that the immigrants are leaving and those that they want to travel to. Because immigrants have been coming to North America for centuries, America is an excellent country to which this method can be applied.

Before the United States, there was the New World, and the early political communities across this region (the modern-day East Coast) were built by and populated by immigrants.

Back in the 1600s and into the 1700s, these immigrants came from Europe, and at this time, there was no real procedure for entry; in fact, many of these immigrants were basically exported by their home countries.[180]

As the New World developed into the United States, the immigration process changed with it, but remained vital as ever. More people came to the country to work and build new lives, and they contributed to the economy by filling new jobs and starting their own businesses. With so much land and opportunity available, America needed labor. It was a perfect match.

Immigrants coming to North America with few to no restraints characterized American immigration until the 1870s. One reason for this is up to that point, America was not exactly a centralized state; another explanation is that there were too many other things going on to focus on immigration, an issue of limited importance to most Americans.

After the Civil War, immigrants remained an important influence on American life, both culturally and economically. At the same time, following a Supreme Court decision[181] that held that the federal government has the sole power to regulate immigration, Washington took a new approach—namely, it began to limit immigration by setting terms for entry.[182]

The common idea behind these regulations was that immigration ought to be to the benefit of American citizens.[183] While on a case-by-case basis, this might prove difficult, the idea behind it is the right one. Immigration should help, or at least not hurt, the interests of existing American citizens.

This means several things; firstly, illegal immigration will *always* conflict with the interest all Americans *should* have to uphold the rule of law. This principle, that the law is sovereign and universally applied, hinges on its enforcement, which is itself contingent on buy-in. In other words, if people do not honor and believe in the rule of law, it ceases to exist.

While no human is illegal in the literal sense, neither is a person a sovereign citizen—a being outside the law—in the legal sense. Countries are sovereign within their borders and have a right to make and enforce their own immigration laws.

The act of illegal entry further erodes the rule of law. In some cases, it can have a geometric effect: a few radical jurisdictions try to get around federal law by sanctioning this illegal activity by providing documentation to illegal immigrants.[184]

As should be clear by now, the current crisis at the border and our broken immigration system are bad for the rule of law (in no small part because it puts strain on the constitutionally demarcated relationship between the states and the federal power in Washington, DC) and is unjust because it rewards antisocial behavior while millions try to enter the country through legal channels[185]—and that is to say nothing of the substantial strain that some illegal immigrants put on American institutions and citizens alike.[186]

While, in many cases, these immigrants come to the US for the right reason, to enjoy our unique system of meritocracy, they break the law to do so. It is unfair to the millions of immigrants who came to the US legally by waiting in line and filling out the paperwork necessary to reward those who flagrantly violated the law by allowing them to work in the US. Plenty can be said about how difficult it can be to come to the US legally, and there exist simple commonsense reforms, but the point here is millions of people do it each year. The US cannot be a country that values the rule of law but then rewards those who break the law.

We are pro-legal immigration when it is built around advancing American interests. We recognize that illegal immigration will always be in tension with core civic values, and we begin this chapter by making this point clear.

Secondly, the legal immigration regime must factor in social and economic considerations. Values including justice, fairness to American citizens, the diversity of immigrants, and social harmony are factors we must consider when crafting immigration policy.

The debate between legal immigration and defense of illegal immigration understandably takes up a large portion of the conversation around this area of public policy. This is however to the detriment of the debate between those who believe that the current legal immigration regime is working fine versus those who think it needs an update from the 1960s.

Specifically, we think that one of the defining features of the Immigration and Nationality Act of 1965, one that was unintended—namely, its provision to prioritize "family unification" but which led to chain migration—needs to be amended to emphasize employability and to serve the economic interests of the US.[187]

The existing law also subjects both low-skilled and certain high-skilled Americans to unfair levels of competition from foreign labor that disproportionately benefits businesses that underpay and often choose *not* to employ Americans.[188] This becomes a race to the bottom that devalues the American meritocracy in the worst way.

We respect the power of market forces and oppose rent-seeking because we value our uniquely American system of meritocracy. We also recognize that there is something inherently wrong with this situation because it arose not from calculated, intended actions but from an unintended policy built into a larger law. Americans did not vote for this, elected officials did not intend it, and we believe that the law ought to be brought into alignment with statutory intent and the will of citizens. And as has been said, but to reinforce the point fully, it also fundamentally undermines our meritocratic system. It devalues those who believe in themselves, work hard, and persevere only to lose out in industries that can substitute with cheap skilled foreign labor instead of paying Americans an honest wage for the same job.

As it stands now, the immigration *status quo* is untenable, and it is simply the inertia of the 1965 law that keeps this regime going. Adjusting an almost sixty-year-old law to do what it was intended to do in the first place is in the interest of

all Americans, from those in the working class to big industries and people across the economic spectrum. As the economist Milton Friedman once argued, you can't have open borders and a welfare state. In his 1978 speech at the University of
Chicago titled "What Is America?", he famously argued that
"it is one thing to have free immigration to jobs, it is another
thing to have free immigration to welfare."[189] Immigration that
does not contribute to the success of America, but rather pulls
vital resources from the welfare system, ultimately harms the
most vulnerable Americans trying to get ahead.

In summary, illegal immigration is bad, and legal immigration is good, as it has been for much of American history.
And when legal immigration is done well, is oriented towards
the American interest, and is endorsed by citizens, it is best.
Right now, the US approach to immigration is out of sync with
the intentions behind the dominant 1965 law and of limited
popularity. We should focus our efforts on amending immigration law to serve the interests of citizens and underscore
our uniquely American system of meritocracy, embracing all
those who want to come to America and positively contribute
to our society.

II. Immigrant Excellence

Across American history, there are few constants. But when
it comes to immigration, the story is pretty consistent: immigrants come here seeking better lives. Usually, they succeed in
that effort—and often, become incredibly rich and influential
on American life in the process. Immigrants come to the US
because of our unique system of meritocracy, where anyone

can come from any background and achieve more than they ever imagined. Our meritocratic system benefits everyone because their gains and contributions matriculate across society and generations, and that is to everyone's benefit.

In the previous chapter, we explained that the special factor that makes this kind of achievement possible is America's meritocratic principle. When it is fairly and consistently applied, it allows people to embrace their gifts and pursue their interests, and everyone benefits as a result.

And the results are striking. America has produced an incredible list of geniuses, innovators, and entrepreneurs who have changed human life for the better. This continues today in the case of perhaps our most successful immigrant yet, Elon Musk of Tesla, who originated from South Africa.

There is a reason that the US is home to the disrupters and risk-takers: its institutions, laws, and norms benefit those who believe in themselves, work hard, and persevere through tough times. Our American system of meritocracy is designed for those people to succeed. Immigrants, in particular, are well suited to this arrangement because many of their personal characteristics, such as industriousness, align with the meritocratic incentive structure.

What is odd to us is that if one were to form an opinion on the relationship between meritocracy, immigration, and excellence in America, that opinion might be very bleak if one looked *only* to media corporations for information about the dynamics of American society.

Indeed, if one believes the pessimistic journalism about American society and the opportunities available, it is likely that they would assume that immigrants—Black immigrants in particular—have no chance of making anything of themselves here.

For the last few years, we have heard a lot about systemic oppression, or the idea that the US—through laws, norms, and customs—is determined to hold Black people back for no reason other than the fact that the American people are inherently racist.

Fortunately, the story of Black immigrants to America—a category that should be uniquely disadvantaged if the systemic oppression theory is to be taken seriously—reveals just how far off the mark this account is.

When it comes to immigrant success in America, including early success, Nigerians do as well as any other group.[190] Consider the following metrics: "29% of Nigerian-Americans over the age of 25 hold a graduate degree…[and are among the] most successful immigrant communities, with a median household income of $62,351, compared to $57,617 nationally."[191]

These are stunning numbers. And they become all the more impressive when one realizes that Nigerians in America outperform many groups of Whites and Asians—two categories thought to outperform everyone and that are derided for benefiting from the privilege allegedly built into our country's laws and institutions.

Some critics might look at the figures and say that, despite what they report, there are no dominant Nigerians in American life while there are immigrants of other ethnicities who get farther ahead and in more prominent positions, e.g., Elon Musk.

To this, we say that the story of Adebayo Ogunlesi serves as a powerful counter-example. Ogunlesi is a Nigerian immigrant who has excelled in everything he has undertaken. As a college student in the UK, he graduated with high honors from Oxford University; in America, he earned a JD and an MBA *at the same time* from Harvard University.[192]

After graduating, Ogunlesi worked as a Supreme Court clerk (these positions are notoriously difficult to get, even for excellent students at top law schools) for Justice Thurgood Marshall. From there, he has worked in the highest levels of law, banking, and education. As a lecturer at Ivy League schools and as a facilitator of billion-dollar, global business deals, where his first-rate financial instincts have made him a legendary figure, Ogunlesi has succeeded like few others have.

To be sure, Ogunlesi succeeded before he arrived in America. However, he has excelled since. But the main point is that he benefited from his experiences in the US, and these experiences further developed his innate gifts, which, in turn, assisted him as he reached dizzying heights in multiple professions. Moreover, the American system of meritocracy allowed him to further excel because of the hard work he put in. Ogunlesi became a billionaire over the last decade by building the firm Global Infrastructure Partners.

The consistent and similar levels of success of other Nigerian immigrants to America demonstrate that Ogunlesi's success, impressive as it is, is no outlier. If systemic oppression rules in the US, then it is not working well. This does not mean that there is no longer racism in America or that we should not strive to be even better. What it does show, however, is that we have made substantial improvements as a country.

The case that America is systemically oppressive gets even worse when one factors in immigrants from East Asia and Southeast Asia.

Whether they are from Japan, South Korea, India, or somewhere else, immigrants from Asia generally outperform native-born White Americans in an assortment of different metrics, from their standard of living to earnings[193] and education outcomes.[194] Look at the stunning success of Asian immigrants when it comes to running prominent organizations and businesses.[195] Look at CEOs of Indian ancestry: they have become more prominent each year, and they are among the most successful young leaders in Silicon Valley.

Race relations have improved and blatant racism has been largely confined to fringe cultures in America. And through our culture of self-healing, we have taken steps to cure these problems. Whether through ratification of the Reconstruction Amendments, or the passage of federal civil rights laws, we have made incredible strides.

What should be clear is that America's meritocratic system works, particularly for the people who are supposedly oppressed by it. To the degree to which it fails to provide opportunities, our self-healing system of government works to self-correct. This means several things, including that the popular account of systemic oppression fails to explain gaps between groups in the US. We will return to this topic in later chapters when we offer a competing and more compelling thesis to explain these variations across groups.

III. Voting for America with Their Feet: American Aspirations

A great way to measure the effectiveness or popularity of a product is to see what lengths people go to get it. The price of a good, while helpful, does not fully express the degree to which a person goes out of his or her way to acquire something.

A fun story that may not be widely known, but which relates very much to this idea, is the Chick-Fil-A campout. For those who do not know, when a new Chick-Fil-A opens, it will provide an incentive to customers: be one of the first people to order and earn free food for a year.[196]

And people show up. If you ever go by a Chick-Fil-A that is scheduled to open soon, you will see people camped out days in advance, no matter the weather or the temperature. Late at night, these scenes look like something out of a zombie movie: people huddled around a dark building waiting for something to kick them into action.

Crazy as that sounds, it gets even wilder: people will travel from states far away to get in on the action. People *really* love Chick-Fil-A, and they are willing to do quite a lot to position themselves to get it at a discount.

Now imagine that the dedication that some people put into securing free Chick-Fil-A is multiplied many times over. At the same time, there is substantial risk, and the reward is more distant (and, in some cases, is not necessarily assured in the way that a year's worth of fried chicken is for the first customers to order from a new Chick-Fil-A).

That sounds like a pretty crazy scenario. But it describes a real phenomenon. Need assistance imagining what that might look like? Here is some help: the hypothetical we are talking about is no hypothetical at all—it is the legal immigration system into the US. People wait on lists to gain legal entry, sometimes for years, and often give up their lives as they know them in their effort to come to America.

While America accepts many immigrants each year—many legal but some illegal—there is nonetheless a higher demand to enter than there is availability.[197] Many people who want to come to the US cannot do so. And even those who do come give up a tremendous number of things, including proximity to their families, communal stability, and the sense of purpose one gets from cultural continuity. That is how important our meritocratic system and the American Dream are to them. They will literally give up everything they have to come here.

In a recent and horrible example, during the American exit from Afghanistan, some people put their lives in harm's way when they tried to hold onto planes headed for the US, and many of them perished.[198] It is a tragedy that these people died in their attempts to come to America. There is no silver lining here. Still, this episode does show how intensely some people—in fact, many, many people—want to come here.

Bill Maher, the host of HBO's *Real Time*, made a dark but very accurate joke about the botched Afghanistan withdrawal in 2021.

Speaking about the ideological inflexibility of progressives and their histrionics in talking about America, he observed that "America may not be the country of your faculty lounge and Twitter dreams, but no one here tries to escape by hanging on to an airplane."[199]

This is a grizzly joke, but the point is well-taken. No one is dying to get out of the US, which underscores a central point that we hope to convey: America's problems, serious as they may be, are not existential to the degree that they are in so many other countries. If people want to leave the US, we do not stop them; they are free to go. This is in direct contrast to other countries where they do not let you leave.

Additionally, something we all ought to give thought to when we talk about immigration is that immigrants have a different perspective on the US. Perhaps it is our affluence or cultural blinders, but all things considered, we have it pretty well in America, and many immigrants understand that. If that wasn't the case, they would not try to get here in any way possible, legally or illegally.

But how is that? How do immigrants see the country positively? We ask this because if one listens to or reads major American media outlets, the overwhelming impression that one comes away with is that America is a pretty rotten country. And yet, here in the case of immigrants, so many of them from places outside of Europe, the opposite appears to be true: they see the country in a more positive light, and indeed many sacrifice everything they have to come here.

If America was founded on racism, if pervasive, prejudiced structures continue to hold back people who are not White, and if the failings of America far outweigh its virtues, we must ask: What gives? Why the optimism on the part of immigrants? Is the media wrong, or are we so biased and immigrants so deluded that we cannot see the truth of the situation?

America is the land of opportunity and still the shining city on the hill. America's detractors fail to see the uniquely American culture of meritocracy. Despite its failings, America routinely comes together in the process of self-healing that allows us to grow stronger as a nation. It is this self-healing combined with meritocracy that sets the United States apart.

Per usual, we think that the best way to determine the truth is to look at what people do in the real world. And in the real world, immigrants—especially immigrants from predominantly non-White countries—want to come to the US in large numbers. So, what do immigrants think about the US once they get here?

III. What Immigrants Think About America

Immigrants want to come to America—that much has been established. Still, we want to say a brief word about *why* they come here. As we see it, there are a few core reasons.

First, America offers an assortment of opportunities that other countries do not because we provide a situation that is close to a true meritocracy—something that is not available across the developed world. If you have talents, a vision, and the resolve to see it through, you can make it in the US.

Second, America offers substantial protections for individual liberties. While the trend has been mixed recently, we still outperform most other countries, which is a testament to how impressive our Constitution was in the first place. In America, people can use the legal process to defend themselves against the encroachments of the state. In many other countries, people get no such recourse.

Third, America's government, while also problematic and at times deeply frustrating, is superior to the governments of most developing countries, where strongmen rule and ordinary people are on their own. In the US, people can elect their own representatives and vote them out when they don't like the job they are doing.

Taken together, these are, in our estimate, the reasons why people come to America. To distill these ideas to a single coherent point, one could say that they embody the spectrum of American values: a system based on meritocracy unlike any other in the world, individual rights for citizens, checks on government, and a system of justice in which everyone has an equal opportunity.

While there are obviously gaps between these principles and the practice of everyday life, it is nonetheless the aspiration to live under these institutions and to believe in these values that pulls immigrants from around the world to come here and to join our political community.

Critics may reject some of these pronouncements. Luckily for us, and unfortunately for them, there is solid, recent polling on these topics (as well as a few adjacent ones) that provide reasons to believe that the positive immigrant experience we described is substantiated by the actual attitudes and beliefs of the people in question.

Some polling indicates that citizen immigrants hold more positive views about America than do citizens, and noncitizen immigrants are not far behind; polling of these same groups on the question of how America compares to other countries delivers similar results.[200]

Elsewhere we see that the American Dream may be especially alive and well for immigrants. Specifically, immigrants, including immigrants in the lowest-income category, experience upward mobility within a generation—something that is not true of native-born citizens.[201]

This is one reason, albeit a very powerful one, that could explain why immigrants see the US so positively. It is worth wondering to what degree this relatively short-term success could inspire the criticism of the US that is so common among native-born progressives, both with regard to those who have achieved a lot and those who have not.

In light of these positive surveys, it is especially frustrating to see those in government and media try to promote the false narrative that immigrants are imposed upon by virtue of their being here, that they are unduly subjected to hardship, or that they are simply unwanted and unwelcome. And while there may be some who would seek to end our tradition of beneficial legal immigration, often through their own prejudice or intolerance, they are a minority.

To be sure, there are some immigrants who come to the US and are deeply resentful of the country, but they are among the minority. And there are still other patriotic, assimilated immigrants whose children and grandchildren—Indians, Africans, East Asians, people of all backgrounds—identify less with America and try to fall back on their cultural ethnicities.[202] But these cases are irregular and thus do not reflect on the broader experience.

In fact, here is a fun experiment to try out: next time you are riding in an Uber, start a conversation with your driver. There is a decent chance that person is an immigrant,[203] and the odds are that you will find this person to be thrilled about his or her experience in America; there is also a great chance that they have more commonsensical social and political views than your average American.

In summary, legal immigrants who come to America: 1) usually hold positive views about the country and its institutions; 2) are optimistic about the prospects of building a better life for themselves and their families; and 3) are often more grounded in their assessments of the country than some existing American citizens, and this is because they have an experience outside of the US, and thus an understanding of many of America's better aspects that others take for granted.

This is not to say that immigrants are inherently "natural conservatives," as some have said in the past, but which is now a punchline. But neither are they necessarily resentful progressives. Rather, we believe that many immigrants see America in a healthy, fair, and overwhelmingly beneficent light, which is a good thing. If they did not see it in this light, it would be a mystery as to why they risked so much to come here.

The degree to which we can change the attitudes of future Americans, both born here and from abroad, is dependent on the organization of and the values presented by our institutions, a topic we discuss in greater detail in the following chapters.

America remains a largely positive beacon of hope for millions around the world because of our unique American way of self-healing and our system based on meritocracy. While our political institutions are imperfect, and though our problems remain substantial, we still outperform many other countries in many other regions, from the Middle East to Europe and Latin America. This is why many immigrants want to come here.

That we remain such a prominent and positive country in the eyes of so many is a testament to the enduring power of our Constitution, undermined as it is and transformed though it was in the previous century.

We should understand that this fact—that we remain desirable even in the face of enduring and existential threats—is a good sign: it means that we have the capacity to arrest bad trends and to rectify our institutions. The future is not inherently doomed to be worse than the present or the past. In the following chapter, we explore and analyze some of these challenges in greater detail.

CHAPTER 8

THREATS TO OUR FUTURE

"Freedom is a fragile thing and it's never more than one generation away from extinction. It is not ours by way of inheritance; it must be fought for and defended constantly by each generation, for it comes only once to a people. And those in world history who have known freedom and then lost it have never known it again."
—Ronald Reagan

I. Optimism and Honesty

We are very optimistic about America's future because when we have had tough times before like those we currently face, America has *always* come back stronger. We have the capital, the brainpower, and the institutions to succeed. These assets helped us reach new heights in every century of America's existence.

Right now, the country faces an assortment of threats— some novel and others recurring, some social and others economic—that must be addressed if we are to avoid potentially existential pitfalls, including insolvency, economic stagnation, and cultural or social balkanization.

Our problems are not rhetorical flourishes or hot-button topics to use in the service of going viral on social media or to raise our profiles. We sincerely believe that America is in a very difficult position right now, and if things go the wrong way, there could be disastrous consequences for you, your family, and future generations of Americans.

Our prosperity isn't guaranteed—it's earned every day by each successive generation that holds power.

And even more broadly, if these problems remain unresolved, they will effectively mark the end of America as we know it today, i.e., our unique culture of self-healing, meritocracy and the promise of the American Dream, and consensus for large changes to our system.

Indeed, if Americans do not wake up and steer the country well clear of these problems, opportunities will dry up, and America will no longer be seen as a desirable place to live and raise a family—for immigrants and citizens alike. Moreover, once our system is gone, it may be gone forever, as history has shown for other nations.

We believe that the country can solve its problems because it has in the past. This is one of the things that makes America so unique. But the threats are real, and they are metastasizing. To combat them, we must understand what they are, why they are bad, and crucially, where they come from.

II. Market Meddling

The first category of threats we will discuss is economic. Some of these problems are novel, but others have been developing for some time. We will move through these issues in chrono-logical order.

The earliest of these economic problems come from the artifacts of FDR's New Deal[204] and Lyndon B. Johnson's Great Society.[205] Specifically, these welfare schemes are unsustainable and have created serious levels of debt that will only increase as the Baby Boomers and Generation X retire. This is because many of these programs operate no differently than Ponzi schemes: people who pay in at first get the benefits of the return from new investors, but the new investors may never see any of the money at all if the system collapses.[206] Millennials and Generation Z are increasingly pessimistic about their chances of receiving Social Security, with one in every four believing they'll never receive anything in the future from the program.[207]

While these programs have worked for decades, the simple mathematical fact is that they are going bankrupt. This is due to the trajectory of demographics in the US, along with the impending retirement of a whole generation of Americans, an increasing lifespan, and decreasing birth rates. These programs are not sustainable. In short, the money will not be there.

This means that a generation of Americans will have paid substantial amounts of money in taxes into programs that they will *never* benefit from. This is tantamount to fraud, and it will have horrible consequences on the American econ-omy and faith in our government, not to mention the lives of millions who will rely on entitlements that will not be there for them.

But this is only half of the economic problem. Washington will not stop spending: it has committed itself to all manner of other spending that is similarly untenable. Where the prior problem began in the past, this issue started decades earlier but continues today.

While we can throw several examples of ridiculous and indefensible government spending programs, the truth is only four matter: Social Security, Medicare, Medicaid, and Defense.[208] These four take up the largest part of the budget by a wide margin. Sixty-five percent of the $6 trillion the US is expected to spend in 2022 will be based solely on Social Security, Medicare, and Medicaid.[209] If serious changes are not made, we will face a bankruptcy crisis that has never been seen before in the US. The US dollar, which facilitates many of the transactions in global markets, could potentially collapse if its stability is in doubt. These programs *must* be reformed.

Interest costs on the debt issued to finance these programs and all others are projected to triple over the next decade, reaching nearly $1 trillion annually by 2030.[210] If left unchecked, by 2050, the percentage of all federal revenues necessary to finance our past spending could reach 45 percent.[211] In other words, nearly $1 in every $2 paid by Americans in the form of taxes would *not* be spent on government programs but on interest payments. This situation is akin to a family trapped in mountains of debt with high interest rates, forced to spend half of their income on the interest payments alone without paying down the principal as they're forced to allocate their remaining income to barely survive.

If Americans are to address this looming problem in earnest, they must find solutions to better manage the tremendous costs associated with Social Security, Medicare, Medicaid, and Defense, lest the burden of debt crush them before they can be reformed.

Welfare is a frequent target for those looking to address our looming debt crisis. Certainly, excesses exist in many programs and should be trimmed as they're identified, such as the fraudulent "business owners" who took advantage of COVID-19 relief funds. According to the *Washington Post*, identity theft and other criminal activity alone resulted in $163 billion in wasted COVID-19-related unemployment benefits.[212] But cutting welfare entirely would only marginally improve the prospects of getting America's spending problem under control, as welfare currently makes up approximately 5 percent of federal expenses.[213] We believe welfare can have a much greater social cost beyond just the financial cost to the American taxpayer, though, and it's the creation of a new class of people exclusively dependent on government support for their continued well-being.

We recognize that welfare has an important role in society, and we are well aware of the tired critiques of those who would seek to reform it as cruel or selfish. Welfare has a place in America, but it should be used to transition people back to work, not as a substitute for a job.

Sadly, for some, welfare has become a lifestyle. One figure, in particular, highlights this problem: roughly four out of every ten Americans on welfare remain on it for multiple years.[214] Living on welfare is becoming normal, and that is not good.

Another statistic, labor force participation, makes it clear that our current trajectory is (and has been) moving in the wrong direction.[215] This figure provides us with a measure of the country's industriousness, and right now, fewer people are working.

Welfare is not a problem confined to a particular race or sex. And at a core level, endless spending cannot be a solution to our social and economic problems.

What many people miss about this problem is that by spending so much money, the government is forced to issue more debt, which will, in turn, devalue the dollar and create anxiety in the market. This is the starting point for so many terrible economic crises, and the danger of uncertainty cannot be overstated.

Indeed, Larry Summers, an eminent economist, former Treasury secretary, and a mainstay advisor in Democratic administrations, has warned that "if price stability is lost and inflation accelerates, sooner or later the consequence will be a severe recession that will hit the poor and middle class hardest and undo recent employment gains."[216]

This is a great risk, particularly when millions of Americans are still in the process of recovering from the economic shock of the COVID-19 recession, while others never fully recovered from the historic recession of 2008. Summers recognizes that creating these problems is easy—just implement bad policies—while rectifying them is much more difficult.

To help avoid this situation, we need to first reinforce the importance of America's pro-work and pro-growth culture. Since before the founding of the country, diligent work has defined the American experience, and it built America into the power that it is today. That same work ethic that guided the earliest among us must guide America today against our current challenges.

Unfortunately, the incentives and messaging of the Biden administration push people away from this great cultural heritage and towards dependency and sloth. This is a new development, and the truth of this statement is most obvious when one looks at the words of the last Democratic president, Barack Obama, who was not exactly a right-wing radical or laissez-faire fundamentalist.

It was not long ago when President Obama observed that "any strategy to reduce intergenerational poverty has to be centered on work, not welfare—not only because work provides independence and income but also because work provides order, structure, dignity, and opportunities for growth in people's lives."[217]

Building wealth is always superior to redistributing the proverbial pie as it exists today, and Obama understood that.

But Biden's government does not share that view, and it appears it may be more committed to the quackery of what has been dubbed "modern monetary theory." The theory suggests that the modern, developed states need not be constrained by revenues when spending.[218] To translate, that means that a country like the US can simply continue printing money because it has a large economy and prestige. The growth in the money supply can be matched or even exceeded by equal growth. This theory suggests government spending can create an infinite fountain of economic growth!

This idea is insane. And it argues that because we are economically dominant now and our dollar is a preferred currency of choice by many across the world, we can afford to do all kinds of things which undermine the fundamentals that account for our present position. Never assume continuity in the face of radical change.

The other issue with modern monetary theory is that it presumes that America's status quo as a world leader will not change based on what economic programs it implements. The success of modern monetary theory largely depends on the stable value globally of the dollar. Any serious understanding of economics should make clear that this theory, if applied, will harm people through inflation and, in turn, harm the broader economy, both of which will cost America its standing in the world, thus undermining its financial situation. This eventually becomes a self-reinforcing and dangerous cycle.

And if that is not convincing enough, just look at what happened to Venezuela when the government turned to a policy of rapid currency devaluation.[219] If you're unfamiliar, let's put it simply: it did not go well for anyone involved.

Our observations of modern monetary theory and America's approach to entitlements should be taken as uncontroversial by anyone looking at these questions honestly. These arguments should not be dismissed or seen as partisan. And yet they are, which is a microcosm of another big issue, namely the politicization of all aspects of American life.

Whether it is sports, television, or even fast food, politics is everywhere in America, and that is a new development and one we should be gravely concerned with. Other societies that underwent a process of ideological escalation and politicization include pre-revolutionary Russia (the 1910s) and France (the 1780s), neither of which are situations we should want to replicate.

III. Pervasive Partisanship and the Fracturing of Civil Society

There are many causes for the spread of politics into every aspect of American life, and in our assessment, the degradation of civil society is one of the biggest forces behind this sad, ongoing trend.

As noted above, politics is everywhere, and a sense of community is seemingly nowhere. People are more atomized than ever, and to the degree that there are common bonds, they break down along political lines. Whether politicization is the cause or the effect of this trend is irrelevant: it is a clear problem.

Moreover, the ascent of this political age has, in turn, contributed to the rise of partisan groups outside of the mainstream, like Antifa or the Proud Boys; the decline of traditional organizations—like social clubs and recreational sporting leagues, to name a few—further highlight this development.

While these are some of the more radical groups (as well as some of the newer ones on the scene), there are many others that are just divisive, including but not limited to groups like Media Matters, the Southern Poverty Law Center, and the collective "woke" Twitter mob—which are committed to punishing people for holding the "wrong" political views with no regard for their reputations or the accuracy of their charges and slurs.

In almost all cases, this attack goes in one direction: against moderates/conservatives to boost progressives.[220] This tattletale culture is unhealthy and reminiscent of the (un)civil societies that characterized communist regimes, especially the censorial, informant culture of the USSR.

Civil society has been subjected to an unrelenting, partisan offensive for years, and the decades in which it has been the front line for culture-war battles have left it badly scarred.

This trend of civil society declining has gone on for some time. Famously and years ago, a political scientist named Robert Putnam wrote a book called *Bowling Alone: The Collapse and Revival of American Community* (2000) to document that very problem.

Putnam's book focuses on the degradation of civil society as measured in social capital (i.e., the bonds and relationships of people in a community upon which that group relies), a trend that he argues began in the middle of the twentieth century and that, if left unchecked, will generate a litany of problems for individual people and for the larger country.[221]

Bowling Alone chronicles the ubiquitous decline of social life in America over the last fifty years, which is captured by two major developments: 1) Americans are less social than they once were; and 2) their levels of civic engagement have fallen off since the 1950s.[222]

Putnam decries this trend as a disaster for American democracy and for the maintenance of any meaningful social sphere. The basic point is that, for there to be continuity within a political community, there must first be community.

Putnam understood that, for America to succeed and continue to function properly, it would need to rely on social institutions and relationships, both to help the market function properly and to ensure that key American traditions are transmitted to younger generations and immigrants. Additionally, these relationships develop a sense of tolerance and understanding, allowing us to see better the perspective of other Americans and how they live their lives.

But this transmission and continuity of values are not guaranteed, and since the 1950s, there are reasons to worry that something integral to America is breaking down. In particular, Putnam highlights the uptick in distrust within the country. Specifically, people are less personally close while, at the same time, they are more skeptical of those around them.

One reason for this that Putnam does not hit on is the celebration of antisocial behavior by large opinion-forming institutions, including the media and entertainment industries. From narcissism to deception and anti-natalism (the belief that no one should have children and is fueled in part by extreme environmentalism), the messages sent through and reinforced by actors within American culture have encouraged very antisocial themes that have contributed to this era of mistrust and isolation.

In its most extreme form, this includes the attempt at normalizing crime. Downplaying the problems with theft and property damage (among other crimes) has contributed to a massive crime spike over the last few years.[223] For instance, the murder rate in 2021 reached its highest in twenty-five years in the US, as almost twenty thousand were murdered.[224] Moreover, a series of major cities had the highest homicide rate they've ever recorded.[225] This is not a trend we want to see accelerating in the future.

Efforts by talking heads and politicians to contextualize the crime wave speaks to the core issue, which is that a small section of American society does not believe crime is a problem—and, for them, it is not, since they have the money to afford private security[226] or gated homes and can write off losses from theft.[227] But for everyone else, it is a serious issue that can destroy lives and fracture communities.[228]

While some of the rising crime is attributable to the so-called Ferguson Effect[229] and efforts to defund police departments from policing crime (or to simply prevent cops from doing their jobs), the bigger problem is the attempt at shifting attitudes on crime, including the attempt to redefine crime as a social problem that can be corrected as opposed to an unfortunate reality that defines human society and that must be responded to accordingly to mitigate its effects. In cases where our criminal justice system fails to provide fair or reasonable punishment for crimes, we should seek to embrace our self-healing nature and improve. But we must not do so at the expense of belittling the damaging effects of crime on society.

A pro-crime society cannot be a pro-community or a pro-trust society. In fact, it will have serious ramifications elsewhere, including in the economy.

Returning to Putnam, he cites several potential culprits for the decaying of American social life, including the availability and use of technology, the changing nature of social relations with time, and a larger general trend towards individualism (more choice translates into more difference).[230]

However, there is a more obvious one that we recognize today, which was not so obvious when Putnam conducted his research. Put simply, this alternative cause is the diffusion of an extremely toxic and pervasive ideology, which is better known today as "wokeness." In short, wokeness is an anathema to our culture of self-healing and meritocracy.

While we think many are familiar with the term (both the *New York Times* and President Trump have talked about it, after all), we want to spell out what it means, where it comes from, how it operates, what it is doing, and what it will do to America in the long term if it is not countered and defeated.

IV. The HR-ization of American Life

As we observed in the previous chapter, civil society was furthered, and America healed under the civil rights laws of the 1960s.

Americans built a consensus that the Jim Crow system in the South was wrong and at odds not only with our founding principles but also with steps America took after the Civil War. As a result, the Civil Rights Act of 1964 was passed to put an end to this egregious discrimination and move us closer to a truly meritocratic society. It is a good reminder that the way America has solved its problems in the past is by recognizing they exist and building a consensus to rectify them, a point we've made often in this book.

Now, for over fifty years, discrimination against individuals on the basis of race has been illegal in every institution in the country, from universities to profit-seeking entities in the private sector. We have done the best we can to enshrine our meritocratic society into law, and there are no threats of Jim Crow returning from the grave, in no small part because attitudes on race have changed.[231] Today, America is finally living in a world remade by these laws in which prejudice against minorities is truly taboo and only accepted in the most fringe cultures of American society.

Unfortunately, despite the many incredible changes in American society since the victory of the civil rights movement, there is a tension between the good aims of the early civil rights laws (to end discrimination) and the modern civil rights agenda. The modern agenda thinks it is possible to transform society to eliminate *all* disparities between groups, something that is impossible given the amount of coercion it would require—not to mention the fact that individuals have distinct talents and career interests, which would also frustrate any efforts at securing total parity. One of the important things that come with a system of meritocracy is embracing the fact that people are different. They have different skill sets, abilities, talents, work ethics, and so on. Our law simply cannot mandate that everyone be equal, in terms of outcomes and not opportunity, regardless of these factors. America would be fundamentally transformed into a completely unrecognizable country if this were to happen.

While we do not pretend to know the exact degree to which wokeness is harming human relations and institutions, we do know that declining social trust is no doubt amplified (if not instigated) by America's new human resources (HR) culture. It takes everyday social interactions and subjects them to never-ending oversight by workplace antagonists who increasingly inhibit offices in firms, schools, and other organizations from operating smoothly.

It is the establishment of and regulation by HR offices (which have ballooned in number and influence over recent decades) that spreads and maintains wokeness via the transformation of civil rights law by judges, bureaucrats, and other politicians. In practical terms, this means HR exerts significant influence over hiring and investing, the policing of language through the imprecision of legal language and the repression of political views,[232] and the imposition of divisive, fringe "work trainings" and other partisan educational programs.[233]

As Vivek Ramaswamy's research in *Woke, Inc.* makes clear, these woke bureaucrats, who use their sway to commandeer the culture of and shape political causes championed by corporations, receive help in the form of the added influence of left-leaning, controlling shareholders who cynically support the ESG evaluation movement—environmental, social, and governance—to atone for other sins, including dubious business practices such as engaging in crony capitalism.[234]

The upshot is that these atonement-seeking businesspeople, often steered by HR employees, drive their companies further into the political arena on the side of progressives, often against the wishes of a numerical majority of shareholders and employees. Ramaswamy argues that this explains the positions of corporations today in their support for extreme environmental solutions, social causes, and political candidates.[235] And all the while, corporations successfully defang challenges to their anticompetitive and other questionable behaviors.

So, where exactly did these entities come from? Sad as it is to say, modern HR departments were born out of mutated federal laws. Federal programs aimed at establishing equity, executive orders dictating hiring practices for contractors, the reinterpretation of civil rights statutes to exclude categories from race-based policies: all of these developments drive the politicization of the country by empowering HR departments to institute "woke" policies and programs throughout the country—in government, education, and business.[236]

These ideas that have pervaded business and other institutions find their origin in academia, though. Much discussion has been had in the past year about critical race theory, but few understand the intellectual history of the ideas that created the broad category of critical theory. James Lindsay and Helen Pluckrose, in their book *Cynical Theories*, dissect the origin of the dominant philosophy informing today's social justice crusade, namely postmodernism, which evolved in leftist circles with the decline of Marxism as the prevailing philosophy (though the two philosophies have many things in common, such as a focus on power and privilege). Postmodern philosophy, according to their analysis, took root primarily in France in the 1960s (although other similar schools of thought originated elsewhere) and was led by philosophers such as Michel Foucault, Jacques Derrida, and Jean-François Lyotard.[237]

While postmodernism can be obtuse and dense (perhaps intentionally), it's most simply understood as a rejection of modernism, i.e., that scientific inquiry can advance society through technological innovation, that social progress can be made through ideas such as representative democracy and classical liberalism, and that objective knowledge is obtainable. French postmodernism focused on deconstruction, specifically as it relates to power and knowledge. In this deconstructive framework, concepts such as the "individual," "facts," and "freedom" are social constructs devoid of real meaning beyond those who have controlled their definitions through positions of power. It should be unsurprising that the modern derivatives of this philosophy reject the societal value of constitutional government and ultimately propagate a form of moral relativism. As the ideas grew in prominence, they began to dominate scholarship in academia, and it should be unsurprising that they've escaped academia and touched almost all facets of American life.

While the origin of these ideas is important to understand the broader social justice movement, the focus of this discussion is specific to the impact on business and the damage created in this institution. It would be one thing if these woke corporate policies actually led to better race relations or even healthier, more productive work environments. Instead, these HR programs and related rules are deliberately divisive and discriminatory: they assume guilt, browbeat particular people while simultaneously trying to erase individual people, and redefine humans in groups; they create disparate standards for people of different lifestyles and ancestries; and they cost institutions tons of money and productivity due to the general (and growing) costs they put on doing business,[238] which cumulatively reduces the GDP.[239] It's important to reiterate that, in the working world, no one should feel intimidated or abused because of their background.

To use one example, let us return to the HR-ization problem. Companies must be in compliance with state and federal rules regulating employment. These rules are complex and subject to constant change, often through non-legislative means (i.e., government agencies can promulgate new rules themselves, which they often do, depending on the political party in power). This creates an untenable situation for businesses that subject them to the threat of massive lawsuits at all times.

To avoid those problems, companies hire loads of people to fill out expensive and robust HR departments to comply with these rules. In fact, many companies now set aside money to pay these people as a cost of doing business, such is the extent to which the HR culture is ingrained in American business and the legal systems that regulate it. It is easy to see how this creates a self-sustaining cycle.

A quick view of stories on this subject shows that these "professionals" earn salaries in the hundreds of thousands at *universities*; other public speakers rake in tens of thousands of dollars *per event*. "Go woke, go broke" could not be further from the truth.

There are many parties at fault for this development. There are activist groups like the ACLU, which has drifted sharply from its legacy as civil libertarians, that actively and intentionally push civil rights law into new directions to promote the interests of its donors and allies. In a 2021 *New York Times* article titled "Once a Bastion of Free Speech, the A.C.L.U. Faces an Identity Crisis," the subtitle frames the shift succinctly: "An organization that has defended the First Amendment rights of Nazis and the Ku Klux Klan is split by an internal debate over whether supporting progressive causes is more important."[240] This is not to say that the ideas of these hateful groups are worth defending, but that the fundamental American right to say them should be protected, regardless of how vile they may be. There are also judges whose activist decisions take the law far outside what the text of the statute provides for, which leads to unintended consequences. And then there are those who one would assume would oppose wokeness, like Republicans, but who ultimately have not touched any (and in some cases issued a few) of the executive orders that give this ideology teeth.[241]

Indeed, one of the most concerning aspects of wokeness is that most politicians either do not understand its genesis, or they do and are unwilling to critically assess, let alone amend, misinterpreted civil rights laws and programs.

The HR-ization of American life and the woke ideology that made this change possible is fundamentally wrong for several reasons. First, this system is unjust because it legalizes disparate treatment. Second, it is based on a lie, namely that all differences between groups are predicated on racial animus. And third, the HR-woke complex rewards bad behaviors—grifting, racial antagonism, victimhood, and scapegoating—and frustrates market efficiency, speech rights, and good business practices. Finally, it is at odds with our unique meritocratic culture. This system promotes nothing of value; it only helps those who push the victim narrative.

In short, Americans pay *a lot* for wokeness and get very little in return—that is, if you are in on the scam, wokeness is great for business because the grift is the business. But for the rest of us, this is not sustainable and is at direct odds with our meritocratic culture. Therefore, we must defeat this ideology before it takes over society at large.

V. Political Myopia and the Big Threat

If the problems of wokeness and our current economic situation are the results of unintended consequences and foolish political trade-offs, then America's inability to address pressing issues is a problem of imagination.

To use one example, since the COVID-19 pandemic began, there has been significantly more concern over opening public schools than in making available resources for alternatives to public schools.[242] When one looks at international[243] educational outcomes, it should be clear that non-public options should be celebrated and promoted, particularly for their ability to improve the lives of poor and non-White students.[244] As it stands, the current system is one of educational apartheid, where geographic location segregates the fortunate from the least fortunate and leaves the neediest children in failing schools without access to other options.

Regrettably, the focus has not been on these larger issues. In our view, this is a mistake that distracts from serious problems. In Washington, there is nothing that politicians and the media do better than distract from a major issue to focus on a smaller one that they, in turn, make into a polarizing political fight. One of the best examples of this category of problems is the Afghanistan War controversy.

In the summer of 2021, President Biden did what President Trump twice campaigned on: extract the US from a protracted and confused war. Prior to withdrawing American troops, the program enjoyed broad, bipartisan support. Troops were taken out of the region, and the local government, which was organized by Washington and whose troops were trained and armed by American military personnel, was left on its own. No sooner had Biden given orders to exit than the mood changed, and it became a partisan issue.[245]

Setting aside that a Democratic president did what a Republican president ran on, the real concern ought to be in the fact that the public and their representatives did not receive accurate information from military brass and the bureaucrats in their assessments of the situation in Afghanistan.

Consider the most absurd example: Mark Milley, the head of the Joint Chiefs of Staff, was supposedly blindsided by the collapse of the Afghanistan government, which, as a reminder, occurred basically overnight.[246] This should have been a huge controversy; instead, the focus was on the young administration's newly partisan action rather than the failures of the entrenched forces that oversaw the war for decades.

Ultimately, Afghanistan is in itself a microcosm of a larger problem, namely the lack of focus on the core interests of the US. In the Middle East, the Far East, and Eurasia, the US has spent billions to police the actions of other states in their own spheres of influence, nominally to prevent bad behavior. But at home, the same politicians shaping these policies will shrug at the fact that so many of America's biggest cities are objectively dangerous and lawless when the sun goes down (and, in some cases, during the day too).

In the final analysis, it may be impossible to determine where this myopic view of politics came from and why it remains with us today (we think some of it is due to the way

information is conveyed in America—largely via television—
and the profit-seeking, politics-selling nature of the medium).
But whatever the cause, the effect is clear: issues that matter
are being ignored while the problems swell.

Consider one other problem: the sustained and serious
challenge to long-standing American political institutions,
which comes predominantly from the left side of the political
spectrum.[247] The Electoral College, the Supreme Court, and
the Bill of Rights (see Appendix B) have been incessantly crit-
icized for at least the last five years.

Taken together, these are the things that determine how
we as Americans engage in the political process. The corollary is that we ought to be keenly focused on strengthening
these institutions and on developing the best arguments in
their favor. Instead, many on the right have spent time doing
other things, including devoting a disproportionate amount
of time and resources to challenging international issues that
are wholly unrelated to these essential domestic problems.[248]

To highlight this growing divide, America today faces
inflation to a degree that hasn't been seen for decades. When
the prices of goods and services rise, Americans can purchase
less with their income and are ultimately poorer as a consequence. In this way, inflation can be also seen as a tax on
the least well-off in society, who spend a greater portion of
their income on necessities. To highlight the economic illit-
eracy currently pervading the public discourse on this issue,
politicians have suggested that the best way to combat rising
gas prices is to provide stimulus checks to individuals and
families with nearly identical income requirements as the
COVID-19 relief effort.[249] While it's easy to be sympathetic

to the COVID-19 relief effort during a time that saw millions forced out of work overnight without warning, the recent discussion of gas price stimulus checks shows that this may become a go-to response to any economic crisis. Increased government spending will accelerate inflation, not mitigate it, as recent economic research has suggested.[250] Putting the middle class on what essentially amounts to welfare for every economic shock will only seek to drive prices higher into the future and further harm the people the policy intends to help.

As with wokeness and economically illiterate policies, this is a major problem and one that must be confronted if we are to avoid the mother of all issues facing America: the end of meritocracy.

If the trends described in this chapter are not stopped and reversed, then America will move further and perhaps irreversibly in a bad direction.

The anti-work, antisocial culture that has been inculcated over the last few decades is an existential threat to the way that Americans have heretofore lived and worked. The challenges to America's core political institutions represent an equally potent threat to the political culture of the country. And finally, the HR-ization of business and life promises to pry apart what remains of civil society and hamstring industry and education.

To reiterate a point we made earlier, there are no good alternatives to meritocracy. On the one hand, there is a spoils system: the rich and the connected do great, and everyone else languishes on the outside. The other option is an equally bad system of privilege, but this would cut along racial lines and breed resentment and economic stagnation.

We discuss meritocracy in greater detail in the following chapter. Before moving to that conversation, we want to impart one last warning. America can be restored, but to do so requires focus, commitment, and leadership on the part of the American people and their representatives to revive the principles and systems that turned our country into a world leader.

To be sure, other countries, like China, are paying close attention to the ugly path that America is walking. Our competitors understand what made us successful and a global leader: namely, our openness to competition, new ideas, new people, and new possibilities—in short, the American system.

These rivals also know that other countries in North America and South America took different paths. It is up to this generation of Americans to decide which road we take, if we embrace the strengths of our past traditions, or if we opt for the Latin American model of limited social mobility, clannishness, and a general decline in community with its attendant higher rates of crime and diminishing social trust. If this sounds unappealing, then our only option is to return to a true meritocracy and accept that equal outcomes and distributions are not possible under such a system—which is okay.

CHAPTER 9

MERITOCRACY

*"Live honestly and honorably within the limits
and to the limits of your own ability—and give thanks
to the men and women whose greater ability has
made such a magnificent world possible for you."*
—Ayn Rand

I. Our Best

No matter what any pundit, political party, or movement says, we believe in a simple truth about our country: at the heart of the American system is the idea that good, effective people should and will be promoted. This truth lies at the core of the American Dream and our unique system of meritocracy. Hopefully, we have demonstrated this in the preceding chapters.

Throughout American history, people have worked hard and persevered to see their ideas and innovations succeed. The harder workers get ahead, their good ideas make themselves and other people wealthy, and often, society benefits in the process. In a nutshell, this is a meritocracy, and for cen-turies (including a few before the American Founding in the late 1700s), it defined American life.

But there is an important and closely related point, a corollary to the meritocratic system upon which America is built, and that is that those who do not produce, those who do not deserve to move ahead, and those ideas that are not worthwhile will often lose out. As we see it, it is the potential for there to be losers that animates so much of the anti-meri-tocracy discourse of our age.

When America is at its best—economically, politically, socially, morally, in every regard—our meritocracy is func-tioning and unrestrained. Whether it was the NASA pro-gram, the country-wide and private-sector-led effort to fight and win World War II, or the rise of Silicon Valley, in each of these cases, market competition and the spirit of individ-ual risk-taking led America to achieve things to which other developed countries only aspire.

Unsurprisingly, we also believe that, when America is not working well, our meritocracy is usually not functioning properly either.

Unfortunately, much of the contemporary debate over racism, privilege, and entitlement comes from a disagree-ment over whether America ought to move towards an equal-ity-of-outcome system rather than an equality-of-opportu-nity system. The contours of this debate were established, and we would argue best articulated, at Harvard University. To be more precise, it was in the form of an argument between pro-fessors in the philosophy department, John Rawls and Robert

Nozick, which is captured in two works, A *Theory of Justice* (1971) and *Anarchy, State, and Utopia* (1974), respectively.

These are both complex books in which the authors present numerous arguments and sub-arguments, so we will stick to the main ideas here for expediency and clarity, beginning with Rawls.

Rawls's A *Theory of Justice* presents an egalitarian view of what justice demands. He famously offered an idea of justice in which differences and inequalities could only be permitted so long as they benefit the worst off in a society—a rule that, if taken seriously, puts both a ceiling and a floor on success.[251]

Rawls did not believe that there could be differences across individuals and groups unless the least well-off people got something out of the achievements of the successful. This is an extreme position that, in practical terms, makes the case for acute redistribution, and that, in turn, requires central planning and a socialist economic model.

Nozick understood the ugly programs Rawls's theory suggested (if not demanded) and set out his own account of what a just government would look like. This argument was captured in his *magnum opus*, a book titled *Anarchy, State, and Utopia*. Towards this end, Nozick offered a defense of liberal principles, including and especially the acceptance of difference, i.e., that people would live with it rather than try to "correct" it.

In a memorable section, Nozick asks the reader to envision a world in which one million people have 25 cents that they all give to the basketball player Wilt Chamberlain, one of the most successful players of all time, over the course of a season to watch him play.[252] After this transfer, Nozick says, Chamberlain is significantly richer than everyone else in society, but per Rawls, this is a just outcome: everyone is better off and received what they wanted, namely to see a star perform at a high level.

The basic point that Nozick makes is that, under Rawls's view, justice would eliminate any semblance of liberty or choice. In such a situation, this idea of justice would pave the way for a nonconsensual society in which the incentive structure would be completely backward, among other undesirable things.

The insight of Nozick's counterargument to Rawls is our best case for meritocracy. To reduce this point to a single sentence, in our estimation, the argument for disparate outcomes, or for the virtue of a dynamic market, is the moral and economic system opposite of socialism or redistributionism. This is the core difference between equality of opportunity and equality of outcome. And there can be no distributive scheme or formula that can overcome the inescapable problem with equality of outcome, namely that it is manifestly unfair—a point that the Chamberlain example succinctly demonstrates.

The last conclusion we draw, no matter how it is dressed up or what flag it sails under, is that redistributionist policies of the Rawlsian variety are never just and are simply incompatible with a free-enterprise system. This implies they are also fundamentally at odds with a meritocratic system. Today, many advocates couch their desires to implement such programs in appeals to the Constitution, religion, and the civil rights movement; in other cases, they simply charge that America is illegitimate due to its past and must atone—which is strangely something that they believe it can never *really do*—by implementing redistributionist policies.

In the end, these are simply attempts to fundamentally change the country and get something out of it via redistribution for groups pandered to by progressives.

Albeit the moral stakes are significantly less, so many of the problems of today—anti-market regulations, bad incentives, and the ascendant HR culture—have their genesis in that same uncompetitive, rent-seeking spirit that Rawls' writings are so often used to justify.

It follows, in our estimation, that to get things back on track, we must commit ourselves to countering this desire on the one hand while reducing existing barriers to a more meritocratic system on the other. We must embrace the market and accept the differences that capitalism reveals and that Nozick defended. To do this, we must be willing to defend the morality of a non-redistributionist, anti-equity system, i.e., the free-enterprise approach based on meritocracy.

Given how powerful the US is, how well integrated its financial system is, and how many strong allies it possesses around the world, it is likely the case that the problems that truly threaten the country in a fundamental and irreversible way likely come from the inside, not the outside.

As we stressed in the last chapter, these threats are real. Be they economic, social, or cultural, the danger is there, and we must take it seriously. In particular, we think that the collection of threats facing the country—the balkanization of American life, the spread of racially divisive outlooks and theories, unsustainable entitlements, massive military spending, untenable commitments abroad, and the declining economic situation—are untenable and need to be rectified before we lose the country for good.

Globally, assimilation and racial harmony are rare and are often the exception. Not enough people recognize or appreciate that, but it is true, and it makes America's relative success even more impressive. But, if our differences do pull us apart, if racial resentment and polarization do fracture the country, then what does that say about democracy as a political system? In our view, it would vindicate China's own chauvinist culture and policies, and that would be a tragedy.

This leads into an even greater question: What can we do? While no solutions are guaranteed to work in every case, we have some ideas.

II. How to Fix This Mess

Before getting to the particular solutions, we will briefly list out the five big threats—some independent, but many interrelated—that we see as posing the gravest challenge to the American way of life:

1. The anti-meritocracy movement
2. HR-ization of business and life
3. Politicization and decline of civil society
4. Counterproductive economic policies
5. Lack of political imagination, resolve, and courage

We believe that the defining characteristic of America is its meritocratic ethos and that its success is built on its pro-risk-taking method.

Before the country was established, hard work and initiative determined a person's success. Without an aristocracy or tradition of nobles, America and its people have always generally relied on the outputs of individuals to determine if and when a person will get ahead. This was true for the political sphere just as much as it was true for the economic realm, and it should always be at the core of how America operates.

Threats to this system come in many forms, from attempts to design a new caste system to boost progressives' favorite groups and to suppress those they dislike to the concentrated movement away from risk. Policies that divide Americans by race are a good example of the former, while the neurosis around COVID-19 safety-ism highlights the latter. In all cases, we have a serious problem, namely an alternative way to live and a competing view of oneself relative to others and their political community.

We think America can live up to its aspirations, as it has in the past, and because of that, we come down hard on the side of meritocracy. In truth, there is no alternative. The HR-ization issue overlaps with the defense of meritocracy. Bureaucratization, grifting, the micromanaging of private business—these all connect to the rise of the HR office. This institution is inefficient and onerous, not to mention unnecessary in too many cases. While HR does perform many important roles, the monolithic role it plays in the office today can be counterproductive and costly at times. Instead of supplementing the culture necessary so businesses can put strong goods and services on the market, HR too often takes steps to make it more difficult for those ideas to see the light of day.

Related to both the attack on meritocracy and the rise of the HR office is the politicization of American life. HR bureaucrats push companies to take sides in partisan disputes and leverage their influence to handicap and punish political rivals in ways that undermine principles of fairness as well as the First Amendment culture that for so long characterized civil society.[253] Unfortunately, HR today sees its job as being the police for every minor office dispute. While HR plays an important role when it investigates allegations of abuse, sexual harassment, fraud, and so on, it moves far away from its mission when it harasses employees on what language should be used in the office to make it more inclusive, assuming said language isn't used in a way to harass or demean a colleague.

The goal of the diversity ideology to make institutions "look more like America" is a strange one, because of the ever-changing demographics of the country.

Does anyone really think it would be just or fair if the federal government or some interest group brought these organizations to court to ensure that their teams promoted proportional representation? Would anyone *want* to watch a professional basketball game in which the best athletes, the most explosive players, most of them Black American and Eastern European players, were limited to a set number of spots per team rather than given time based on their aptitude?

The result would be a mediocre league and an unjust situation in which people are selected not for their talents but for what boxes they can be put into, depending on their skin tone or country of origin. This is what the law currently does through incorrect legal interpretations and the power of rapacious HR departments, and it must stop.

The economically ruinous policies of the federal government are no better. Decades of mismanagement, an unwillingness to confront long-standing fiscal problems, and the arrival of a slew of bad programs have created a situation in which inflation is up and unemployment may soon follow.[254] The economic growth of the Trump years has been followed by the slowdown of the Biden tenure. Even controlling for the COVID-19 pandemic, the unprecedented uptick in spending suggests that this change could be fundamental.

There are no new ideas anymore in Washington, only half-hearted arguments over issues that were resolved (or became unresolvable) long ago. Washington must catch up to the problems of the present, and it must commit itself to seeing them addressed in a sensible, realistic manner. This requires creativity to imagine new solutions and the courage to implement them, even and especially when doing so may not be politically rewarding in the short term.

With these problems sketched out, we can now look at a few realistic solutions that would go a long way toward improving the country in the immediate and over time.

The lowest hanging fruit, or the most achievable goals, would do quite a lot to restore our meritocracy while empowering businesses and deescalating cultural and political disputes. Specifically, courts could enforce the actual language of the 1964 Civil Rights Act to prohibit intentional discrimination on the basis of race in all facets of employment.

In practice, this would mean the end of racial preferences and a substantive clampdown on efforts to institutionalize "equity" and other social justice (i.e., anti-meritocratic) schemes. This would level the playing field in hiring and admissions and would translate to better outputs and less contentious professional and academic environments.

To prevent future manipulation of the law, legislators should be very clear in the text of a bill before it becomes law to lessen the chance of misinterpretation.

After all, what is the end goal of affirmative action policies? At certain moments in American history, they've helped open doors to opportunities that were previously unavailable to some people. So, when do we reach the point that these policies have had their intended effect of creating equal opportunity for every American? It should be clear at this stage that we believe some would set that goal at complete parity among all groups (i.e., half of all CEOs are women, and half are men). This focus on outcome over opportunity creates an ever-shifting goal in need of continuous tinkering controlled by government elites. When a day comes that 51 percent of women are CEOs, do we begin to fire that 1 percent in order to reach total parity across sexes? This is why we believe that a better measure will always be opportunity through a meritocratic process, and in cases where individuals are barred from competition with others, barriers should be torn down.

The president, now or in the future, could do a lot on this front. He or she should rescind coercive and misguided executive orders that tell private businesses and government contractors how to run their enterprises, which, in the real world, translates to picking winners and losers based on their commitment to the political views of bureaucrats, as well as their ethnic backgrounds.[255] The government should not micromanage personnel decisions. Companies know their own interests best, and social engineering is wrong.

Come the October 2022 term, the Supreme Court will also have an opportunity to end discriminatory admissions practices in colleges and universities. The court has agreed to review the constitutionality of Harvard University and the University of North Carolina's race-based admissions systems to see whether they are consistent with the Fourteenth Amendment's equal protection clause.[256] While some might note that Harvard is a private university and is not subject to the equal protection clause, because Harvard receives federal funds, it is subject to federal law that prohibits discrimination on the basis of race.[257] In short, the court has a historic opportunity to correct its own past wrong in allowing colleges and universities to use race as a plus factor when considering applicants, but to also fulfill the central command of the equal protection clause, which is race neutrality.[258] If the court rules the right way, it will bring America another step closer to a system based on meritocracy. If it rules the wrong way, it will tell millions of Americans that race is one of the most important defining characteristics of applicants, not hard work or perseverance.

Legislators could also create incentives for government workers to keep people away from government dependence. For instance, they might reward those that are better at getting individuals off government programs and into paying jobs. This would be good for the individuals steered into employment, as there is a pride and dignity that comes from work, while also ensuring that they aren't smothered by government programs, but it would also be good for people in the second category of welfare (we mentioned this very early in the book). Specifically, this would open up funds for the truly mentally or physically disabled who rely on welfare just to live.

Another significant reform would be mandating a sunset period of five or ten years for major pieces of legislation that become law. For example, imagine if in the next few years there is still unspent COVID-19 relief or unspent dollars for the recent infrastructure bill. If the government could not find a way to spend the billions and billions of dollars in that time period, why should it continue to get the chance after the moment has passed? It is nothing short of crazy to say that if the government hasn't spent all the COVID-19 relief funds in the next ten years, it should continue to get another chance.

Republicans are out of the White House, but assuming they win the House back in 2022, they could opt to limit funding to the partisan tools of the state. The concept here is that they could reduce the influence of wokeness and the ascendant politically correct culture. This would be tantamount to disarming one's rival.

But control of political institutions in Washington is subject to the vicissitudes of public opinion and elections. Republicans should adopt a new outlook on politics, one with a more long-term focus. Being more aggressive in the immediate on a particular issue may change the contours of the debate in the aggregate, which could make unimaginable goals attainable in the future.

Dr. Richard Hanania, a prominent public intellectual and researcher, has offered a few more difficult to achieve but infinitely more impactful solutions, including the elimination of the "disparate impact" legal standard (i.e., that gaps between groups prove discrimination of one or more groups) as well as the narrowing of the "hostile work environment" concept so that it does not cut against conservative political speech and culture.[259]

These admittedly would not fix things immediately, but over time, they would lead to a transformation in the culture of businesses, academia, and other influential institutions. As their corruption took decades, so too will their renewal.

This is a crucial point. Something we believe that moderates, conservatives, and liberals who worry about the long-term trajectory of the woke/politically correct (PC)/identity politics movement must keep in mind is that there is no one policy goal and no single election that can arrest and reverse this force in American politics. Unfortunately, this means that whether it is in the school system or in the military, the craziness of woke policies will require years of committed, serious effort to overturn. Campaigning on pushing back, tweeting about it, or issuing statements will do nothing without diligent, substantive work.

We turn now to the environment. We believe that resolving problems associated with balancing energy needs and sustainability concerns can be addressed in part through the depoliticization of civil society and private-sector actors. This depoliticization would hopefully bring companies back into the mainstream on a host of other issues.

But these are long-term goals. To address the environment in the immediate, elected leaders and civilians alike must do several things. First, they must defend and advance pro-energy policies. People do not benefit from high costs on energy, as it is an invaluable resource for individuals and for our economy.[260] Wealthy people and urban dwellers can afford exorbitant energy costs because they have alternatives, such as walking to work, teleworking, or public transportation. Working or rural Americans often do not have that luxury.

Second, to skeptics of the energy industry, one can point out that innovations in energy, which are essential if humanity is to move away from fossil fuels in a realistic and sustainable manner, are not possible without the existing revenues generated by and power available through such resources. We would like to add that experimentation with new energy sources is a good thing, whether one is certain we face environmental Armageddon or not.

To be sure, some of these programs and schemes are costly; some experiments fail. But so long as people retain access to affordable sources of energy, and on the condition that the market—not the federal government (its record[261] is shoddy at best)—leads in the innovation effort, then we should all be in favor of research into cheaper, more effective sources of energy. We are confident that new technologies will reduce the usage of fossil fuels in the long run and that the free-enterprise system will play an integral role in reaching that resolution.

To leave a final word on this topic, we want to clarify that, contrary to how companies are (or have been) portrayed, they are not disinterested in, and are certainly not aligned against, the natural environment.

In David's experience, his own company did substantial work to provide safe, affordable energy to Americans. On top of that, due to its successes, the company invested money into research and development that eventually led to the efficient use of wind turbines, which, in turn, shifted the one-third of the energy produced by the company to wind. This is an important reminder of how the relationship between energy, investment, and innovation is best pursued in the private sector.

We also believe that other enduring problems, particularly poverty, can and will be solved through the same approach of unleashing private sector forces. We must also not forget the role that charities play in combating poverty. We are one of the most generous nations in the history of the world when it comes to giving resources to those who need help. Not to be too dramatic, but all these factors are our best hope, as the last sixty years demonstrate the expensive futility of the state-run approach to combating poverty.[262]

This comes back to our idea of thinking big, of discarding yesterday's ideas and looking for new solutions. Government is not going to shrink rapidly, and individual people from difficult financial backgrounds are not going to be wholly independent right away. We believe that some of the existing federal programs aimed at poverty can be helpful. At the same time, we are adamant in our belief that these programs should not be solutions themselves, but are a means to a better end, namely self-sufficiency. The goal of these programs should be to help those in need and to help them achieve a new skill that can advance them in the market. It should *not* be to keep them dependent on government benefits with no pathway to help themselves.

Building wealth in the private sector and encouraging innovation and work—these are things the state can do largely by getting out of the way, and this is especially true in the case of fighting poverty.

America's historic commitment to the market and the individuals who revolutionized it has paid off for everyone, and it has directly led to the impressive economic situation that we all enjoy today. Innovation and competition translate to lower costs for goods for American families.[263] This is good for parties on both ends of the exchange, and it ensures that technologies become available to a greater number of people. And for those who want to see increased and sustainable government revenue, economic growth provides a path to increased tax revenue without increasing the percentage of American private wealth extracted from the economy.

In the case of the oven, microwave, and the vacuum cleaner—and any other household appliance one can think of—these innovations transformed hundreds of thousands (if not millions) of people's lives for the better. By cutting the time of chores, these devices opened up new possibilities for men, women, and children, including the chance to pursue an education or to take another job.

To fight poverty, to streamline innovation, to improve the lives of American citizens, we must promote meritocracy, risk-taking, investment, and the other forces that contribute to the country's productive output. When output increases, so does America's economic dynamism, which has characterized our country since before its official founding. If we do this, we will further reduce poverty in America while simultaneously increasing the standard of living for millions of Americans.

Turning to our final topics in this chapter, we will return to a proposed law called the Regulations from the Executive in Need of Scrutiny Act, or REINS Act for short.[264] Today, agencies within the executive branch are allowed to promulgate new regulations to enforce federal law. However, there are only two real checks on this process. The first is a new presidential administration rescinding bad regulations. The other is a plaintiff bringing a successful lawsuit that prevents a regulation from being enforced because it is against the law (i.e., the law does not allow for the regulation). Sadly, Congress has completely ceded its role in this area.

Under the REINS Act,[265] the executive branch would need to get approval from Congress before it enacts major regulations, specifically ones that cost more than $100 million to the economy, ones that create a major increase in costs or prices for consumers, or ones that have a significant adverse effect on competition, employment, investment, productivity, and so on. The REINS Act is a good piece of legislation because it shows Congress is serious about its constitutional role of lawmaker and a desire to take power back it wrongly ceded to the executive branch.

While it may seem innocuous to want branches of the federal government to do the jobs they are required by law to do, and not to do those that are outside of their domain, this proposition is actually quite controversial. Indeed, disagreement over the proposed law turns on whether one believes that the Constitution is the final arbiter of the law or if experts in agencies ought to be the deciding force in politics.

Another important issue in administrative law (also known as regulations agencies promulgate to enforce federal law) is *Chevron* deference. In *Chevron*, the Supreme Court held that when an agency interprets a law that Congress has instructed it to interpret (i.e., the Department of Homeland Security interprets immigration laws), the agency receives judicial deference on its interpretation of the law as long as its interpretation is reasonable.[266]

While *Chevron* might sound complex, the important thing is that it gives agencies free rein when it promulgates regulations if Congress instructs the agency to enforce the law at issue. That means, if a plaintiff brings a lawsuit challenging the legality of the regulation in court, the court will defer to an agency instead of doing what courts are supposed to do— say what the law is.[267] Under a judicial system that doesn't give deference to agencies, challengers have a fair chance in court. Unfortunately, until the Supreme Court or Congress[268] overturns *Chevron*, the judicial system will *always* have a thumb on the scale in favor of the government and against the people.

The dirty secret about *Chevron* deference is that Congress agrees with it. Congress is rewarded under *Chevron* because it is not required to write tightly worded statutes, which allows them to avoid accountability to their constituents on important matters of government. Instead, agencies fill out those details. And when an agency does something that Congress does not like, Congress does nothing of any real substance. In response to a harmful regulation, members of Congress issue press releases, give speeches, and campaign on rescinding the regulation, but nothing happens. *Chevron* gives Congress an issue that sounds good on the campaign trail, but in Washington, Congress never does anything to rescind the regulation. Regulations pick winners and losers—there is no way around it. This translates into harming and hurting people arbitrarily, and when done intentionally, it's almost always in favor of the wealthy and well-connected elite. Thankfully, the REINS Act is a good first step, but much more must be done to get our country back on track.

There must also be a more forceful defense of the virtue of work. No matter what one does, working is itself a virtue. As humans, we find meaning in our work; it is what sustains us and allows us access to attempt greater goals and more important pursuits in our lives. Be it marriage, a business venture, or a vacation, it is the work we do and the money and connections we make through it that help give our lives purpose among our many experiences.

Work is essential, particularly if we want our country to do as well in the future as it did in the past. In this regard, we actually agree with President Biden, who once tweeted, "[a] job is about a lot more than a paycheck. It's about dignity...."[269]

We also worry that too many Americans wrongly believe that a "good" or "meaningful" job is attainable only with a college degree. This is nonsense. Though opinion-forming institutions celebrate and glamorize college (and mostly for its social aspects, not the educational experience), it is not at all true that this is the only path to happiness or wealth. As a matter of fact, almost two-thirds of people in the labor force today do *not* have a college degree.[270]

College is a huge investment, and despite the fact that universities are fundamentally profit-seeking creatures, they are exempted from many of the information-sharing requirements of private-sector enterprises, meaning that students and aspiring students alike are not given access to pertinent information about what they are paying for.

This means that college can be more of a gamble than many realize. We do not believe that all Americans should feel inclined to make this potentially risky bet, particularly because college is not always essential, but a good education is. By education, we mean a desire to better understand things as they are and actively seeking answers to questions. This type of education is equally important to the medical doctor and the plumber. There are many other reasons to be skeptical of a college education aside from the uncertain outcomes, including the partisan slant[271] of the university system and the ever-rising and often superfluous costs associated with earning a college degree.[272]

Instead, there are other paths, many of them better, and there must be a concerted effort to emphasize other routes and explain their virtues. Attending trade schools is a great option as many jobs open up after graduation that pay substantially better[273] than the average opening job after college.[274] There is also the added benefit of little to no debt upon graduation from one of these programs, which is not true for the average person who takes out student loans.[275]

All of this is to say that Americans still have options, and we believe that more young people ought to consider an alternative path. It is wrong to think that one can only achieve success and a meaningful job with a college education. Sadly, our culture and education system too often convince young people that the only path toward a respectable career is college.

Lastly, and in the same vein, it is imperative that the federal government step back from its aggressive posture vis-à-vis small businesses. Costly requirements, labyrinthian regulations and requirements, and the constant need to check in with new rules out of Washington serve to make it more difficult for entrepreneurs to go to work and follow their dreams.

If Washington is to have any role in shaping the actions of small businesses and in influencing the actions of those seeking to start them, it should be offering assistance, not creating headaches. To restore the American Dream and for us to come closer to a society that embraces meritocracy, the government must give people a fair shot, and that starts with reducing costs on business. We discuss this and more in the book's final chapter.

CHAPTER 10

RESTORE THE
AMERICAN DREAM

*"I say to you today, my friends, so even though we face the
difficulties of today and tomorrow, I still have a dream. It
is a dream deeply rooted in the American dream. I have
a dream that one day this nation will rise up and live
out the true meaning of its creed: "We hold these truths
to be self-evident: that all men are created equal."*
—Martin Luther King Jr. (see Appendix D)

I. Defining the Dream

In the first chapter, we discussed what the American Dream is,
and we return to that discussion now. We said that, at a basic
level, the American Dream is about working hard with the
talents you were born with or cultivate, persevering through
difficult times, and achieving more success and prosperity
than past generations. We also said that this society is *only*
possible in our uniquely meritocratic system.

To an incredible degree, America achieved this because there was consensus among its people that these values were foundational to the American success story. But if we go awry, if we turn our back on what worked, then what will historians say? What will they blame? And what, in turn, will that say about our multiracial, multiethnic experiment in self-rule?

For some, the American Dream might only mean higher wages or greater wealth than their parents, but we believe that the definition is also understood as encompassing a meaningful increase in personal freedom, typically made possible by better financial security and success.

We believe that the American Dream is more than just wealth because money is not the be-all and end-all for many people. Rather, it is often a means to an end, e.g., to start a family, build a business, perfect a skill or hobby, or develop new relationships and goals. And it's also about the liberty to do all of these things with very few restrictions.

Indeed, we believe that it is the American way to provide a means for people to follow those goals and passions via a meritocratic system in which traits and talents are rewarded as opposed to specific people, relationships, and social classes. This is what makes our country special, and it is time to return to those virtues and renew our commitment to them.

Before our founding, America was a large and intimidating landmass of deep forests, cold winters, and unknown paths. It was a place for those who wanted things not attainable in Europe, be they religious toleration, higher wages, or something else. And once founded, America formally became a land of new beginnings and the realization of dreams.

If one phrase from our foundational documents had to represent what the American experiment is about, it would not be the First or Second Amendment or even excerpts from *The Federalist Papers*. Instead, it would be something simple and powerful, namely, the key line from the Declaration of Independence, "[w]e hold these truths to be self-evident, that all men are created equal, that they are endowed by their Creator with certain unalienable Rights, that among these are life, liberty, and the pursuit of happiness."

Security, independence, and choice—these are the values that make America, America. While we have strayed from these bedrock features, and though change has reoriented the country's priorities, we still believe in these values. Our country can flourish if we pursue policies that better support these ideals.

While we were specific in our explanations of the existential problems America faces, and though we did not hold back in describing their origins and the serious nature of these threats, we are still optimistic about the future. America is a self-healing country—we get better when faced with problems, and we have always risen to challenges. This is not true of most other countries, and it is crucial to keep that in mind.

And when we mess up, we are honest about it. We reflect, study, and experiment with solutions. This is as true of America's business history as it is with our sociopolitical experiences. America overcame slavery, Jim Crow, communist and fascist dictators abroad, and a litany of environmental, social, educational, and economic challenges for one simple reason: it built an internal consensus there was a problem, came up with a solution to rectify the problem that united rather than divided Americans, and implemented the solution.

But this process of learning, discourse, and problem-solving is only possible when we collectively speak the same moral language and when we adhere to a shared commitment to good faith and reason.

We must commit ourselves to a few baseline ideas, including (but not limited to) the principle that the Constitution is the supreme law of the land; that everyone deserves an equal opportunity, not an equal outcome; that discrimination is fundamentally wrong; that, cliché though it may be, we are all in it together; and that we should pursue policies that will best allow people the ability to live their lives as they wish, to the degree that they do not encroach on the freedom of others, so as to maximize their ability to follow their particular dreams without limitations.

This is not a partisan outlook. Unfortunately, philosophies that cannot coexist with America's meritocratic ethos, predicated on equal rights and responsibilities for citizens, have been amplified by media corporations and academics and, in turn, adopted by political figures and movements.

However one wants to define them, ideologies predicated on jealousy, resentment, and radical self-interest predominate in America today in a way that was not true only a few decades ago. The effects of these trends are tragic. One is especially concerning: not only are people now talking past each other, but there is also no longer a common moral and political dialect in which everyone speaks. We don't think there will be a civil war, but there will be a growing fracture of American society that does not bode well. To remedy that, it will require a genuine and good faith attempt to understand those who disagree or differ from us, even though we may all fail to live up to this aspiration at times.

Understanding this ugly reality is essential for making sense of the fact that America's problems today are so often misconstrued, arguments deliberately misrepresented, and ideas "memed" into caricatures of themselves. While these things are all conducive to comedy, page views, and going viral online, they are extremely destructive to the goal of building relationships, sharing ideas, and, ultimately, solving problems and ameliorating the suffering in the lives of fellow citizens. In short, these things divide Americans further apart instead of bringing Americans closer together through a shared sense of ideas and a hopeful outlook for the country.

We believe strongly in discussion and open dialogue, and we think that compromise is most often necessary for any large political project. At the same time, there are certain issues that we believe cannot be up for debate. These include the principles that discrimination is wrong, that all Americans deserve an equal opportunity to get ahead, and that the country's political culture of building consensus is worth preserving.

Of course, there are other issues we feel similarly strongly about. With this outlook in mind, let us talk briefly about just a few real-world cases to give this framework some color. First, providing children the best education possible and giving their parents the tools and resources to make these decisions for their children are things we should all agree on. For example, charter schools are often the only institutions that poor children in tough neighborhoods can rely on to learn and escape from poverty. Currently, there exists a system of education apartheid that determines the quality of education a child has available to them by geographic zip code, and that must end. We can debate specific policy solutions to advance charter schools, but there currently exists a broad consensus in America that all children should receive a quality education, and charter schools have a demonstrated track record that they can do just that.

Reforming the HR culture that has commandeered American business and higher education is another. This has been a terrible development that has raised the proverbial temperature in politics and civil society; it has raised the cost of a college education; and it has undermined the efficiency of every organization it has touched. HR plays an important role in every business, but its job is not to police daily employee interactions or try to indoctrinate employees with the newest diversity, equity, and inclusion talking points. Institutions suffer when factors other than merit are key factors in recruiting, hiring, or promotion.

Finally, there is the issue of entitlements. Millions and millions of Americans are paying into well-intentioned programs that are going bankrupt. While beneficiaries today are doing okay, in the near term, these programs will not be doing okay. In fact, the Medicare Board of Trustees went on record in early 2021 that the program will become insolvent in 2026.[276] We must make fundamental changes to all our entitlement programs to prevent events like this from happening.

While our personal commitment to certain principles defines our position on particular political issues that perhaps are not currently supported among Americans broadly, it is our objective to build consensus on those ideas and solutions through a free and open debate. Returning to this once bedrock principle of American politics will ensure our institutions, such as government, retain the legitimacy necessary to lead.

II. Restore Our Institutions

As Sir Winston Churchill once said, "democracy is the worst form of government except for all those other forms that have been tried from time to time."[277] He understood that no government created by man could be perfect. Importantly, no other form of government has matched the economic, multicultural, or technological inventiveness of American democracy.

Our meritocratic and freedom-based society is founded upon a fundamental principle that our Founders held dear when they formulated our Constitution. This fundamental principle is consensus. While we have talked about consensus a lot in this book, we have not spelled out in what ways the Constitution requires consensus in our system through checks and balances.

Consensus and plurality are too often confused today. Consensus requires a burden beyond a simple majority. It forces us to not just compromise, but to build support broadly and bridge divides. The Founders' intent when writing our Constitution was that it would provide a foundation through which the country could adapt to modern times. They desired this foundation to be structurally sound, resistant to fleeting political sentiment, amended from time to time, and built upon consensus. Why? Because foundational elements of our society should require consensus.

The Founders understood that a simple plurality could cause a constant back and forth that threatens the stability and effectiveness of our government. They recognized that this would put minority rights at risk. As a result, our Constitution requires that before a new amendment can become law, it must be adopted by 67 percent of both houses of Congress and then 75 percent of the states. Appropriately, they established a very high bar so that consensus would be required to amend our Constitution.

Similarly, our founders placed a two-thirds senatorial voting requirement in the Constitution to convict (remove) during an impeachment trial. While the Constitution allows the Senate to come up with its own rules outside of qualifications, impeachment, and treaties, senators in both parties still recognized the importance of consensus. Beginning in the 1850s, the Senate has consistently adopted rules in each succeeding Senate that require a greater than majority threshold to proceed to a vote on legislation.[278] Today, that number is sixty. As a matter of practice, if a senator vehemently opposes the legislation under consideration, they may delay the vote through a filibuster and force their colleagues to reach consensus and move past those concerns to move to a simple majority vote. In today's partisan Congress, we've seen a rise in the use of reconciliation, a legislative budget process, to pack all of the ambitions of the majority party to avoid the filibuster and the consensus that's required to achieve legislative victory.

This foundational principle of consensus has served our country extremely well for over 240 years. Only recently have we seen attempts to diminish this consensus requirement and only require a simple majority vote in the Senate. Such a change, while perhaps being expedient to the party in power, could destroy the strength of our country's foundation. President Biden's ill-fated attempt to end the filibuster in January 2022 was only defeated by two votes. Senators Joe Manchin and Krysten Sinema, both Democrats, should be praised for having the courage to stand against the president of their own party. The people Senator Manchin represents in West Virginia appreciated his stand, as his approval rating with his constituents rose significantly after the decision.[279] To best protect all our citizens, we must always require a consensus before we attempt to make major changes to our government. Doing away with such protections will be the first step toward authoritarianism in America.

Abortion is perhaps the most divisive issue in America. We don't intend to make a case for either side and will leave that discussion to others, not because we don't have our own personal perspective, but because the process for which decisions are made on abortion laws is flawed, and we believe our concerns should be shared by both perspectives on this issue.

In 1973, the Supreme Court took the issue of abortion away from the American people. In *Roe v. Wade*, the court held for the first time that the Fourteenth Amendment protects a woman's right to have an abortion.[280] By basing its decision on the Constitution, the court *removed* the ability of states to pass their own abortion laws.

However, the court missed a key fact: when the Fourteenth Amendment was ratified in 1868, thirty of the thirty-seven states that ratified it had criminal laws against abortion.[281] In short, the framers of the Fourteenth Amendment knew that abortion was an issue that belonged in the democratic arena. But the court decided that after one hundred years of states experimenting with their own abortion laws, it was time to take the issue away from them.

There are two other episodes in the court's history that are instructive with *Roe* in mind. As in *Roe*, the court has a long history of reading the liberty provision of the Fourteenth Amendment's due process clause broadly. Throughout the early 1900s, the court held that the clause created an unenumerated individual right to contract free from government regulation.[282] In *Lochner v. New York*, the court invalidated a New York statute that prohibited employees who work in bakeries from working more than sixty hours a week.[283] In *Adkins v. Children's Hospital*, the court invalidated a minimum wage law for women and children under the same doctrine.[284]

After decades of experimenting with the unenumerated right to contract, the court ultimately reversed course. In *West Coast Hotel Co. v. Parrish*, the court overruled *Adkins* and held that legislatures are entitled to great deference when they consider issues in the economic arena.[285] In other words, the court recognized these questions are better resolved by the American people in their respective states, not unelected and unaccountable justices. Today, state and local legislatures are free to enact their own minimum wage laws, maximum work hour laws, and unemployment compensation programs.

Unfortunately, *Roe* incentivized lawyers to come up with novel legal theories that result in the court creating unenumerated rights and taking issues away from the American people. Thankfully, the test the court has traditionally used to find unenumerated rights has been a difficult one to pass. For an unenumerated right to receive constitutional protection, it must be objectively deeply rooted in our nation's history and tradition, and there must be a careful description of the fundamental liberty interest.[286] When the court applied this test in *Washington v. Glucksberg*, it held that the right to assisted suicide was *not* objectively deeply rooted in our nation's history and tradition.[287] As a result, it did not receive constitutional protection and was left for the American people to consider through the democratic process.

In *West Coast Hotel* and *Glucksberg*, the court recognized that it should be very careful before providing constitutional protections to rights not found in the Constitution. In *Roe*, the court was not so careful. And abortion has been taken away from the democratic process for almost fifty years. But, if the American people really want an issue taken away from the democratic process, the Constitution provides a process. It does not involve the Supreme Court finding unenumerated rights. Rather, Article V of the Constitution spells out how amendments can be adopted. In our nation's history, the Constitution has been amended twenty-seven times. By taking issues away from the democratic process, the court increases its own power and makes the Article V process irrelevant. The real losers end up being the American people.

While some might argue the Article V process is too difficult, it is difficult because a large consensus is needed to amend the Constitution to take issues away from the democratic process. When an unelected body like the Supreme Court takes issues away from the democratic process, there is no consensus, and it only further divides the American people. It destroys our system of checks and balances because there is no effective way to check the Supreme Court when it bases its decisions on the Constitution. Moreover, the consensus needed for Article V underscores our system of checks and balances because it requires the American people to widely agree before an issue receives constitutional protection.

The late Justice Scalia understood all this, as he also touched on another major constitutional law subject in a speech given at Brown University in 1991 that adds to this discussion. Scalia said that while the importance of the separation of powers is bandied around a lot, it is often poorly defined. In its simplest terms, the doctrine holds that different branches of government and different levels of government each enjoy their own powers under the Constitution. Because government power is so diffused across the system, it actually increases our liberty.

Under the doctrine, there are two different types of federalism: horizontal and vertical. Horizontal federalism deals with the different powers of the federal legislature (Congress), executive branch (the president), and judicial branch (Supreme Court). Vertical federalism deals with the different powers of the federal, state, and local governments. In our constitutional system, each branch, and each government, has a unique and distinct role to play.

Because no branch can constitutionally usurp the authority of the other, our liberty increases. For example, in our constitutional system, the president (executive) cannot make the law, enforce the law, and then determine that you broke the law. If it did, it would unconstitutionally usurp the roles of both the legislative and judicial branches. Our system is unique because, in many countries, there is only one government, and it plays all three roles.

Justice Scalia hammered this point home when he noted that many countries have a Bill of Rights, but in reality, that legally means *nothing*. When the government prosecuting you is self-interested in that it wrote the law, is bringing the lawsuit, and controls the judges or judicial system, your legal protections mean nothing. This kind of government doesn't care about the legal protections you have on a piece of paper, it cares about making a statement that it thinks you broke the law, and it will make sure all citizens understand that.

Our separation of powers is also important because it requires consensus. For Congress to pass a law, it must go through both houses, and it must be signed by the president. If the president vetoes the bill, Congress must override the veto with a two-thirds vote in both houses. There are many barriers before the law even goes into enactment. Then, the executive branch must determine that you violated the law egregiously enough to actually bring an enforcement action. And finally, the executive branch has the burden of proving beyond a reasonable doubt in a criminal case, or by a preponderance of the evidence in a civil case, that the defendant is guilty of the accusation. All the while, the defendant is free to argue that the government's action is unconstitutional or illegal, and an independent judge or jury (for jury trials) has the authority to check the government's action. In other words, there are a number of sign-offs necessary before your liberty can be taken away by the government. In most, if not all other countries, this is not the case.

We see this destruction of checks and balances as well in the increased use of executive orders in lieu of building consensus and passing legislation. When the White House switches control between Republicans and Democrats, the new president launches a series of executive orders to undo the policies of their predecessor and implement their own objectives. The process is inherently unstable and ultimately leads to confusion and frustration for those who seek to comply with the ever-evolving rules.

The above cases should show by now the importance of building a consensus. For major changes to our government, politicians must convince *more than* a simple majority of the American people before they can go into effect. In that way, the Senate filibuster and Article V process work hand in hand. For major pieces of legislation to be passed through Congress, sixty senators must agree to proceed to the vote. Any changes to our Constitution must be adopted by two-thirds of both houses of Congress, and then three-quarters of the states. Forcing majorities to build a consensus is the best way to protect minority rights. In addition, the special separation of powers system we have in the US requires consensus across multiple branches of government before the government can take away your liberty. Congress must reestablish its role in the creation of law and not defer that authority to the president or Supreme Court for our system to get back on track. To achieve this, Congress must not just do what is politically advantageous, but work hard to build consensus across ideological divides.

III. Clashing Outlooks

Thomas Sowell is one of the most perceptive and important thinkers of the last fifty years, and we believe that one of his books is extremely relevant today. Titled *Conflict of Visions* (1987), Sowell's book seeks to answer the question as to why the same people tend to be opposed on issues that vary as widely as taxing schemes to gun control. So, what gives?

According to Sowell, the bifurcated nature of politics in America (and elsewhere) is due to the fact that people largely hold two distinct and uncompromising views of human nature, one optimistic and the other less so. He dubs these the "unconstrained" and the "constrained" outlooks, the former being more utopian and the latter more realistic.

At the root of this disagreement is a dispute over what human nature is. The unconstrained and hopeful see it as good and, to a large degree, malleable, meaning it can become better with time and effort as its downsides are mitigated.[288] The constrained hold a more tragic view of human nature: they see it as self-interested and stable if not resistant to change.[289]

Related, the unconstrained believe that there are some who have overcome the moral limitations of humanity and are therefore better positioned to rule. Emotional appeals are often used to substantiate the preferred programs of the utopians. The constrained disagree and believe that the only solution is a system in which ambitions can be checked to construct an uneasy but workable balance. And for those who hold this tragic view, empirical evidence is essential.

If this sounds familiar, that is because it is. This disagreement parallels many controversies in America today, namely whether America will return to a constitutional government, built around the idea that human nature is tragic, or if it will complete its metamorphosis into a new regime predicated on a more utopian view, in which the state is led by the morally superior who nudge[290] citizens towards a particular end.

In practice, the "nudge" necessary to bring about this new world would be far stronger and more impactful than a simple push. Moreover, it would require an even stronger, more relentless, and more anti-constitutional government than we have now. In other words, the utopians require a level of power unknown to the United States, and that is something we should all fear and reject.

Still, we do not want to sound as if we are opposed to the country. Far from it: we love America, and we are proud of our history. But we are also protective of our status as citizens, and we do not want to lose it or see it transformed.

There is a great comment by Mark Twain about how "patriotism is supporting your country all the time and your government when it deserves it." We will always support and believe in America; we will do the same for the state, or the government, when its behavior warrants it—and the same is true of the politicians who run it.

IV. Resolve Through Reform and Return

The defining characteristic of America is our economic dynamism, and our greatest cultural artifact is the Constitution. But perhaps the greatest aspect of our country is its ability to heal and correct its errors.

Whether it was in the colonial period, during the Revolution or the Civil War, in the effort against authoritarianism in World War II, or in the struggle for civil rights, Americans have always solved problems via social participation and community-led efforts.

While we outlined problems within the political and legal spheres, and though we offered ideas on how to fix them, we believe that quite a lot can be improved through participation in civil society. This can mean many things, but for us, we think that one of the best options is to engage in activism.

Taking a stand on an issue is hard, but in our experience, all it takes is for one person to articulate his or her views. Once this hard part is done, more people will join in. After all, humans are social creatures: we interact with others and like company, and humans for all of history have found ways to cooperate with each other to reach larger goals.

If more Americans stand up for and support historical American virtues and values—fairness, the equal application of the law, prosocial behaviors and attitudes, and defending interests common to all—then America will be well on its way to a healthier shared civic culture, which the country desperately needs.

But to do this, to reach the largest number of people, citizens must be sure to embrace those around them to the best of their ability. In practice, this means avoiding the demonizing language that so often predominates in our political discourse.

Equally important is the effort that must be made to emphasize the things that we have in common, such as our mutual status as citizens and our shared interest in seeing the US remain a nice place where families can thrive and individuals can get ahead.

But to do this and to make a real difference, we must be vigilant in our effort to lower the proverbial temperature in American life. This means that we have a duty to push back on efforts to tribalize and divide citizens.

For instance, we must demand serious evidence from incendiary arguments, e.g., that all gaps between groups are due to discrimination and inegalitarian institutions or laws. We must also reject demagoguery, be it a claim that a politician will single-handedly fix all of our problems or that the country has not changed and made progress on past failures.

In closing, we believe that America can heal itself again— even at a time when such a situation may seem impossible. We believe this is possible because this is the American story: a series of improbable but ultimately realized efforts at self-correction, for which we are all better off. Americans solve hard problems. This is what we do.

And if we can keep Dr. Martin Luther King's observation that "injustice anywhere is a threat to justice everywhere... [because] we are caught in an inescapable network of mutuality, tied in a single garment of destiny...[and that] whatever affects one directly, affects all indirectly," then we can overcome the struggles of the present to secure even greater achievement for the next generation of Americans.

But to do this, we must have the will, and that necessitates a vision and the capacity to organize—both of which fall on the shoulders of ordinary citizens. We hope this book provides a sketch of what such a vision might entail. Now it is up to you to complement that vision and begin the arduous task of organizing and engaging your local communities.

Especially *after* elections, when the talking ends and the work needs to be done.

AFTERWORD BY DICK STEPHENSON

3/10/22

It's not uncommon these days for a positive, hopeful vision of the future to be dismissed as naive and unattainable. For many, this reaction is almost reflexive, especially in many of our nation's young people. But I'd like to think that my experience could serve as an example and maybe hold a special weight in breaking through this bleak and reductionist attitude about not only what lies ahead, but what could lie ahead—that is, the power we have as individuals to be real movers and shakers in our society, if only we take that first terrifying step and try.

In America, if we don't presently "see" the future we want for ourselves, we have the glorious opportunity to create it. In fact, we're the only ones who can! As my friends, David Sokol and Adam Brandon, have brilliantly argued in this book, this opportunity sets America apart from any other country in the world. Failure here is not the same as failure elsewhere. Anyone can try to build something for themselves (and others) if only they summon the courage to fail and fail again until failure morphs into success. The founding spirit of our nation, which primarily embraced personal freedom, liberty for all, and encouraged tenacity and hard work, immediately created a unique environment in which this rocky road to success is open not just to the high born and wealthy, but to anyone with the gumption and vision to try.

Have you ever met an American who doesn't love a good success story?

My story is a testament to the enduring and tangible ideals that David and Adam have written about; hopefully, it can also serve as encouragement for others to embark upon that sometimes rocky road.

When my mother was diagnosed with cancer, any optimism I had for the future was shattered. What's the future supposed to look like without your mother? Lonely, half-full. I was crushed with despair, especially when I looked around and saw a pitiful lack of compassionate care and advanced treatment and hopeful options for her.

Following my mother's death, I made a vow that I would never let another cancer patient suffer without hope for the future. This personal tragedy became the impetus for me and my family to found Cancer Treatment Centers of America. The goal of CTCA is to empower patients and their caregivers with the most innovative and promising programs and practices on the market so that they can maintain a high quality of life during and after treatment. This vow introduced a new paradigm into cancer treatment, in which patients would receive the kind of warm care and consideration they might receive from a loved one.

This new paradigm was called the "Mother Standard" of care and featured concepts such as "Patient Empowerment Medicine," "It's Always and Only About the Patient," and "Care that Never Quits."

While continuing my long-standing global merchant banking career, a couple of years after founding CTCA, I also started Gateway for Cancer Research, which has raised nearly one hundred million dollars to fund clinical cancer treatment trials around the world and helps to fulfill the vow I made to mitigate the sufferings and improve the quality of life for adult cancer patients.

Though my more recent "life's work" has been inspired by a deeply personal experience, I am humbled when I think about how none of my work could have been possible if not for an accident of birth. I owe it to our nation's founding virtue, which reminds us that in freedom, where the fruit of a man's productive labor is protected by the "rule of law," anyone with a good idea has a chance to see it through. These principles have guided me throughout my life, and many call me a "self-made" man because I was born into a rural Indiana family that had no money; we moved from one rented house to another nine times before I was twelve years old. But we lived in a nation that allowed me to keep the fruits of my labor and my private property and that's all I needed.

David and Adam are correct to point out that the detractors—those who think that the American Dream is dead—do not have the final word here. It is more important than ever to lift up and shine a light on the true success stories of today's America, of which there are an astonishing number. We would do a disservice to these individuals who work hard to better themselves and their fellow citizens if we let the creeping malaise of today overcome us, and succumb to the grossly errant and fatal belief that big government is the solution to all of our personal woes and anxieties about the future.

The American Dream can die only if we choose to kill it.

So, let's not. To keep it alive, first, we have to mend our attitudes and remain optimistic about the future. We have to reject the popular but bankrupt and simply untrue belief that our best days are behind us. If we lose our sense of optimism, we begin to lose what truly makes this country great. History tells us this, and my friends who wrote this book remind us that millions upon millions of success stories have been made possible thanks to both hard work and the idea that the future for all of us in this country is always brighter.

Second, we need to move toward a collective understanding that endless growth in the size and scope of government harms all of us and imposes barriers to American success stories like mine. My success came not through government action, but through individual freedom. The freedom for an individual to take risks must be protected by the rule of law, not imperiled and taken from us by government. This means far less government spending, less regulatory burdens, and more incentives and support of the entrepreneurial spirit that lives inside so many Americans, whether dormant or active. In America, freedom is synonymous with the opportunity to try and succeed.

As we move on from the COVID-19 pandemic, a tumultuous and divided time in our nation's history made more tumultuous and threatening by governmental mandates, et al, America's remarkable ability to heal itself and move on from this tragedy will be of great value. Though it's easy to succumb to despair, I remain optimistic—and you should too—about the future not only because of my past but because of America's past. Think about all we've gone through to get to today—that alone should give us hope that our brightest days are still ahead. Just like our talented and insightful authors, I also will always remain optimistic that brighter days are ahead for America.

APPENDICES

THE DECLARATION OF INDEPENDENCE

IN CONGRESS, JULY 4, 1776

The unanimous Declaration of the thirteen United States of America

When in the Course of human events it becomes necessary for one people to dissolve the political bands which have connected them with another and to assume among the powers of the earth, the separate and equal station to which the Laws of Nature and of Nature's God entitle them, a decent respect to the opinions of mankind requires that they should declare the causes which impel them to the separation.

We hold these truths to be self-evident, that all men are created equal, that they are endowed by their Creator with certain unalienable Rights, that among these are Life, Liberty and the pursuit of Happiness.—That to secure these rights, Governments are instituted among Men, deriving their just powers from the consent of the governed,—That whenever any Form of Government becomes destructive of these ends, it is the Right of the People to alter or to abolish it, and to institute new Government, laying its foundation on such principles and organizing its powers in such form, as to them shall seem most likely to effect their Safety and Happiness. Prudence, indeed, will dictate that Governments long established should not be changed for light and transient causes; and accordingly all experience hath shewn that mankind are more disposed to suffer, while evils are sufferable than to right themselves by abolishing the forms to which they are accustomed. But when a long train of abuses and usurpations, pursuing invariably the same Object evinces a design to reduce them under absolute Despotism, it is their right, it is their duty, to throw off such Government, and to provide new Guards for their future security.—Such has been the patient sufferance of these Colonies; and such is now the necessity which constrains them to alter their former Systems of Government. The history of the present King of Great Britain is a history of repeated injuries and usurpations, all having in direct object the establishment of an absolute Tyranny over these States. To prove this, let Facts be submitted to a candid world.

He has refused his Assent to Laws, the most wholesome and necessary for the public good.

He has forbidden his Governors to pass Laws of immediate and pressing importance, unless suspended in their operation till his Assent should be obtained; and when so suspended, he has utterly neglected to attend to them.

He has refused to pass other Laws for the accommodation of large districts of people, unless those people would relinquish the right of Representation in the Legislature, a right inestimable to them and formidable to tyrants only.

He has called together legislative bodies at places unusual, uncomfortable, and distant from the depository of their Public Records, for the sole purpose of fatiguing them into compliance with his measures.

He has dissolved Representative Houses repeatedly, for opposing with manly firmness his invasions on the rights of the people.

He has refused for a long time, after such dissolutions, to cause others to be elected, whereby the Legislative Powers, incapable of Annihilation, have returned to the People at large for their exercise; the State remaining in the mean time exposed to all the dangers of invasion from without, and convulsions within.

He has endeavoured to prevent the population of these States; for that purpose obstructing the Laws for Naturalization of Foreigners; refusing to pass others to encourage their migrations hither, and raising the conditions of new Appropriations of Lands.

He has obstructed the Administration of Justice by refusing his Assent to Laws for establishing Judiciary Powers.

He has made Judges dependent on his Will alone for the tenure of their offices, and the amount and payment of their salaries.

He has erected a multitude of New Offices, and sent hither swarms of Officers to harass our people and eat out their substance.

He has kept among us, in times of peace, Standing Armies without the Consent of our legislatures.

He has affected to render the Military independent of and superior to the Civil Power.

He has combined with others to subject us to a jurisdiction foreign to our constitution, and unacknowledged by our laws; giving his Assent to their Acts of pretended Legislation:

For quartering large bodies of armed troops among us:

For protecting them, by a mock Trial from punishment for any Murders which they should commit on the Inhabitants of these States:

For cutting off our Trade with all parts of the world:

For imposing Taxes on us without our Consent:

For depriving us in many cases, of the benefit of Trial by Jury:

For transporting us beyond Seas to be tried for pretended offences:

For abolishing the free System of English Laws in a neighbouring Province, establishing therein an Arbitrary government, and enlarging its Boundaries so as to render it at once an example and fit instrument for introducing the same absolute rule into these Colonies

For taking away our Charters, abolishing our most valuable Laws and altering fundamentally the Forms of our Governments:

For suspending our own Legislatures, and declaring themselves invested with power to legislate for us in all cases whatsoever.

He has abdicated Government here, by declaring us out of his Protection and waging War against us.

He has plundered our seas, ravaged our coasts, burnt our towns, and destroyed the lives of our people.

He is at this time transporting large Armies of foreign Mercenaries to compleat the works of death, desolation, and tyranny, already begun with circumstances of Cruelty & Perfidy scarcely paralleled in the most barbarous ages, and totally unworthy the Head of a civilized nation.

He has constrained our fellow Citizens taken Captive on the high Seas to bear Arms against their Country, to become the executioners of their friends and Brethren, or to fall themselves by their Hands.

He has excited domestic insurrections amongst us, and has endeavoured to bring on the inhabitants of our frontiers, the merciless Indian Savages whose known rule of warfare, is an undistinguished destruction of all ages, sexes and conditions.

In every stage of these Oppressions We have Petitioned for Redress in the most humble terms: Our repeated Petitions have been answered only by repeated injury. A Prince, whose character is thus marked by every act which may define a Tyrant, is unfit to be the ruler of a free people.

Nor have We been wanting in attentions to our British brethren. We have warned them from time to time of attempts by their legislature to extend an unwarrantable jurisdiction over us. We have reminded them of the circumstances of our emigration and settlement here. We have appealed to their native justice and magnanimity, and we have conjured them by the ties of our common kindred to disavow these usurpations, which would inevitably interrupt our connections and correspondence. They too have been deaf to the voice of justice and of consanguinity. We must, therefore, acquiesce in the necessity, which denounces our Separation, and hold them, as we hold the rest of mankind, Enemies in War, in Peace Friends.

We, therefore, the Representatives of the united States of America, in General Congress, Assembled, appealing to the Supreme Judge of the world for the rectitude of our intentions, do, in the Name, and by Authority of the good People of these Colonies, solemnly publish and declare, That these united Colonies are, and of Right ought to be Free and Independent States, that they are Absolved from all Allegiance to the British Crown, and that all political connection between them and the State of Great Britain, is and ought to be totally dissolved; and that as Free and Independent States, they have full Power to levy War, conclude Peace, contract Alliances, establish Commerce, and to do all other Acts and Things which Independent States may of right do.—And for the support of this Declaration, with a firm reliance on the protection of Divine Providence, we mutually pledge to each other our Lives, our Fortunes, and our sacred Honor.[291]

THE CONSTITUTION OF THE UNITED STATES, BILL OF RIGHTS, AND SUBSE- QUENT AMENDMENTS

We the People of the United States, in Order to form a more perfect Union, establish Justice, insure domestic Tranquility, provide for the common defence, promote the general Welfare, and secure the Blessings of Liberty to ourselves and our Posterity, do ordain and establish this Constitution for the United States of America.

The Constitutional Convention

Article I

Section 1: Congress

All legislative Powers herein granted shall be vested in a Congress of the United States, which shall consist of a Senate and House of Representatives.

Section 2: The House of Representatives

The House of Representatives shall be composed of Members chosen every second Year by the People of the several States, and the Electors in each State shall have the Qualifications requisite for Electors of the most numerous Branch of the State Legislature.

No Person shall be a Representative who shall not have attained to the Age of twenty five Years, and been seven Years a Citizen of the United States, and who shall not, when elected, be an Inhabitant of that State in which he shall be chosen.

Representatives and direct Taxes shall be apportioned among the several States which may be included within this Union, according to their respective Numbers, which shall be determined by adding to the whole Number of free Persons, including those bound to Service for a Term of Years, and excluding Indians not taxed, three fifths of all other Persons. The actual Enumeration shall be made within three Years after the first Meeting of the Congress of the United States, and within every subsequent Term of ten Years, in such Manner as they shall by Law direct. The number of Representatives shall not exceed one for every thirty Thousand, but each State shall have at Least one Representative; and until such enumeration shall be made, the State of New Hampshire shall be entitled to chuse three, Massachusetts eight, Rhode-Island and Providence Plantations one, Connecticut five, New-York six, New Jersey four, Pennsylvania eight, Delaware one, Maryland six, Virginia ten, North Carolina five, South Carolina five, and Georgia three.

When vacancies happen in the Representation from any State, the Executive Authority thereof shall issue Writs of Election to fill such Vacancies.

The House of Representatives shall chuse their Speaker and other Officers; and shall have the sole Power of Impeachment.

Section 3: The Senate

The Senate of the United States shall be composed of two Senators from each State, chosen by the Legislature thereof, for six Years; and each Senator shall have one Vote.

Immediately after they shall be assembled in Consequence of the first Election, they shall be divided as equally as may be into three Classes. The Seats of the Senators of the first Class shall be vacated at the Expiration of the second Year, of the second Class at the Expiration of the fourth Year, and of the third Class at the Expiration of the sixth Year, so that one third may be chosen every second Year; and if Vacancies happen by Resignation, or otherwise, during the Recess of the Legislature of any State, the Executive thereof may make temporary Appointments until the next Meeting of the Legislature, which shall then fill such Vacancies.

No Person shall be a Senator who shall not have attained to the Age of thirty Years, and been nine Years a Citizen of the United States, and who shall not, when elected, be an Inhabitant of that State for which he shall be chosen.

The Vice President of the United States shall be President of the Senate, but shall have no Vote, unless they be equally divided.

The Senate shall chuse their other Officers, and also a President pro tempore, in the Absence of the Vice President, or when he shall exercise the Office of President of the United States.

The Senate shall have the sole Power to try all Impeachments. When sitting for that Purpose, they shall be on Oath or Affirmation. When the President of the United States is tried, the Chief Justice shall preside: And no Person shall be convicted without the Concurrence of two thirds of the Members present.

Judgment in Cases of Impeachment shall not extend further than to removal from Office, and disqualification to hold and enjoy any Office of honor, Trust or Profit under the United States: but the Party convicted shall nevertheless be liable and subject to Indictment, Trial, Judgment and Punishment, according to Law.

Section 4: Elections

The Times, Places and Manner of holding Elections for Senators and Representatives, shall be prescribed in each State by the Legislature thereof; but the Congress may at any time by Law make or alter such Regulations, except as to the Places of chusing Senators.

The Congress shall assemble at least once in every Year, and such Meeting shall be on the first Monday in December, unless they shall by Law appoint a different Day.

Section 5: Powers and Duties of Congress

Each House shall be the Judge of the Elections, Returns and Qualifications of its own Members, and a Majority of each shall constitute a Quorum to do Business; but a smaller Number may adjourn from day to day, and may be authorized to compel the Attendance of absent Members, in such Manner, and under such Penalties as each House may provide.

Each House may determine the Rules of its Proceedings, punish its Members for disorderly Behaviour, and, with the Concurrence of two thirds, expel a Member.

Each House shall keep a Journal of its Proceedings, and from time to time publish the same, excepting such Parts as may in their Judgment require Secrecy; and the Yeas and Nays of the Members of either House on any question shall, at the Desire of one fifth of those Present, be entered on the Journal.

Neither House, during the Session of Congress, shall, without the Consent of the other, adjourn for more than three days, nor to any other Place than that in which the two Houses shall be sitting.

Section 6: Rights and Disabilities of Members

The Senators and Representatives shall receive a Compensation for their Services, to be ascertained by Law, and paid out of the Treasury of the United States. They shall in all Cases, except Treason, Felony and Breach of the Peace, be privileged from Arrest during their Attendance at the Session of their respective Houses, and in going to and returning from the same; and for any Speech or Debate in either House, they shall not be questioned in any other Place.

No Senator or Representative shall, during the Time for which he was elected, be appointed to any civil Office under the Authority of the United States, which shall have been created, or the Emoluments whereof shall have been encreased during such time; and no Person holding any Office under the United States, shall be a Member of either House during his Continuance in Office.

Section 7: Legislative Process

All Bills for raising Revenue shall originate in the House of Representatives; but the Senate may propose or concur with Amendments as on other Bills.

Every Bill which shall have passed the House of Representatives and the Senate, shall, before it become a Law, be presented to the President of the United States; If he approve he shall sign it, but if not he shall return it, with his Objections to that House in which it shall have originated, who shall enter the Objections at large on their Journal, and proceed to reconsider it. If after such Reconsideration two thirds of that House shall agree to pass the Bill, it shall be sent, together with the Objections, to the other House, by which it shall likewise be reconsidered, and if approved by two thirds of that House, it shall become a Law. But in all such Cases the Votes of both Houses shall be determined by Yeas and Nays, and the Names of the Persons voting for and against the Bill shall be entered on the Journal of each House respectively. If any Bill shall not be returned by the President within ten Days (Sundays excepted) after it shall have been presented to him, the Same shall be a Law, in like Manner as if he had signed it, unless the Congress by their Adjournment prevent its Return, in which Case it shall not be a Law.

Every Order, Resolution, or Vote to which the Concurrence of the Senate and House of Representatives may be necessary (except on a question of Adjournment) shall be presented to the President of the United States; and before the Same shall take Effect, shall be approved by him, or being disapproved by him, shall be repassed by two thirds of the Senate and House of Representatives, according to the Rules and Limitations prescribed in the Case of a Bill.

Section 8: Powers of Congress

The Congress shall have Power To lay and collect Taxes, Duties, Imposts and Excises, to pay the Debts and provide for the common Defence and general Welfare of the United States; but all Duties, Imposts and Excises shall be uniform throughout the United States;

To borrow Money on the credit of the United States;

To regulate Commerce with foreign Nations, and among the several States, and with the Indian Tribes;

To establish a uniform Rule of Naturalization, and uniform Laws on the subject of Bankruptcies throughout the United States;

To coin Money, regulate the Value thereof, and of foreign Coin, and fix the Standard of Weights and Measures;

To provide for the Punishment of counterfeiting the Securities and current Coin of the United States;

To establish Post Offices and post Roads;

To promote the Progress of Science and useful Arts, by securing for limited Times to Authors and Inventors the exclusive Right to their respective Writings and Discoveries;

To constitute Tribunals inferior to the supreme Court;

To define and punish Piracies and Felonies committed on the high Seas, and Offenses against the Law of Nations;

To declare War, grant Letters of Marque and Reprisal, and make Rules concerning Captures on Land and Water;

To raise and support Armies, but no Appropriation of Money to that Use shall be for a longer Term than two Years;

To provide and maintain a Navy;

To make Rules for the Government and Regulation of the land and naval Forces;

To provide for calling forth the Militia to execute the Laws of the Union, suppress Insurrections and repel Invasions;

To provide for organizing, arming, and disciplining, the Militia, and for governing such Part of them as may be employed in the Service of the United States, reserving to the States respectively, the Appointment of the Officers, and the Authority of training the Militia according to the discipline prescribed by Congress;

To exercise exclusive Legislation in all Cases whatsoever, over such District (not exceeding ten Miles square) as may, by Cession of particular States, and the Acceptance of Congress, become the Seat of the Government of the United States, and to exercise like Authority over all Places purchased by the Consent of the Legislature of the State in which the Same shall be, for the Erection of Forts, Magazines, Arsenals, dock-Yards and other needful Buildings;-And

To make all Laws which shall be necessary and proper for carrying into Execution the foregoing Powers, and all other Powers vested by this Constitution in the Government of the United States, or in any Department or Officer thereof.

Section 9: Powers Denied Congress

The Migration or Importation of such Persons as any of the States now existing shall think proper to admit, shall not be prohibited by the Congress prior to the Year one thousand eight hundred and eight, but a Tax or duty may be imposed on such Importation, not exceeding ten dollars for each Person.

The Privilege of the Writ of Habeas Corpus shall not be suspended, unless when in Cases of Rebellion or Invasion the public Safety may require it.

No Bill of Attainder or ex post facto Law shall be passed.

No Capitation, or other direct, Tax shall be laid, unless in Proportion to the Census or Enumeration herein before directed to be taken.

No Tax or Duty shall be laid on Articles exported from any State.

No Preference shall be given by any Regulation of Commerce or Revenue to the Ports of one State over those of another: nor shall Vessels bound to, or from, one State, be obliged to enter, clear, or pay Duties in another.

No Money shall be drawn from the Treasury, but in Consequence of Appropriations made by Law; and a regular Statement and Account of the Receipts and Expenditures of all public Money shall be published from time to time.

No Title of Nobility shall be granted by the United States: And no Person holding any Office of Profit or Trust under them, shall, without the Consent of the Congress, accept of any present, Emolument, Office, or Title, of any kind whatever, from any King, Prince, or foreign State.

Section 10: Powers Denied to the States

No State shall enter into any Treaty, Alliance, or Confederation; grant Letters of Marque and Reprisal; coin Money; emit Bills of Credit; make any Thing but gold and silver Coin a Tender in Payment of Debts; pass any Bill of Attainder, ex post facto Law, or Law impairing the Obligation of Contracts, or grant any Title of Nobility.

No State shall, without the Consent of the Congress, lay any Imposts or Duties on Imports or Exports, except what may be absolutely necessary for executing it's inspection Laws: and the net Produce of all Duties and Imposts, laid by any State on Imports or Exports, shall be for the Use of the Treasury of the United States; and all such Laws shall be subject to the Revision and Controul of the Congress.

No State shall, without the Consent of Congress, lay any Duty of Tonnage, keep Troops, or Ships of War in time of Peace, enter into any Agreement or Compact with another State, or with a foreign Power, or engage in War, unless actually invaded, or in such imminent Danger as will not admit of delay.

Article II

Section 1

The executive Power shall be vested in a President of the United States of America.

He shall hold his Office during the Term of four Years, and, together with the Vice President, chosen for the same Term, be elected, as follows:

Each State shall appoint, in such Manner as the Legislature thereof may direct, a Number of Electors, equal to the whole Number of Senators and Representatives to which the State may be entitled in the Congress: but no Senator or Representative, or

Person holding an Office of Trust or Profit under the United States, shall be appointed an Elector.

The Electors shall meet in their respective States, and vote by Ballot for two Persons, of whom one at least shall not be an Inhabitant of the same State with themselves. And they shall make a List of all the Persons voted for, and of the Number of Votes for each; which List they shall sign and certify, and transmit sealed to the Seat of the Government of the United States, directed to the President of the Senate. The President of the Senate shall, in the Presence of the Senate and House of Representatives, open all the Certificates, and the Votes shall then be counted. The Person having the greatest Number of Votes shall be the President, if such Number be a Majority of the whole Number of Electors appointed; and if there be more than one who have such Majority, and have an equal Number of Votes, then the House of Representatives shall immediately chuse by Ballot one of them for President; and if no Person have a Majority, then from the five highest on the List the said House shall in like Manner chuse the President. But in chusing the President, the Votes shall be taken by States, the Representation from each State having one Vote; A quorum for this Purpose shall consist of a Member or Members from two thirds of the States, and a Majority of all the States shall be necessary to a Choice. In every Case, after the Choice of the President, the Person having the greatest Number of Votes of the Electors shall be the Vice President. But if there should remain two or more who have equal Votes, the Senate shall chuse from them by Ballot the Vice President.

The Congress may determine the Time of chusing the Electors, and the Day on which they shall give their Votes; which Day shall be the same throughout the United States.

No Person except a natural born Citizen, or a Citizen of the United States, at the time of the Adoption of this Constitution, shall be eligible to the Office of President; neither shall any person be eligible to that Office who shall not have attained to the Age of thirty five Years, and been fourteen Years a Resident within the United States.

In Case of the Removal of the President from Office, or of his Death, Resignation, or Inability to discharge the Powers and Duties of the said Office, the Same shall devolve on the Vice President, and the Congress may by Law provide for the Case of Removal, Death, Resignation or Inability, both of the President and Vice President, declaring what Officer shall then act as President, and such Officer shall act accordingly, until the Disability be removed, or a President shall be elected.

The President shall, at stated Times, receive for his Services, a Compensation, which shall neither be increased nor diminished during the Period for which he shall have been elected, and he shall not receive within that Period any other Emolument from the United States, or any of them.

Before he enter on the Execution of his Office, he shall take the following Oath or Affirmation:–"I do solemnly swear (or affirm) that I will faithfully execute the Office of President of the United States, and will to the best of my Ability, preserve, protect and defend the Constitution of the United States."

Section 2

The President shall be Commander in Chief of the Army and Navy of the United States, and of the Militia of the several States, when called into the actual Service of the United States; he may require the Opinion, in writing, of the principal Officer in each of the executive Departments, upon any Subject relating to the Duties of their respective Offices, and he shall have Power to grant Reprieves and Pardons for Offenses against the United States, except in Cases of Impeachment.

He shall have Power, by and with the Advice and Consent of the Senate, to make Treaties, provided two thirds of the Senators present concur; and he shall nominate, and by and with the Advice and Consent of the Senate, shall appoint Ambassadors, other public Ministers and Consuls, Judges of the supreme Court, and all other Officers of the United States, whose Appointments are not herein otherwise provided for, and which shall be established by Law:

but the Congress may by Law vest the Appointment of such inferior Officers, as they think proper, in the President alone, in the Courts of Law, or in the Heads of Departments.

The President shall have Power to fill up all Vacancies that may happen during the Recess of the Senate, by granting Commissions which shall expire at the End of their next Session.

Section 3

He shall from time to time give to the Congress Information of the State of the Union, and recommend to their Consideration such Measures as he shall judge necessary and expedient; he may, on extraordinary Occasions, convene both Houses, or either of them, and in Case of Disagreement between them, with Respect to the Time of Adjournment, he may adjourn them to such Time as he shall think proper; he shall receive Ambassadors and other public Ministers; he shall take Care that the Laws be faithfully executed, and shall Commission all the Officers of the United States.

Section 4

The President, Vice President and all civil Officers of the United States, shall be removed from Office on Impeachment for, and Conviction of, Treason, Bribery, or other high Crimes and Misdemeanors.

Article III

Section 1

The judicial Power of the United States, shall be vested in one supreme Court, and in such inferior Courts as the Congress may from time to time ordain and establish. The Judges, both of the supreme and inferior Courts, shall hold their Offices during good Behaviour, and shall, at stated Times, receive for their Services, a Compensation, which shall not be diminished during their Continuance in Office.

Section 2

The judicial Power shall extend to all Cases, in Law and Equity, arising under this Constitution, the Laws of the United States, and Treaties made, or which shall be made, under their Authority;—to all Cases affecting Ambassadors, other public Ministers and Consuls;—to all Cases of admiralty and maritime Jurisdiction;—to Controversies to which the United States shall be a Party;—to Controversies between two or more States;—between a State and Citizens of another State;—between Citizens of different States;—between Citizens of the same State claiming Lands under Grants of different States, and between a State, or the Citizens thereof, and foreign States, Citizens or Subjects.

In all Cases affecting Ambassadors, other public Ministers and Consuls, and those in which a State shall be Party, the supreme Court shall have original Jurisdiction. In all the other Cases before mentioned, the supreme Court shall have appellate Jurisdiction, both as to Law and Fact, with such Exceptions, and under such Regulations as the Congress shall make.

The Trial of all Crimes, except in Cases of Impeachment; shall be by Jury; and such Trial shall be held in the State where the said Crimes shall have been committed; but when not committed within any State, the Trial shall be at such Place or Places as the Congress may by Law have directed.

Section 3

Treason against the United States, shall consist only in levying War against them, or in adhering to their Enemies, giving them Aid and Comfort. No Person shall be convicted of Treason unless on the Testimony of two Witnesses to the same overt Act, or on Confession in open Court.

The Congress shall have Power to declare the Punishment of Treason, but no Attainder of Treason shall work Corruption of Blood, or Forfeiture except during the Life of the Person attainted.

Article IV

Section 1

Full Faith and Credit shall be given in each State to the public Acts, Records, and judicial Proceedings of every other State. And the Congress may by general Laws prescribe the Manner in which such Acts,

Records and Proceedings shall be proved, and the Effect thereof.

Section 2

The Citizens of each State shall be entitled to all Privileges and Immunities of Citizens in the several States.

A Person charged in any State with Treason, Felony, or other Crime, who shall flee from Justice, and be found in another State, shall on Demand of the executive Authority of the State from which he fled, be delivered up, to be removed to the State having Jurisdiction of the Crime.

No Person held to Service or Labour in one State, under the Laws thereof, escaping into another, shall, in Consequence of any Law or Regulation therein, be discharged from such Service or Labour, but shall be delivered up on Claim of the Party to whom such Service or Labour may be due.

Section 3

New States may be admitted by the Congress into this Union; but no new State shall be formed or erected within the Jurisdiction of any other State; nor any State be formed by the Junction of two or more States, or Parts of States, without the Consent of the Legislatures of the States concerned as well as of the Congress.

The Congress shall have Power to dispose of and make all needful Rules and Regulations respecting the Territory or other Property belonging to the United States; and nothing in this Constitution shall be so construed as to Prejudice any Claims of the United States, or of any particular State.

Section 4

The United States shall guarantee to every State in this Union a Republican Form of Government, and shall protect each of them against Invasion; and on Application of the Legislature, or of the Executive (when the Legislature cannot be convened) against domestic Violence.

Article V

The Congress, whenever two thirds of both Houses shall deem it necessary, shall propose Amendments to this Constitution, or, on the Application of the Legislatures of two thirds of the several States, shall call a Convention for proposing Amendments, which, in either Case, shall be valid to all Intents and Purposes, as Part of this Constitution, when ratified by the Legislatures of three fourths of the several States, or by Conventions in three fourths thereof, as the one or the other Mode of Ratification may be proposed by the Congress; Provided that no Amendment which may be made prior to the Year One thousand eight hundred and eight shall in any Manner affect the first and fourth Clauses in the Ninth Section of the first

Article; and that no State, without its Consent, shall be deprived of its equal Suffrage in the Senate.

Article VI

All Debts contracted and Engagements entered into, before the Adoption of this Constitution, shall be as valid against the United States under this Constitution, as under the Confederation.

This Constitution, and the Laws of the United States which shall be made in Pursuance thereof; and all Treaties made, or which shall be made, under the Authority of the United States, shall be the supreme Law of the Land; and the Judges in every State shall be bound thereby, any Thing in the Constitution or Laws of any State to the Contrary notwithstanding.

The Senators and Representatives before mentioned, and the Members of the several State Legislatures, and all executive and judicial Officers, both of the United States and of the several States, shall be bound by Oath or Affirmation, to support this Constitution; but no religious Test shall ever be required as a Qualification to any Office or public Trust under the United States.

Article VII

The Ratification of the Conventions of nine States, shall be sufficient for the Establishment of this Constitution between the States so ratifying the Same.

First Amendment

Congress shall make no law respecting an establishment of religion, or prohibiting the free exercise thereof; or abridging the freedom of speech, or of the press; or the right of the people peaceably to assemble, and to petition the Government for a redress of grievances. (December 15, 1791)

Second Amendment

A well regulated Militia, being necessary to the security of a free State, the right of the people to keep and bear Arms, shall not be infringed. (December 15, 1791)

Third Amendment

No Soldier shall, in time of peace be quartered in any house, without the consent of the Owner, nor in time of war, but in a manner to be prescribed by law. (December 15, 1791)

Fourth Amendment

The right of the people to be secure in their persons, houses, papers, and effects, against unreasonable searches and seizures, shall not be violated, and no Warrants shall issue, but upon probable cause, supported by Oath or affirmation, and particularly describing the place to be searched, and the persons or things to be seized. (December 15, 1791)

Fifth Amendment

No person shall be held to answer for a capital, or otherwise infamous crime, unless on a presentment or indictment of a Grand Jury, except in cases arising in the land or naval forces, or in the Militia, when in actual service in time of War or public danger; nor shall any person be subject for the same offence to be twice put in jeopardy of life or limb; nor shall be compelled in any criminal case to be a witness against himself, nor be deprived of life, liberty, or property, without due process of law; nor shall private property be taken for public use, without just compensation. (December 15, 1791)

Sixth Amendment

In all criminal prosecutions, the accused shall enjoy the right to a speedy and public trial, by an impartial jury of the State and district wherein the crime shall have been committed, which district shall have been previously ascertained by law, and to be informed of the nature and cause of the accusation; to be confronted with the witnesses against him; to have compulsory process for obtaining witnesses in his favor, and to have the Assistance of Counsel for his defence. (December 15, 1791)

Seventh Amendment

In Suits at common law, where the value in controversy shall exceed twenty dollars, the right of trial by jury shall be preserved, and no fact tried by a jury, shall be otherwise reexamined in any Court of the United States, than according to the rules of the common law. (December 15, 1791)

Eighth Amendment

Excessive bail shall not be required, nor excessive fines imposed, nor cruel and unusual punishments inflicted. (December 15, 1791)

Ninth Amendment

The enumeration in the Constitution, of certain rights, shall not be construed to deny or disparage others retained by the people. (December 15, 1791)

10th Amendment

The powers not delegated to the United States by the Constitution, nor prohibited by it to the States, are reserved to the States respectively, or to the people. (December 15, 1791)

11th Amendment

The Judicial power of the United States shall not be construed to extend to any suit in law or equity, commenced or prosecuted against one of the United States by Citizens of another State, or by Citizens or Subjects of any Foreign State. (February 7, 1795)

12th Amendment

The Electors shall meet in their respective states and vote by ballot for President and Vice-President, one of whom, at least, shall not be an inhabitant of the same state with themselves; they shall name in their ballots the person voted for as President, and in distinct ballots the person voted for as Vice-President, and they shall make distinct lists of all persons voted for as President, and of all persons voted for as Vice-President, and of the number of votes for each, which lists they shall sign and certify, and transmit sealed to the seat of the government of the United States, directed to the President of the Senate;—The President of the Senate shall, in the presence of the Senate and House of Representatives, open all the certificates and the votes shall then be counted;—The person having the greatest number of votes for President, shall be the President, if such number be a majority of the whole number of Electors appointed; and if no person have such majority, then from the persons having the highest numbers not exceeding three on the list of those voted for as President, the House of Representatives shall choose immediately, by ballot, the President. But in choosing the President, the votes shall be taken by states, the representation from each state having one vote; a quorum for this purpose shall consist of a member or members from two-thirds of the states, and a majority of all the states shall be necessary to a choice. And if the House of Representatives shall not choose a President whenever the right of choice shall devolve upon them, before the fourth day of March next following, then the Vice-President shall act as President, as in case of the death or other constitutional disability of the President.—The person having the greatest number of votes as Vice-President, shall be the Vice-President, if such number be a majority of the whole number of Electors appointed, and if no person have a majority, then from the two highest numbers on the list, the Senate shall choose the Vice-President; a quorum for the purpose shall consist of two-thirds of the whole number of Senators, and a majority of the whole number shall be necessary to a choice. But no person constitutionally ineligible to the office of President shall be eligible to that of Vice-President of the United States. (June 15, 1804)

13th Amendment

Section 1

Neither slavery nor involuntary servitude, except as a punishment for crime whereof the party shall have been duly convicted, shall exist within the United States, or any place subject to their jurisdiction.

Section 2

Congress shall have power to enforce this article by appropriate legislation. (December 6, 1865)

14th Amendment

Section 1

All persons born or naturalized in the United States, and subject to the jurisdiction thereof, are citizens of the United States and of the State wherein they reside. No State shall make or enforce any law which shall abridge the privileges or immunities of citizens of the United States; nor shall any State deprive any person of life, liberty, or property, without due process of law; nor deny to any person within its jurisdiction the equal protection of the laws.

Section 2

Representatives shall be apportioned among the several States according to their respective numbers, counting the whole number of persons in each State, excluding Indians not taxed. But when the right to vote at any election for the choice of electors for President and Vice-President of the United States, Representatives in Congress, the Executive and Judicial officers of a State, or the members of the Legislature thereof, is denied to any of the male inhabitants of such State, being twenty-one years of age, and citizens of the United States, or in any way abridged, except for participation in rebellion, or other crime, the basis of representation therein shall be reduced in the proportion which the number of such male citizens shall bear to the whole number of male citizens twenty-one years of age in such State.

Section 3

No person shall be a Senator or Representative in Congress, or elector of President and Vice-President, or hold any office, civil or military, under the United States, or under any State, who, having previously taken an oath, as a member of Congress, or as an officer of the United States, or as a member of any State legislature, or as an executive or judicial officer of any State, to support the Constitution of the United States, shall have engaged in insurrection or rebellion against the same, or given aid or comfort to the enemies thereof. But Congress may by a vote of two-thirds of each House, remove such disability.

Section 4

The validity of the public debt of the United States, authorized by law, including debts incurred for payment of pensions and bounties for services in suppressing insurrection or rebellion, shall not be questioned. But neither the United States nor any State shall assume or pay any debt or obligation incurred in aid of insurrection or rebellion against the United States, or any claim for the loss or emancipation of any slave; but all such debts, obligations and claims shall be held illegal and void.

Section 5

The Congress shall have the power to enforce, by appropriate legislation, the provisions of this article. (July 9, 1868)

15th Amendment

Section 1

The right of citizens of the United States to vote shall not be denied or abridged by the United States or by any State on account of race, color, or previous condition of servitude.

Section 2

The Congress shall have the power to enforce this article by appropriate legislation. (February 3, 1870)

16th Amendment

The Congress shall have power to lay and collect taxes on incomes, from whatever source derived, without apportionment among the several States, and without regard to any census or enumeration. (February 3, 1913)

17th Amendment

The Senate of the United States shall be composed of two Senators from each State, elected by the people thereof, for six years; and each Senator shall have one vote. The electors in each State shall have the qualifications requisite for electors of the most numerous branch of the State legislatures.

When vacancies happen in the representation of any State in the Senate, the executive authority of such State shall issue writs of election to fill such vacancies: Provided, That the legislature of any State may empower the executive thereof to make temporary appointments until the people fill the vacancies by election as the legislature may direct.

This amendment shall not be so construed as to affect the election or term of any Senator chosen before it becomes valid as part of the Constitution. (April 8, 1913)

18th Amendment

Section 1

After one year from the ratification of this article the manufacture, sale, or transportation of intoxicating liquors within, the importation thereof into, or the exportation thereof from the United States and all territory subject to the jurisdiction thereof for beverage purposes is hereby prohibited.

Section 2

The Congress and the several States shall have concurrent power to enforce this article by appropriate legislation.

Section 3

This article shall be inoperative unless it shall have been ratified as an amendment to the Constitution by the legislatures of the several States, as provided in the Constitution, within seven years from the date of the submission hereof to the States by the Congress. (January 16, 1919; repealed December 5, 1933)

19th Amendment

The right of citizens of the United States to vote shall not be denied or abridged by the United States or by any State on account of sex.

Congress shall have power to enforce this article by appropriate legislation. (August 18, 1920)

20th Amendment

Section 1

The terms of the President and the Vice President shall end at noon on the 20th day of January, and the terms of Senators and Representatives at noon on the 3d day of January, of the years in which such terms would have ended if this article had not been ratified; and the terms of their successors shall then begin.

Section 2

The Congress shall assemble at least once in every year, and such meeting shall begin at noon on the 3d day of January, unless they shall by law appoint a different day.

Section 3

If, at the time fixed for the beginning of the term of the President, the President elect shall have died, the Vice President elect shall become President. If a President shall not have been chosen before the time fixed for the beginning of his term, or if the President elect shall have failed to qualify, then the Vice President elect shall act as President until a President shall have qualified; and the Congress may by law provide for the case wherein neither a President elect nor a Vice President shall have qualified, declaring who shall then act as President, or the manner in which one who is to act shall be selected, and such person shall act accordingly until a President or Vice President shall have qualified.

Section 4

The Congress may by law provide for the case of the death of any of the persons from whom the House of Representatives may choose a President whenever the right of choice shall have devolved upon them, and for the case of the death of any of the persons from whom the Senate may choose a Vice President whenever the right of choice shall have devolved upon them.

Section 5

Sections 1 and 2 shall take effect on the 15th day of October following the ratification of this article.

Section 6

This article shall be inoperative unless it shall have been ratified as an amendment to the Constitution by the legislatures of three-fourths of the several States within seven years from the date of its submission. (January 23, 1933)

21st Amendment

Section 1

The eighteenth article of amendment to the Constitution of the United States is hereby repealed.

Section 2

The transportation or importation into any State, Territory, or Possession of the United States for delivery or use therein of intoxicating liquors, in violation of the laws thereof, is hereby prohibited.

Section 3

This article shall be inoperative unless it shall have been ratified as an amendment to the Constitution by conventions in the several States, as provided in the Constitution, within seven years from the date of the submission hereof to the States by the Congress. (December 5, 1933)

22nd Amendment

Section 1

No person shall be elected to the office of the President more than twice, and no person who has held the office of President, or acted as President, for more than two years of a term to which some other person was elected President shall be elected to the office of President more than once. But this Article shall not apply to any person holding the office of President when this Article was proposed by Congress, and shall not prevent any person who may be holding the office of President, or acting as President, during the term within which this Article becomes operative from holding the office of President or acting as President during the remainder of such term.

Section 2

This article shall be inoperative unless it shall have been ratified as an amendment to the Constitution by the legislatures of three-fourths of the several States within seven years from the date of its submission to the States by the Congress. (February 27, 1951)

23rd Amendment

Section 1

The District constituting the seat of Government of the United States shall appoint in such manner as Congress may direct:

A number of electors of President and Vice President equal to the whole number of Senators and Representatives in Congress to which the District would be entitled if it were a State, but in no event more than the least populous State; they shall be in addition to those appointed by the States, but they shall be considered, for the purposes of the election of President and Vice President, to be electors appointed by a State; and they shall meet in the District and perform such duties as provided by the twelfth article of amendment.

Section 2

The Congress shall have power to enforce this article by appropriate legislation. (March 29, 1961)

24th Amendment

Section 1

The right of citizens of the United States to vote in any primary or other election for President or Vice President, for electors for President or Vice President, or for Senator or Representative in Congress, shall not be denied or abridged by the United States or any State by reason of failure to pay poll tax or other tax.

Section 2

The Congress shall have power to enforce this article by appropriate legislation. (January 23, 1964)

25th Amendment

Section 1

In case of the removal of the President from office or of his death or resignation, the Vice President shall become President.

Section 2

Whenever there is a vacancy in the office of the Vice President, the President shall nominate a Vice President who shall take office upon confirmation by a majority vote of both Houses of Congress.

Section 3

Whenever the President transmits to the President pro tempore of the Senate and the Speaker of the House of Representatives his written declaration that he is unable to discharge the powers and duties of his office, and until he transmits to them a written declaration to the contrary, such powers and duties shall be discharged by the Vice President as Acting President.

Section 4

Whenever the Vice President and a majority of either the principal officers of the executive departments or of such other body as Congress may by law provide, transmit to the President pro tempore of the Senate and the Speaker of the House of Representatives their written declaration that the President is unable to discharge the powers and duties of his office, the Vice President shall immediately assume the powers and duties of the office as Acting President.

Thereafter, when the President transmits to the President pro tempore of the Senate and the Speaker of the House of Representatives his written declaration that no inability exists, he shall resume the powers and duties of his office unless the Vice President and a majority of either the principal officers of the executive department or of such other body as Congress may by law provide, transmit within four days to the President pro tempore of the Senate and the Speaker of the House of Representatives their written declaration that the President is unable to discharge the powers and duties of his office. Thereupon Congress shall decide the issue, assembling within forty-eight hours for that purpose if not in session. If the Congress,

within twenty-one days after receipt of the latter written declaration, or, if Congress is not in session, within
twenty-one days after Congress is required to assemble, determines by two-thirds vote of both Houses
that the President is unable to discharge the powers and duties of his office, the Vice President shall
continue to discharge the same as Acting President;
otherwise, the President shall resume the powers and
duties of his office. (February 10, 1967)

26th Amendment

Section 1

The right of citizens of the United States, who are
eighteen years of age or older, to vote shall not be
denied or abridged by the United States or by any
State on account of age.

Section 2

The Congress shall have power to enforce this article
by appropriate legislation. (July 1, 1971)

27th Amendment

No law, varying the compensation for the services of
the Senators and Representatives, shall take effect,
until an election of representatives shall have inter-
vened. (May 7, 1992)[292]

APPENDIX C

THE GETTYSBURG ADDRESS

Four score and seven years ago our fathers brought forth on this continent, a new nation, conceived in Liberty, and dedicated to the proposition that all men are created equal.

Now we are engaged in a great civil war, testing whether that nation, or any nation so conceived and so dedicated, can long endure. We are met on a great battle-field of that war. We have come to dedicate a portion of that field, as a final resting place for those who here gave their lives that that nation might live. It is altogether fitting and proper that we should do this.

But, in a larger sense, we can not dedicate—we can not consecrate—we can not hallow—this ground. The brave men, living and dead, who struggled here, have consecrated it, far above our poor power to add or detract. The world will little note, nor long remember what we say here, but it can never forget what they did here. It is for us the living, rather, to be dedicated here to the unfinished work which they who fought here have thus far so nobly advanced. It is rather for us to be here dedicated to the great task remaining before us—that from these honored dead we take increased devotion to that cause for which they gave the last full measure of devotion—that we here highly resolve that these dead shall not have died in vain—that this nation, under God, shall have a new birth of freedom—and that government of the people, by the people, for the people, shall not perish from the earth.[293]

"I HAVE A DREAM"

Five score years ago, a great American, in whose symbolic shadow we stand today, signed the Emancipation Proclamation. This momentous decree came as a great beacon light of hope to millions of Negro slaves who had been seared in the flames of withering injustice. It came as a joyous daybreak to end the long night of their captivity.

But 100 years later, the Negro still is not free. One hundred years later, the life of the Negro is still sadly crippled by the manacles of segregation and the chains of discrimination. One hundred years later, the Negro lives on a lonely island of poverty in the midst of a vast ocean of material prosperity. One hundred years later the Negro is still languished in the corners of American society and finds himself in exile in his own land. And so we've come here today to dramatize a shameful condition. In a sense we've come to our nation's capital to cash a check.

When the architects of our republic wrote the magnificent words of the Constitution and the Declaration of Independence, they were signing a promissory note to which every American was to fall heir. This note was a promise that all men—yes, Black men as well as white men—would be guaranteed the unalienable rights of life, liberty and the pursuit of happiness.

It is obvious today that America has defaulted on this promissory note insofar as her citizens of color are concerned. Instead of honoring this sacred obligation, America has given the Negro people a bad check, a check which has come back marked insufficient funds.

But we refuse to believe that the bank of justice is bankrupt.

We refuse to believe that there are insufficient funds in the great vaults of opportunity of this nation. And so we've come to cash this check, a check that will give us upon demand the riches of freedom and the security of justice.

We have also come to his hallowed spot to remind America of the fierce urgency of now. This is no time to engage in the luxury of cooling off or to take the tranquilizing drug of gradualism.

Now is the time to make real the promises of democracy. Now is the time to rise from the dark and desolate valley of segregation to the sunlit path of racial justice. Now is the time to lift our nation from the quick sands of racial injustice to the solid rock of brotherhood. Now is the time to make justice a reality for all of God's children.

It would be fatal for the nation to overlook the urgency of the moment. This sweltering summer of the Negro's legitimate discontent will not pass until there is an invigorating autumn of freedom and equality. 1963 is not an end, but a beginning. Those who hope that the Negro needed to blow off steam and will now be content will have a rude awakening if the nation returns to business as usual.

There will be neither rest nor tranquility in America until the Negro is granted his citizenship rights. The whirlwinds of revolt will continue to shake the foundations of our nation until the bright day of justice emerges.

But there is something that I must say to my people who stand on the warm threshold which leads into the palace of justice. In the process of gaining our rightful place, we must not be guilty of wrongful deeds. Let us not seek to satisfy our thirst for freedom by drinking from the cup of bitterness and hatred.

We must forever conduct our struggle on the high plane of dignity and discipline. We must not allow our creative protest to degenerate into physical violence. Again and again, we must rise to the majestic heights of meeting physical force with soul force. The marvelous new militancy which has engulfed the Negro community must not lead us to a distrust of all white people, for many of our white brothers, as evidenced by their presence here today, have come to realize that their destiny is tied up with our destiny.

And they have come to realize that their freedom is inextricably bound to our freedom. We cannot walk alone. And as we walk, we must make the pledge that we shall always march ahead. We cannot turn back.

There are those who are asking the devotees of civil rights, when will you be satisfied? We can never be satisfied as long as the Negro is the victim of the unspeakable horrors of police brutality. We can never be satisfied as long as our bodies, heavy with the fatigue of travel, cannot gain lodging in the motels of the highways and the hotels of the cities.

We cannot be satisfied as long as the Negro's basic mobility is from a smaller ghetto to a larger one. We can never be satisfied as long as our children are stripped of their selfhood and robbed of their dignity by signs stating: for whites only.

We cannot be satisfied as long as a Negro in Mississippi cannot vote and a Negro in New York believes he has nothing for which to vote.

No, no, we are not satisfied, and we will not be satisfied until justice rolls down like waters, and righteousness like a mighty stream.

I am not unmindful that some of you have come here out of great trials and tribulations. Some of you have come fresh from narrow jail cells. Some of you have come from areas where your quest for freedom left you battered by the storms of persecution and staggered by the winds of police brutality. You have been the veterans of creative suffering. Continue to work with the faith that unearned suffering is redemptive. Go back to Mississippi, go back to Alabama, go back to South Carolina, go back to Georgia, go back to Louisiana, go back to the slums and ghettos of our Northern cities, knowing that somehow this situation can and will be changed.

Let us not wallow in the valley of despair, I say to you today, my friends.

So even though we face the difficulties of today and tomorrow, I still have a dream. It is a dream deeply rooted in the American dream. I have a dream that one day this nation will rise up and live out the true meaning of its creed: We hold these truths to be self-evident, that all men are created equal.

I have a dream that one day on the red hills of Georgia, the sons of former slaves and the sons of former slave owners will be able to sit down together at the table of brotherhood.

I have a dream that one day even the state of Mississippi, a state sweltering with the heat of injustice, sweltering with the heat of oppression will be transformed into an oasis of freedom and justice.

I have a dream that my four little children will one day live in a nation where they will not be judged by the color of their skin but by the content of their character. I have a dream today.

I have a dream that one day down in Alabama with its vicious racists, with its governor having his lips dripping with the words of interposition and nullification, one day right down in Alabama little Black boys and Black girls will be able to join hands with little white boys and white girls as sisters and brothers. I have a dream today.

I have a dream that one day every valley shall be exalted, every hill and mountain shall be made low, the rough places will be made plain, and the crooked places will be made straight, and the glory of the Lord shall be revealed, and all flesh shall see it together.

This is our hope. This is the faith that I go back to the South with. With this faith, we will be able to hew out of the mountain of despair a stone of hope. With this faith we will be able to transform the jangling discords of our nation into a beautiful symphony of brotherhood. With this faith we will be able to work together, to pray together, to struggle together, to go to jail together, to stand up for freedom together, knowing that we will be free one day.

This will be the day when all of God's children will be able to sing with new meaning: My country, 'tis of thee, sweet land of liberty, of thee I sing. Land where my fathers died, land of the pilgrims' pride, from every mountainside, let freedom ring.

And if America is to be a great nation, this must become true. And so let freedom ring from the prodigious hilltops of New Hampshire. Let freedom ring from the mighty mountains of New York. Let freedom ring from the heightening Alleghenies of Pennsylvania. Let freedom ring from the snow-capped Rockies of Colorado. Let freedom ring from the curvaceous slopes of California. But not only that, let freedom ring from Stone Mountain of Georgia. Let freedom ring from Lookout Mountain of Tennessee. Let freedom ring from every hill and molehill of Mississippi. From every mountainside, let freedom ring.

And when this happens, and when we allow freedom ring, when we let it ring from every village and every hamlet, from every state and every city, we will be able to speed up that day when all of God's children, Black men and white men, Jews and Gentiles, Protestants and Catholics, will be able to join hands and sing in the words of the old Negro spiritual: Free at last. Free at last. Thank God almighty, we are free at last.[294]

ENDNOTES

Introduction

[1] Tanza Loudenback, "Spanx founder Sara Blakely learned an important lesson about failure from her dad — now she's passing it on to her 4 kids," Yahoo! Sports, October 14, 2016, https://ca.sports.yahoo.com/news/spanx-founder-sara-blakely-learned-164500101.html (accessed March 1, 2022).

[2] Ibid.

[3] Gillian Zoe Segal, "This self-made billionaire failed the LSAT twice, then sold fax machines for 7 years before hitting big—here's how she got there," CNBC, April 3, 2019, https://www.cnbc.com/2019/04/03/self-made-billionaire-spanx-founder-sara-blakely-sold-fax-machines-before-making-it-big.html/ (accessed May 19, 2022).

[4] Rachel Makinson, "How Spanx Founder Sara Blakely Created a Billion-Dollar Brand," *CEO Today*, October 28, 2021, https://www.ceotodaymagazine.com/2021/10/how-spanx-founder-sara-blakely-created-a-billion-dollar-brand/ (accessed February 10, 2022).

[5] Eric Jackson, "Coronavirus: Atlanta billionaire to donate $5 million to female business owners," *Atlanta Business Chronicle*, April 5, 2020, https://www.bizjournals.com/atlanta/news/2020/04/05/coronavirusatlanta-billionaire-to-donate-5-million.html (accessed February 10, 2022).

[6] Clare Kelly, "Lighting the course for female entrepreneurs," Virgin, January 19, 2020, https://www.virgin.com/virgin-unite/latest/lighting-the-course-for-female-entrepreneurs/ (accessed February 11, 2022).

[7] William V. Wenger, "How the Americans defeated the British in the Revolutionary War," The Past, November 10, 2021, https://the-past.com/feature/how-the-americans-defeated-the-british-in-the-revolutionary-war/.

8   A. E. Dick Howard, "America's Constitution Inspired the World," *American Heritage*, Winter 2020, Vol. 64, Issue 1, https://www. americanheritage.com/americas-constitution-inspired-world.

9   Edward L. Glaeser, Rafael Di Tella, and Lucas Llach, "Introduction to Argentine exceptionalism," *Latin American Economic Review* 27, 1 (2018), https://doi.org/10.1007/s40503-017-0055-4.

10   Rok Spruk, "The rise and fall of Argentina," *Latin American Economic Review* 28, 16 (2019), https://doi.org/10.1186/s40503-019-0076-2.

11   "Argentina 1853 (reinst. 1983, rev. 1994)," translated by Jonathan M. Miller and Fang-Lian Liao, Oxford University Press, Inc., Constitute: The World's Constitutions to Read, Search, and Compare, https:// www.constituteproject.org/constitution/Argentina_1994.

12   Eric R. Wolf and Edward C. Hansen, "Caudillo Politics: A Structural Analysis," *Comparative Studies in Society and History*, Volume 9, Issue 2 (January 1967), 168–179, http://www. latinamericanstudies.org/19-century/caudillo-politics.pdf.

13   Anne L. Potter, "The Failure of Democracy in Argentina 1916-1930: An Institutional Perspective." *Journal of Latin American Studies* 13, no. 1 (1981): 83–109, http://www.jstor.org/stable/156340.

14   Rok Spruk, "The rise and fall of Argentina," *Latin American Economic Review* 28, 16 (2019), https://doi.org/10.1186/s40503-019-0076-2.

15   Ibid.

16   Yair Mundlak, Domingo Cavallo, and Roberto Domenech, "Agriculture and economic growth in Argentina, 1913-84," Research reports 76, International Food Policy Research Institute (IFPRI), 1989.

17   Ibid.

18   Rok Spruk, "The rise and fall of Argentina," *Latin American Economic Review* 28, 16 (2019), https://doi.org/10.1186/s40503-019-0076-2.

19   Ibid.

20   Ibid.

21   William Ratliff and Luis Fernando Calviño, "20th Century Argentina in the Hoover Institution Archives," Hoover Institution Archives, September 2007, https://www.hoover.org/sites/default/ files/library/docs/hoover_argentina_guide_eng.pdf.

22   Ibid.

23   Naomi Schaefer Riley, "'The 1619 Project' Enters American Classrooms: Adding new sizzle to education about slavery— but at a significant cost," *Education Next* 20(4), 34-44 (2020),

https://www.educationnext.org/1619-project-enters-american-classrooms-adding-new-sizzle-slavery-significant-cost/.

24 James Madison, "Federalist Papers No. 51 (1788)," Bill of Rights Institute, https://billofrightsinstitute.org/primary-sources/federalist-no-51.

25 James Madison, "Federalist Papers No. 10 (1787)," Bill of Rights Institute, https://billofrightsinstitute.org/primary-sources/federalist-no-10.

26 Ibid.

27 Alexander Hamilton, "Federalist Papers No. 70 (1788)," Bill of Rights Institute, https://billofrightsinstitute.org/primary-sources/federalist-no-70.

28 "Magna Carta: Muse and Mentor — Magna Carta and the U.S. Constitution," The Library of Congress, https://www.loc.gov/exhibits/magna-carta-muse-and-mentor/magna-carta-and-the-us-constitution.html; Hilary Bok, "Baron de Montesquieu, Charles-Louis de Secondat," The Stanford Encyclopedia of Philosophy (Winter 2018 Edition), Edward N. Zalta (ed.), published July 18, 2003, revised April 2, 2014, https://plato.stanford.edu/archives/win2018/entries/montesquieu/.

29 Gareth Davey, Chuan De Lian, and Louise Higgins, "The university entrance examination system in China," *Journal of Further and Higher Education*, 31:4, 385-396 (2007), https://www.tandfonline.com/doi/abs/10.1080/03098770701625761; John Osburg, *Anxious Wealth: Money and Morality Among China's New Rich* (Stanford: Stanford University Press, 2013).

30 Neha L., "Affirmative Action: Equity or Inequality?" Students 4 Social Change, September 12, 2020, https://students4sc.org/2020/09/12/affirmative-action-equity-or-inequality/.

31 Daniel E. Slotnik, "Whistle-Blower Unites Democrats and Republicans in Calling for Regulation of Facebook," *New York Times*, October 5, 2021, updated October 26, 2021, https://www.nytimes.com/live/2021/10/05/technology/facebook-whistleblower-frances-haugen.

32 "Annotated Guide to the For the People Act of 2021," Brennan Center for Justice at NYU Law, January 20, 2021, updated March 18, 2021, https://www.brennancenter.org/our-work/policy-solutions/annotated-guide-people-act-2021.

Chapter 1

33 Jamie Ballard, "In 2020, do people see the American Dream as attainable?" YouGovAmerica, July 18, 2020, https://today.

yougov.com/topics/politics/articles-reports/2020/07/18/
american-dream-attainable-poll-survey-data.

34   Karlyn Bowman, "Another Poll On The American Dream? Here's
One With New Insights," *Forbes*, January 19, 2021, https://www.
forbes.com/sites/bowmanmarsico/2021/01/19/another-poll-on-the-
american-dream-heres-one-with-new-insights/?sh=7ceee4cc1964.

35   CNN, "YIR/ELECTION: OBAMA 'YOU DIDN'T
BUILD THAT,'" YouTube, July 21, 2016, video, https://
www.youtube.com/watch?v=9GjqdP6KSOE.

36   Alexis de Tocqueville, *Democracy in America* (G. Dearborn & Co., 1838).

37   Megan Brenan, "U.S. National Pride Falls to Record
Low," Gallup, June 15, 2020, https://news.gallup.com/
poll/312644/national-pride-falls-record-low.aspx.

Chapter 2

38   "European Migrations to American Colonies, 1492–1820."
Encyclopedia of Western Colonialism since 1450, Encyclopedia.
com, October 25, 2021, https://www.encyclopedia.com/
history/encyclopedias-almanacs-transcripts-and-maps/
european-migrations-american-colonies-1492-1820.

39   Ibid., 15–28.

40   Antolini, Paola. "1492: The Role of Women." Women of Europe
Supplements, 1992, 35, http://aei.pitt.edu/34007/1/A484.pdf.

41   "The Colonies: 1690-1715," National Humanities Center,
Toolbox Library: Primary Resources in U.S. History and
Literature, rev. September 2009, http://nationalhumanitiescenter.
org/pds/becomingamer/growth/text1/text1read.htm.

42   Joseph Postell, "Regulation in Early America," *American
Affairs*, Spring 2018, https://americanaffairsjournal.
org/2018/02/regulation-early-america/.

43   Alan Greenspan and Adrian Wooldridge, *Capitalism in
America: A History* (New York City: Penguin Press, 2018).

44   Ibid.

45   Jen Deaderick, "What we get wrong about taxes and the American
Revolution," PBS, December 26, 2016, https://www.pbs.org/newshour/
economy/what-we-get-wrong-about-taxes-american-revolution.

46   Stephen Hopkins, "The Rights of the Colonies Examined," The
Harlan Institute, September 9, 2021, https://harlaninstitute.

org/wp-content/uploads/2021/09/Stephen-Hopkins-The-Rights-of-the-Colonies-Examined-21t4yte.pdf.

47 Ibid.

48 Hillsdale College, *American Heritage: A Reader* (Hillsdale, MI: Hillsdale Press, 2011).

49 "Natural Rights: The Declaration of Independence and Natural Rights," Constitutional Rights Foundation, 2001, https://www.crf-usa.org/foundations-of-our-constitution/natural-rights.html.

50 Robert L. Heilbroner, "Adam Smith: Wealth of Nations," *Encyclopedia Britannica*, https://www.britannica.com/biography/Adam-Smith/The-Wealth-of-Nations.

51 "The Theory of Moral Sentiments," Adam Smith Institute, https://www.adamsmith.org/the-theory-of-moral-sentiments.

52 Ibid.

53 Ibid.

54 C.I. Jones, "Chapter 1 - The Facts of Economic Growth," in *Handbook of Macroeconomics, Volume 2A* (Elsevier B.V., 2016), https://web.stanford.edu/~chadj/facts.pdf.

55 Roger Pilon, "Cato Handbook for Policymakers — 16. Property Rights and the Constitution," Cato Institute, 2017, https://www.cato.org/cato-handbook-policymakers/cato-handbook-policy-makers-8th-edition-2017/property-rights-constitution.

56 Brenda Erickson, "Amending the U.S. Constitution," National Conference of State Legislatures, August 2017, https://www.ncsl.org/research/about-state-legislatures/amending-the-u-s-constitution.aspx.

57 Marc Bouloiseau, "The Committee of Public Safety and the Reign of Terror," *Encyclopedia Britannica*, https://www.britannica.com/biography/Maximilien-Robespierre/The-Committee-of-Public-Safety-and-the-Reign-of-Terror.

58 Richard Hofstadter, "The Myth of the Happy Yeoman," *American Heritage*, April 1956, https://www.americanheritage.com/myth-happy-yeoman.

59 Noble E. Cunningham, *The Jeffersonian Republicans in Power: Party Operations, 1801–1809* (Chapel Hill, N.C.: Univ. of North Carolina Press, 2013).

60 "The Federalist and the Republican Party," PBS: American Experience, https://www.pbs.org/wgbh/americanexperience/features/duel-federalist-and-republican-party/.

[61]   Mark Maloy, "The Founding Fathers Views of Slavery," American
      Battlefield Trust, December 8, 2020, updated February 1, 2022,
      https://www.battlefields.org/learn/articles/founding-fathers-views-
      slavery; Daryl Austin, "Anti-slavery revolutionaries who practiced
      what they preached," *The Hill*, July 10, 2020, https://thehill.com/
      changing-america/opinion/506782-anti-slavery-revolutionaries-
      who-practiced-what-they-preached (accessed February 14, 2022).
[62]   J. Gordon Hylton, "Before there were 'red' and 'blue' states, there
      were 'free' states and 'slave' states," Marquette University Law
      School Faculty Blog, December 20, 2012, https://law.marquette.edu/
      facultyblog/2012/12/before-there-were-red-and-blue-states-there-
      were-free-states-and-slave-states/ (accessed February 14, 2022).
[63]   John W. York, "What Our Founders Really Thought of Slavery — And
      Why *The New York Times* Is Wrong," Heritage Foundation, September
      27, 2019, https://www.heritage.org/american-founders/commentary/
      what-our-founders-really-thought-slavery-and-why-the-new-york-times.
[64]   "Founding of Pennsylvania Abolition Society," PBS,
      https://www.pbs.org/wgbh/aia/part3/3p249.html.

Chapter 3

[65]   American Anthropological Association, "1800s-1850s:
      Expansion of slavery in the U.S.," NBC News, May 27,
      2008, https://www.nbcnews.com/id/wbna24714472.
[66]   C.E. Merriam, "The Political Theory of Calhoun,"
      American Journal of Sociology, Vol. 7, No. 5 (1902), 577-
      594, https://www.jstor.org/stable/pdf/2762212.pdf.
[67]   The Editors of the Encyclopedia Britannica, "Anti-
      Federalists." *Encyclopedia Britannica*, September 24, 2021,
      https://www.britannica.com/topic/Anti-Federalists.
[68]   C.E. Merriam, "The Political Theory of Calhoun,"
      American Journal of Sociology, Vol. 7, No. 5 (1902), 577-
      594, https://www.jstor.org/stable/pdf/2762212.pdf.
[69]   John McCormack, "Weekly Standard: Founding Fathers Opposed
      Slavery," NPR, July 6, 2011, https://www.npr.org/2011/07/06/137647715/
      weekly-standard-founding-fathers-opposed-slavery.
[70]   NCC Staff, "The cotton gin: A game-changing social
      and economic invention," National Constitution Center,

March 14, 2022, https://constitutioncenter.org/blog/
the-cotton-gin-a-game-changing-social-and-economic-invention.

71 The Editors of the Encyclopedia Britannica, "Missouri
Compromise." *Encyclopedia Britannica*, July 31, 2019, https://
www.britannica.com/event/Missouri-Compromise.

72 60 U.S. 19 How. 393, 452-53 (1856).

73 *Id.* at 451.

74 Mintz, S. and McNeil, S, "Lincoln's Stand on Slavery in the 1858
Illinois Senate Campaign," Digital History, 2018, https://www.
digitalhistory.uh.edu/disp_textbook.cfm?smtID=3&psid=367.

75 Frank J. Williams, "Abraham Lincoln, Chief Justice Roger
B. Taney, and the *Dred Scott* Case," OUPblog, March 4,
2015, https://blog.oup.com/2015/03/abraham-lincoln-
roger-taney-dred-scott/ (accessed February 15, 2022).

76 Robert F. Durden, "The American Revolution as Seen by Southerners
in 1861." *Louisiana History: The Journal of the Louisiana Historical
Association* 19, no. 1 (1978): 33–42, http://www.jstor.org/stable/4231754.

77 "The Civil War By the Numbers," PBS: American Experience,
https://www.pbs.org/wgbh/americanexperience/features/
death-numbers/ (accessed February 15, 2022).

78 Henry Louis Gates Jr., "Which Slave Sailed Himself to Freedom?"
PBS, 2013, https://www.pbs.org/wnet/african-americans-
many-rivers-to-cross/history/which-slave-sailed-himself-
to-freedom/ (accessed February 16, 2022); "Robert Smalls,"
American Battlefield Trust, https://www.battlefields.org/learn/
biographies/robert-smalls (accessed February 16, 2022).

79 "Booth's Reason for Assassination," Teachinghistory.
org, https://teachinghistory.org/history-content/ask-a-
historian/24242 (accessed February 15, 2022).

80 Robert Purvis, "Appeal of Forty Thousand Citizens, Threatened
with Disfranchisement, to the People of Pennsylvania
(Philadelphia: 1838), 1-18," The American Yawp Reader, https://
www.americanyawp.com/reader/democracy-in-america/
black-philadelphians-defend-their-voting-rights-1838/.

81 U.S. Const. amend. XIV, § 1.

82 U.S. Const. amend. XV, § 1.

83 Isaac Chotiner, "The Buried Promise of the Reconstruction
Amendments," *The New Yorker*, September 9,

2019, https://www.newyorker.com/news/q-and-a/
the-buried-promise-of-the-reconstruction-amendments.

[84] History.com Editors, "Jim Crow Laws," History.com, February 28, 2018, updated January 11, 2022, https://www.history.com/topics/early-20th-century-us/jim-crow-laws (accessed February 8, 2022).

[85] "Robert E. Lee After the War," Virginia Museum of History and Culture, https://virginiahistory.org/learn/robert-e-lee-after-war.

[86] Ibid.

[87] Robert L. Glaze, "Nathan Bedford Forrest," *Encyclopedia Britannica*, October 25, 2021, https://www.britannica.com/biography/Nathan-Bedford-Forrest (accessed February 8, 2022).

Chapter 4

[88] Jack Leach, "The Scientific Revolution, the Enlightenment, and the Industrial Revolution," Merchants and Mechanics: The History of Economic Growth, https://merchantsandmechanics.com/2017/12/25/two-revolutions-and-an-enlightenment/.

[89] Joel Mokyr, *The Enlightened Economy: An Economic History of Britain, 1700-1850* (New Haven: Yale University Press, 2009).

[90] Alan Greenspan and Adrian Wooldridge, "The Triumph of Capitalism: 1865-1914," in *Capitalism in America: A History*, essay (Penguin Books, 2018).

[91] P.J. Hill, "Market Conditions in the Late 19th Century," Hillsdale College, 2006, https://www.hillsdale.edu/educational-outreach/free-market-forum/2006-archive/market-conditions-in-the-late-19th-century/.

[92] Alan Greenspan and Adrian Wooldridge, "The Triumph of Capitalism: 1865-1914," in *Capitalism in America: A History*, essay (Penguin Books, 2018).

[93] Ibid.

[94] Ibid.

[95] Aaron O' Neill, "Life expectancy (from birth) in the United States, from 1860 to 2020," Statista, February 3, 2021, https://www.statista.com/statistics/1040079/life-expectancy-united-states-all-time/.

[96] Erik Haagensen, "Who Was Hetty Green?" Investopedia, January 24, 2022, https://www.investopedia.com/hetty-green-5214747 (accessed February 17, 2022).

[97] Kat Eschner, "The Peculiar Story of the Witch of Wall Street," *Smithsonian Magazine*, November 21, 2017, https://www. smithsonianmag.com/smart-news/peculiar-story-hetty-green-aka-witch-wall-street-180967258/ (accessed February 17, 2022).

[98] Erik Haagensen, "Who Was Hetty Green?" Investopedia, January 24, 2022, https://www.investopedia.com/hetty-green-5214747 (accessed February 17, 2022).

[99] The Editors of Encyclopedia Britannica, "Hetty Green," *Encyclopedia Britannica*, November 17, 2021, https://www.britannica.com/biography/Hetty-Green (accessed February 17, 2022).

[100] Ibid.

[101] Alan Greenspan and Adrian Wooldridge, "The Triumph of Capitalism: 1865-1914," in *Capitalism in America: A History*, essay (Penguin Books, 2018).

[102] Ibid.

[103] Judson MacLaury, "Government Regulation of Workers' Safety and Health, 1877-1917," United States Department of Labor, https://www.dol.gov/general/aboutdol/history/mono-regsafeintrotoc (accessed February 9, 2022).

[104] Olivier Zunz, *Philanthropy in America: A History* (Princeton, N.J: Princeton University Press, 2012).

[105] Jan L. van Zanden, "Wages and the standard of living in Europe, 1500–1800," *European Review of Economic History*, Volume 3, Issue 2, August 1999, Pages 175–197, https://doi.org/10.1017/S136149169900009X.

[106] Karl R. Popper, *The Open Society and Its Enemies* (Princeton, NJ: Princeton University Press, 1971).

[107] Karl Marx, *The Communist Manifesto* (London; Chicago, IL: Pluto Press, 1996).

[108] Ibid.

[109] Ronald Grigor Suny, *The Soviet Experiment: Russia, the USSR, and the Successor States* (New York: Oxford University Press, 1998).

[110] George Frost Kennan, *Russia and the West Under Lenin and Stalin.* (Boston; Toronto: Little, Brown and Company, 1961).

[111] Ibid.

[112] David Winner, "How the left enabled fascism," *The New Statesman*, October 3, 2018, updated September 9, 2021, https://www.newstatesman.com/world/europe/2018/10/how-left-enabled-fascism.

113   Tania Branigan, "China's Great Famine: the true story," *The Guardian*, January 1, 2013, https://www.theguardian.com/world/2013/jan/01/china-great-famine-book-tombstone.

114   Ibid.

115   Evan Osnos, "The Cost of the Cultural Revolution, Fifty Years Later," *The New Yorker*, May 6, 2016, https://www.newyorker.com/news/daily-comment/the-cost-of-the-cultural-revolution-fifty-years-later.

Chapter 5

116   Alan Greenspan and Adrian Wooldridge, *Capitalism in America: A History* (New York City: Penguin Press, 2018).

117   Ibid.

118   William E. Leuchtenberg, "Franklin D. Roosevelt: Campaigns and Elections," University of Virginia: The Miller Center, https://millercenter.org/president/fdroosevelt/campaigns-and-elections.

119   Naftali Bendavid, "FDR's Popularity Helped Power New Deal," *Wall Street Journal*, January 6, 2009, https://www.wsj.com/articles/SB123121393429656673.

120   Ibid.

121   Richard A. Epstein, *The Classical Liberal Constitution: The Uncertain Quest for Limited Government* (Harvard University Press, 2017).

122   Charles Lipson, "Packing the Court, Then and Now," *Discourse Magazine*, April 21, 2021, https://www.discoursemagazine.com/politics/2021/04/21/packing-the-court-then-and-now/.

123   Ibid.

124   Ibid.

125   Richard A. Epstein, *The Classical Liberal Constitution: The Uncertain Quest for Limited Government* (Harvard University Press, 2017).

126   *Wickard v. Filburn*, 317 U.S. 111 (1942).

127   *Id.* at 114-15.

128   U.S. Const. art. 1, § 8.

129   *Wickard v. Filburn*, 317 U.S. at 119-20.

130   *Id.* at 128-29.

131   *United States v. Lopez*, 514 U.S. 549 (1995).

132   Michael A. Bernstein, *The Great Depression: Delayed Recovery and Economic Change in America, 1929-1939* (New York: Cambridge University Press, 1987).

133 Burton W. Folsom Jr., *The New Deal or Raw Deal? How FDR's Economic Legacy Has Damaged America* (New York: Threshold Editions, 2008).

134 Alan Greenspan and Adrian Wooldridge, *Capitalism in America: A History* (New York City: Penguin Press, 2018).

135 Suzanne Mettler, *Soldiers to Citizens: The G.I. Bill and the Making of the Greatest Generation, Illustrated Edition* (Oxford University Press, 2005).

136 Alan Greenspan and Adrian Wooldridge, *Capitalism in America: A History* (New York City: Penguin Press, 2018).

137 Marilyn Geewax, "JFK's Lasting Economic Legacy: Lower Tax Rates," NPR, November 14, 2013, https://www.npr.org/2013/11/12/244772593/jfks-lasting-economic-legacy-lower-tax-rates.

138 Richard Epstein, "American Workers Do Not Need Unions," Law & Liberty, July 1, 2020, https://lawliberty.org/forum/american-workers-do-not-need-unions/.

139 Matthew Fleischer, "Op-Ed: Two L.A. Rams desegregated football. They've never been given the credit they deserve," *Los Angeles Times*, February 3, 2019, https://www.latimes.com/opinion/op-ed/la-oe-fleischer-nfl-football-desegregation-rams-20190203-story.html.

140 Gene Roberts and Hank Klibanoff, *The Race Beat: The Press, the Civil Rights Struggle, and the Awakening of a Nation* (New York: Vintage, 2007).

141 Robert D. Loevy (ed.), *The Civil Rights Act of 1964: The Passage of the Law That Ended Racial Segregation* (New York: State University of the New York Press, 1997).

142 Paul Rockwell, "How Media Turned Dr. King into an Opponent of Affirmative Action," *In Motion Magazine*, October 20, 1996, https://www.inmotionmagazine.com/king2.html.

143 Frank Newport, "In U.S., 87% Approve of Black-White Marriage, vs. 4% in 1958," Gallup, July 25, 2013, https://news.gallup.com/poll/163697/approve-marriage-blacks-whites.aspx.

144 Richard Hanania, "Woke Institutions is Just Civil Rights Law," Richard Hanania's Newsletter: Substack, June 1, 2021, https://richardhanania.substack.com/p/woke-institutions-is-just-civil-rights.

145 *Regents of Univ. of California v. Bakke*, 438 U.S. 265, 316-18 (1978).

146 Alan Greenspan and Adrian Wooldridge, *Capitalism in America: A History* (New York City: Penguin Press, 2018).

147 Ibid.

148 Ibid.

149 Gary Claxton, et al., "How have healthcare prices grown in the U.S. over time?" Peterson-KFF: Health System Tracker, May 8,

2018, https://www.healthsystemtracker.org/chart-collection/
how-have-healthcare-prices-grown-in-the-u-s-over-time/.

[150] James Pethokoukis, "Why does the US spend so much on health
care? My long-read Q&A with Amitabh Chandra," American
Enterprise Institute (AEI): AEIdeas, December 14, 2020, https://
www.aei.org/economics/why-does-the-us-spend-so-much-
on-health-care-my-long-read-qa-with-amitabh-chandra/.

Chapter 6

[151] *Brown v. Board of Education of Topeka*, 349 U.S. 294 (1955).

[152] Alexis Clark, "Why Eisenhower Sent the 101st Airborne to
Little Rock After Brown v. Board," History.com, April 8, 2020,
https://www.history.com/news/little-rock-nine-brown-v-board-
eisenhower-101-airborne (accessed February 23, 2022).

[153] Dwight D. Eisenhower, "Farewell Address," Dwight D. Eisenhower
Presidential Library, Museum, and Boyhood Home, https://
www.eisenhowerlibrary.gov/sites/default/files/research/
online-documents/farewell-address/reading-copy.pdf.

[154] Richard Hanania, "The Weakness of Conservative Anti-
Wokeness," *American Affairs*, Winter 2021, Volume
V, No. 4, https://americanaffairsjournal.org/2021/11/
the-weakness-of-conservative-anti-wokeness/.

[155] Dwight D. Eisenhower, "Farewell Address," Dwight D. Eisenhower
Presidential Library, Museum, and Boyhood Home, https://
www.eisenhowerlibrary.gov/sites/default/files/research/
online-documents/farewell-address/reading-copy.pdf.

[156] Richard Epstein, "The Deserved Demise of EFCA (and Why the
NLRA Should Share Its Fate)," in *Research Handbook on the Economics
of Labor and Employment Law*, ed. Cynthia L. Estlund and Michael
L. Wachter, pp. 177–208, essay (Edward Elgar Publishing, 2014).

[157] Frank Dobbin, *Inventing Equal Opportunity* (Princeton: Princeton
University Press, 2009), https://doi.org/10.1515/9781400830893.

[158] W. Mark Crain and Nicole V. Crain, "The Cost of Federal
Regulation," National Association of Manufacturers, September
10, 2014, https://www.nam.org/the-cost-of-federal-regulation/.

[159] Richard Hanania, "The Weakness of Conservative Anti-
Wokeness," *American Affairs*, Winter 2021, Volume

V, No. 4, https://americanaffairsjournal.org/2021/11/
the-weakness-of-conservative-anti-wokeness/.

160 "Congress and the Public," Gallup, https://news.
gallup.com/poll/1600/congress-public.aspx.

161 Bradley A. Smith, "The Unresolved IRS Scandal," *The
Wall Street Journal*, May 9, 2018, https://www.wsj.com/
articles/the-unresolved-irs-scandal-1525905500.

162 Michael Ginsberg, "Judge Orders FBI To Halt 'Extraction'
From James O'Keefe's Phone Amid Leaks To NYT," *The Daily
Caller*, November 12, 2021, https://dailycaller.com/2021/11/12/
federal-judge-fbi-james-okeefe-phone-leaks-new-york-times/.

163 Robert Levinson, "Fiscal 2020 Pentagon Contracting Hits Record
$445 Billion," Bloomberg Government, January 6, 2021, https://
about.bgov.com/news/fiscal-2020-pentagon-contracting-
hits-record-445-billion/ (accessed February 24, 2022).

164 Ryan Summers, "The Pentagon's Revolving Door Keeps Spinning:
2021 in Review," Project on Government Oversight, January 20, 2022,
https://www.pogo.org/analysis/2022/01/the-pentagons-revolving-
door-keeps-spinning-2021-in-review/ (accessed February 24, 2022).

165 Konstantin Toropin, "Navy Wants to Scrap 9 Littoral Combat Ships
Along with 15 Others to Pay for New Carriers and Submarines,"
Military.com, March 28, 2022, https://www.military.com/daily-
news/2022/03/28/navy-wants-scrap-9-littoral-combat-ships-
along-15-others-pay-new-carriers-and-submarines.html.

166 Oren Liebermann, Ellie Kaufman, and Brad Lendon, "US Navy chief
defends plan to scrap troubled warships even though some are less
than 3 years old," CNN Politics, May 12, 2022, https://www.cnn.
com/2022/05/12/politics/us-navy-scrap-warships/index.html.

167 Craig Whitlock, "At War with the Truth — The Afghanistan Papers:
A Secret History of the War," *Washington Post*, December 9, 2019,
https://www.washingtonpost.com/graphics/2019/investigations/
afghanistan-papers/afghanistan-war-confidential-documents/.

168 Muqtedar Khan, "Is American Foreign Policy a Threat to American
Security?" Brookings Institute, June 1, 2003, https://www.brookings.edu/
opinions/is-american-foreign-policy-a-threat-to-american-security/.

169 Christopher Chantrill, "Entitlement Spending," USGovernmentSpending.
com, http://www.usgovernmentspending.com/entitlement_spending.

170 Paul Attewell and Katherine S. Newman, *Growing gaps: Educational
Inequality around the World* (Oxford University Press, 2010).

171   Michael R. Strain, "Biden's Unemployment Checks Would Harm Economy," *Bloomberg*, February 11, 2021, https://www.bloomberg.com/opinion/articles/2021-02-11/biden-s-unemployment-checks-are-too-high.

172   "Charitable Giving Statistics," National Philanthropic Trust, https://www.nptrust.org/philanthropic-resources/charitable-giving-statistics/.

173   "Most Charitable Countries 2022," World Population Review, https://worldpopulationreview.com/country-rankings/most-charitable-countries; Sintia Radu, "Measuring the World's Most Generous Countries," December 20, 2019, https://www.usnews.com/news/best-countries/articles/2019-12-20/the-worlds-most-generous-countries.

174   Indermit Gill, "Deep-sixing poverty in China," Brookings Institution, January 25, 2021, https://www.brookings.edu/blog/future-development/2021/01/25/deep-sixing-poverty-in-china/.

175   Oiwan Lam, "China, USA: Comparing Poverty Lines," Global Voices, https://globalvoices.org/2011/12/01/china-usa-comparing-poverty-lines/.

176   Rav Aurora, "More Equal Than Others," *City Journal*, July 29, 2021, https://www.city-journal.org/the-systemic-racism-of-the-biden-equity-agenda.

177   "Obama's Father's Day Remarks," *New York Times*, June 15, 2008, https://www.nytimes.com/2008/06/15/us/politics/15text-obama.html.

178   Aaron O' Neill, "Estimated share of African slaves who did not survive the Middle Passage journey to the Americas each year from 1501 to 1866," Statista, February 24, 2021, https://www.statista.com/statistics/1143458/annual-share-slaves-deaths-during-middle-passage/.

179   "What is India's caste system?" BBC News, June 19, 2019, https://www.bbc.com/news/world-asia-india-35650616.

Chapter 7

180   R.J. Clarke, "The land of the 'free': Criminal transportation to America," The History Press, https://www.thehistorypress.co.uk/articles/the-land-of-the-free-criminal-transportation-to-america/.

181   *Chy Lung v. Freeman Et Al.*, 92 U.S. 295 (1875).

182   "Early Immigration Policies," U.S. Citizenship and Immigration Services, last updated July 30, 2020, https://www.uscis.gov/about-us/our-history/overview-of-ins-history/early-american-immigration-policies.

183   Ibid.

184 "States Offering Driver's Licenses to Immigrants," National Conference of State Legislatures, August 9, 2021, https://www.ncsl.org/research/immigration/states-offering-driver-s-licenses-to-immigrants.aspx.

185 Jessica M. Vaughan, "Waiting List for Legal Immigrant Visas Keeps Growing," Center for Immigration Studies, April 16, 2015, https://cis.org/Vaughan/Waiting-List-Legal-Immigrant-Visas-Keeps-Growing#:~:text=More%20than%204.4%20million%20people,member%20in%20the%20United%20States.

186 "Criminal Noncitizen Statistics Fiscal Year 2022," U.S. Customs and Border Protection, last updated April 18, 2022, https://www.cbp.gov/newsroom/stats/cbp-enforcement-statistics/criminal-noncitizen-statistics.

187 Jia Lynn Yang, "How a forgotten 1965 law paved the way for today's battles over immigration," Marketplace, June 23, 2020, https://www.marketplace.org/2020/06/23/how-a-forgotten-1965-law-paved-the-way-for-todays-battles-over-immigration/.

188 George J. Borjas, "Yes, Immigration Hurts American Workers," *Politico Magazine*, September/October 2016, https://www.politico.com/magazine/story/2016/09/trump-clinton-immigration-economy-unemployment-jobs-214216/.

189 Milton Friedman, "What Is America?" filmed October 3, 1977, at the University of Chicago, video, https://miltonfriedman.hoover.org/objects/57282/what-is-america.

190 "The Nigerian Diaspora in the United States," Migration Policy Institute, June 2015, https://www.migrationpolicy.org/sites/default/files/publications/RAD-Nigeria.pdf.

191 Molly Fosco, "The Most Successful Ethnic Group in the U.S. May Surprise You," OZY, June 6, 2018, https://www.ozy.com/around-the-world/the-most-successful-ethnic-group-in-the-u-s-may-surprise-you/86885/.

192 Sean Gregory, "TIME: 2002 Global Influentials — Adebayo Ogunlesi," *Time Magazine*, November 22, 2002, retrieved from The Internet Archive Wayback Machine, https://web.archive.org/web/20070530062727/http://www.time.com/time/2002/globalinfluentials/gbiogunlesi.html.

193 Reginald A. Noël, "Race, Economics, And Social Status," U.S. Bureau of Labor Statistics, May 2018, https://www.bls.gov/spotlight/2018/race-economics-and-social-status/pdf/race-economics-and-social-status.pdf.

194 Martin Carnoy and Emma García, "Five key trends in U.S. student performance," Economic Policy Institute, January 12, 2017, https://www.epi.org/publication/

five-key-trends-in-u-s-student-performance-progress-by-blacks-and-hispanics-the-takeoff-of-asians-the-stall-of-non-english-speakers-the-persistence-of-socioeconomic-gaps-and-the-damaging-effect/.

195 A.B. Wire, "Meet the top 7 Indian Americans CEOs in corporate America," *The American Bazaar*, November 30, 2021, https://www.americanbazaaronline.com/2021/11/30/meet-the-top-7-indian-american-ceos-in-corporate-america-447884/.

196 Sadee Hanson, "Things You'll See at a First 100 Campout," Chick-fil-A, March 17, 2017, https://thechickenwire.chick-fil-a.com/inside-chick-fil-a/things-youll-see-at-a-first-100-campout.

197 Neli Esipova, Anita Pugliese, and Julie Ray, "More Than 750 Million Worldwide Would Migrate If They Could," Gallup, December 10, 2018, https://news.gallup.com/poll/245255/750-million-worldwide-migrate.aspx.

198 "Video shows desperate Afghans climbing US jet to escape," *Associated Press*, August 16, 2021, https://apnews.com/article/afghanistan-kabul-taliban-79d677c29b1e134437842217e469b481.

199 Lexi Lonas, "Maher: Afghanistan shows 'woke' Americans 'what real oppression looks like,'" *The Hill*, August 28, 2021, https://thehill.com/homenews/media/569833-maher-afghanistan-shows-woke-americans-what-real-oppression-looks-like.

200 Alex Nowrasteh and Andrew C. Forrester, "Immigrants Recognize American Greatness: Immigrants and Their Descendants Are Patriotic and Trust America's Governing Institutions," Cato Institute, Immigration Research and Policy Brief No. 10, February 4, 2019, https://www.cato.org/publications/immigration-research-policy-brief/immigrants-recognize-american-greatness-immigrants#methodology-and-data.

201 Nicole Narea, "A new study shows that even the poorest immigrants lift themselves up within a generation," *Vox*, November 1, 2019, https://www.vox.com/policy-and-politics/2019/11/1/20942642/study-paper-american-dream-economic-mobility-immigrant-income-boustan-abramitzky-jacome-perez.

202 Arthur M. Schlesinger Jr. (Arthur Meier), *The Disuniting of America* (New York: Norton, 1992).

203 Erick Burgueño Salas, "Uber: U.S. employees by ethnicity 2017-2020," Statista, October 20, 2021, https://www.statista.com/statistics/693838/uber-employee-ethnicity-us/ (accessed February 26, 2022).

Chapter 8

204   Tara Siegel Bernard, "What the Debt Ceiling Means for Social Security and More," *New York Times*, October 6, 2021, updated October 8, 2021, https://www.nytimes.com/2021/10/06/business/debt-ceiling-social-security-medicare.html.

205   James Piereson, "A Not-So-Great Society," *Washington Examiner*, from the archives of *The Weekly Standard*, September 30, 2016, https://www.washingtonexaminer.com/weekly-standard/a-not-so-great-society.

206   Richard W. Rahn, "Social Security, a government Ponzi scheme, headed for collapse," *The Washington Times*, August 9, 2021, https://www.washingtontimes.com/news/2021/aug/9/social-security-a-government-ponzi-scheme-headed-f/.

207   Megan Leonhardt, "Roughly 1 in 4 younger Americans believe Social Security won't be available when they retire," CNBC, January 6, 2021, https://www.cnbc.com/2021/01/06/social-security-gen-z-millennials-say-its-unlikely-theyll-get-it.html.

208   Kimberly Amadeo, "U.S. Federal Budget Breakdown," The Balance, February 18, 2022, https://www.thebalance.com/u-s-federal-budget-breakdown-3305789 (accessed February 28, 2022).

209   Ibid.

210   "Interest Costs on the National Debt Projected to Nearly Triple over the Next Decade," Peter G. Peterson Foundation, July 21, 2021, https://www.pgpf.org/blog/2021/07/interest-costs-on-the-national-debt-projected-to-nearly-triple-over-the-next-decade.

211   Ibid.

212   Tony Romm and Yeganeh Torbati, "'A magnet for rip-off artists': Fraud siphoned billions from pandemic unemployment benefits," *Washington Post*, May 15, 2022, https://www.washingtonpost.com/us-policy/2022/05/15/unemployment-pandemic-fraud-identity-theft/.

213   G. Dautovic, "Straight Talk on Welfare Statistics," Fortunly, December 9, 2021, https://fortunly.com/statistics/welfare-statistics/#gref.

214   Ibid.

215   "United States Labor Force Participation Rate, April 2022 Data - 1948-2021 Historical," Trading Economics, https://tradingeconomics.com/united-states/labor-force-participation-rate.

216   Lawrence H. Summers, "On inflation, it's past time for team 'transitory' to stand down," *Washington Post*, November 15,

2021, https://www.washingtonpost.com/opinions/2021/11/15/
inflation-its-past-time-team-transitory-stand-down/.

[217] Barack Obama, *The Audacity of Hope: Thoughts on Reclaiming the American Dream* (New York: Crown Publishers, 2006).

[218] Deborah D'Souza, "Modern Monetary Theory (MMT)," Investopedia, updated April 12, 2022, https://www.investopedia.com/modern-monetary-theory-mmt-4588060.

[219] Fabiola Zerpa and Nicolle Yapur, "Bankrupted by Socialism, Venezuela Cedes Control of Companies," Bloomberg, February 12, 2021, https://www.bloomberg.com/news/articles/2021-02-12/bankrupt-by-socialism-venezuela-hands-over-control-of-companies.

[220] Emily Ekins, "Poll: 62% of Americans Say They Have Political Views They're Afraid to Share," Cato Institute, July 22, 2020, https://www.cato.org/survey-reports/poll-62-americans-say-they-have-political-views-theyre-afraid-share.

[221] Robert D. Putnam, *Bowling Alone: The Collapse and Revival of American Community* (New York: Simon & Schuster, 2000).

[222] Ibid.

[223] Rafael A. Mangual, "Yes, the Crime Wave Is as Bad as You Think," *Wall Street Journal*, December 8, 2021, https://www.wsj.com/articles/yes-the-crime-wave-is-as-bad-as-you-think-murder-rate-violent-killings-shootings-defund-police-11638988699.

[224] Stephanie Pagones, "US murder rate highest it's been in 25 years as big cities shatter records," Fox News, January 18, 2022, https://www.foxnews.com/us/us-murder-rate-violence-big-cities-records (accessed February 28, 2022).

[225] Bill Hutchinson, "'It's just crazy': 12 major cities hit all-time homicide records," ABC News, December 8, 2021, https://abcnews.go.com/US/12-major-us-cities-top-annual-homicide-records/story?id=81466453 (accessed February 28, 2022).

[226] Thomas Adjadj, "Is Kalorama a gated community?" GotThisNow, updated March 31, 2021, https://gotthisnow.com/is-kalorama-a-gated-community; Emily Crane, "Cori Bush will pay $200K for private security — but still wants to defund police," *New York Post*, August 5, 2021, https://nypost.com/2021/08/05/cori-bush-will-pay-200k-for-private-security-but-still-wants-to-defund-police/.

[227] Jolie Lash, "Seth Rogen Flamed for Dismissing LA Car Break-Ins as Just the Result of 'Living in a Big City,'" *The Wrap*, November 26, 2021, https://www.thewrap.com/seth-rogen-la-car-break-ins/.

228 Scott Cummings, *Left Behind in Rosedale: Race Relations and the Collapse of Community Institutions* (Boulder, Colo: Westview Press, 1998).

229 Heather Mac Donald, "The unwinding of law and order in our cities has happened with stunning speed," *City Journal*, July 1, 2020, https://www.city-journal.org/ferguson-effect-inner-cities.

230 Robert D. Putnam, *Bowling Alone: The Collapse and Revival of American Community* (New York: Simon & Schuster, 2000).

231 Gretchen Livingston and Anna Brown, "Intermarriage in the U.S. 50 Years After Loving v. Virginia," Pew Research Center, May 18, 2017, https://www.pewresearch.org/social-trends/2017/05/18/intermarriage-in-the-u-s-50-years-after-loving-v-virginia/.

232 Eugene Volokh, "What Speech Does 'Hostile Work Environment' Harassment Law Restrict?" *85 Georgetown Law Journal 627*, 1997, retrieved from https://www2.law.ucla.edu/Volokh/harassg.htm.

233 Paul Kiernan, "Conservative Activist Grabbed Trump's Eye on Diversity Training," *Wall Street Journal*, October 9, 2020, https://www.wsj.com/articles/conservative-activist-grabbed-trumps-eye-on-diversity-training-11602242287.

234 MoneyWeek, "Vivek Ramaswamy: beware of the 'woke industrial complex,'" *MoneyWeek*, November 26, 2021, https://moneyweek.com/investments/investment-strategy/604164/vivek-ramaswamy-beware-of-the-woke-industrial-complex.

235 Vivek Ramaswamy, *Woke, Inc: Inside Corporate America's Social Justice Scam* (Center Street, 2021).

236 Richard Hanania, "Woke Institutions is Just Civil Rights Law," Richard Hanania's Newsletter: Substack, June 1, 2021, https://richardhanania.substack.com/p/woke-institutions-is-just-civil-rights.

237 Helen Pluckrose and James Lindsay, *Cynical Theories: How Activist Scholarship Made Everything about Race, Gender, and Identity* (Durham, North Carolina: Pitchstone Publishing, 2020).

238 "Average Human Resources (HR) Manager Salary," Payscale, https://www.payscale.com/research/US/Job=Human_Resources_(HR)_Manager/Salary.

239 Edwin Rubenstein, "Diversity's Economic Downside," *The Social Contract*, Volume 25, Number 4 (Summer 2015), https://www.thesocialcontract.com/artman2/publish/tsc_25_4/tsc_25_4_rubenstein_printer.shtml.

240   Michael Powell, "Once a Bastion of Free Speech, the A.C.L.U. Faces an
      Identity Crisis," *New York Times*, June 6, 2021, updated September 28,
      2021, https://www.nytimes.com/2021/06/06/us/aclu-free-speech.html.

241   Richard Hanania, "Woke Institutions is Just Civil Rights Law,"
      Richard Hanania's Newsletter: Substack, June 1, 2021, https://
      richardhanania.substack.com/p/woke-institutions-is-just-civil-rights.

242   Lauren Camera, "Schools Reopen But Obstacles Remain as
      COVID-19 Surges," *U.S. News & World Report*, September 17, 2021,
      https://www.usnews.com/news/the-report/articles/2021-09-17/
      schools-reopen-but-obstacles-remain-as-covid-19-surges.

243   "Highlights of U.S. PISA 2018 Results Web Report (NCES 2020-
      166 and 2020-072)," U.S. Department of Education, Institute of
      Education Sciences, National Center for Education Statistics,
      https://nces.ed.gov/surveys/pisa/pisa2018/#/math/intlcompare.

244   Ian Rowe, "The unwelcome success of charter schools," American
      Enterprise Institute, October 5, 2020, https://www.aei.org/
      articles/the-unwelcome-success-of-charter-schools/.

245   Ted Van Green and Carroll Doherty, "Majority of U.S. public
      favors Afghanistan troop withdrawal; Biden criticized for
      his handling of situation," Pew Research Center, August 31,
      2021, https://www.pewresearch.org/fact-tank/2021/08/31/
      majority-of-u-s-public-favors-afghanistan-troop-withdrawal-
      biden-criticized-for-his-handling-of-situation/.

246   "Top US General Milley calls Afghanistan a 'strategic failure,'" Al Jazeera,
      September 28, 2021, https://www.aljazeera.com/news/2021/9/28/
      us-military-officials-to-testify-on-afghanistan-withdrawal.

247   Kermit Roosevelt III, "I Spent 7 Months Studying Supreme Court
      Reform. We Need to Pack the Court Now," *Time*, December 10,
      2021, https://time.com/6127193/supreme-court-reform-expansion/;
      Darrell M. West, "It's time to abolish the Electoral College," Brookings
      Institution, October 15, 2019, https://www.brookings.edu/policy2020/
      bigideas/its-time-to-abolish-the-electoral-college/; Mary Anne Franks,
      "Redo the First Two Amendments," *The Boston Globe*, December
      2021, https://apps.bostonglobe.com/ideas/graphics/2021/12/
      editing-the-constitution/redo-the-first-two-amendments/.

248   Daniel Flatley and Tony Czuczka, "Don't Rejoin Iran Nuclear
      Deal, GOP Lawmakers Tell Biden," *Bloomberg*, February 28,
      2021, https://www.bloomberg.com/news/articles/2021-02-28/
      don-t-rejoin-iran-nuclear-deal-republican-lawmakers-tell-biden.

[249] Aimee Picchi, "Stimulus checks for gas? Here's what could be coming your way," CBS News, March 25, 2022, https://www.cbsnews.com/news/stimulus-check-gas-prices-coming/.

[250] Tunku Varadarajan, "How Government Spending Fuels Inflation," *Wall Street Journal*, February 18, 2022, https://www.wsj.com/articles/government-spending-fuels-inflation-covid-relief-pandemic-debt-federal-reserve-stimulus-powell-biden-stagflation-11645202057.

Chapter 9

[251] John Rawls, *A Theory of Justice* (Belknap Press, 2005).

[252] Robert Nozick, *Anarchy, State, and Utopia* (New York: Basic Books, 1974).

[253] Richard Hanania, "The Problems with Anti-Wokeness," Richard Hanania's Newsletter: Substack, November 20, 2021, https://richardhanania.substack.com/p/the-problems-with-anti-wokeness.

[254] Bill Conerly, "No Recession In 2022—But Watch Out In 2023," *Forbes*, November 2, 2021, https://www.forbes.com/sites/billconerly/2021/11/02/no-recession-in-2022-but-watch-out-in-2023/?sh=39d9d5553555.

[255] "Executive Order 12432," Social Policy: Essential Primary Sources, Encyclopedia.com, April 25, 2022, https://www.encyclopedia.com/social-sciences/applied-and-social-sciences-magazines/executive-order-12432.

[256] See *Students for Fair Admissions Inc. v. President & Fellows of Harvard College; Students for Fair Admissions, Inc. v. University of North Carolina.*

[257] 42 U.S.C. § 2000d.

[258] *Richmond v. J. A. Croson Co.*, 48 U.S. 469, 518 (1989) (Kennedy, J., concurring).

[259] Richard Hanania, "Woke Institutions is Just Civil Rights Law," Richard Hanania's Newsletter: Substack, June 1, 2021, https://richardhanania.substack.com/p/woke-institutions-is-just-civil-rights.

[260] "High Energy Prices to Increase Costs for America's Commercial and Industrial Companies by $41 Billion in 2022, CEA Analysis Finds," Consumer Energy Alliance, December 16, 2021, https://consumerenergyalliance.org/2021/12/high-energy-prices-increase-costs-americas-commercial-industrial-companies-41-billion-2022-cea-analysis-finds/.

[261] Adam Andrzejewski, "Remembering 'Solyndra' – How Many $570M Green Energy Failures Are Hidden Inside Biden's Infrastructure Proposal?" *Forbes*, April 12, 2021, https://www.

forbes.com/sites/adamandrzejewski/2021/04/12/remembering-solyndra--how-many-570m-green-energy-failures-are-hidden-inside-bidens-instructure-proposal/?sh=5c6a738d2672.

262 "Poverty and Spending over the Years," Federal Safety Net, http://federalsafetynet.com/poverty-and-spending-over-the-years.html; Michael D. Tanner, "What's Missing in the War on Poverty?" Cato Institute, January 23, 2019, https://www.cato.org/commentary/whats-missing-war-poverty.

263 Alan Greenspan and Adrian Wooldridge, *Capitalism in America: A History* (New York City: Penguin Press, 2018).

264 "REINS Act," Ballotpedia, https://ballotpedia.org/REINS_Act#Background.

265 Regulations from the Executive in Need of Scrutiny Act of 2021, S. 68, 117th Cong. § 1 (2021).

266 *Chevron, U.S.A., Inc. v. Nat. Res. Def. Council, Inc.*, 467 U.S. 837, 842–43 (1984).

267 *Marbury v. Madison*, 5 U.S. 137, 177 (1803).

268 Separation of Powers Restoration Act of 2021, H.R. 3494,117th Cong. § 1 (2021).

269 @JoeBiden (Joe Biden). "A job is about a lot more than a paycheck. It's about dignity. It's about being able to look your kid in the eye and say everything is going to be okay—and mean it. Too many people today can't do that. We have to rebuild an inclusive middle class and restore the dignity of work." Twitter, December 6, 2019, 10:25 a.m., https://twitter.com/joebiden/status/1202972212384288768?lang=en.

270 Robert E. Scott and David Cooper, "Almost two-thirds of people in the labor force do not have a college degree," Economic Policy Institute, March 16, 2016, https://www.epi.org/publication/almost-two-thirds-of-people-in-the-labor-force-do-not-have-a-college-degree/ (accessed March 2, 2022).

271 Samuel J. Abrams and Amna Khalid, "Are colleges and universities too liberal? What the research says about the political composition of campuses and campus climate," American Enterprise Institute, October 21, 2020, https://www.aei.org/articles/are-colleges-and-universities-too-liberal-what-the-research-says-about-the-political-composition-of-campuses-and-campus-climate/.

272 "Fast Facts: Tuition costs of colleges and universities," U.S. Department of Education. Institute of Education Sciences, National Center for Education Statistics, https://nces.ed.gov/fastfacts/display.asp?id=76.

[273] Michael d'Estries and the SkillPointe Editorial Team, "The 24 Highest-Paying Trade Jobs — No Bachelor's Degree Required," SkillPointe, June 3, 2021, updated October 8, 2021, https://skillpointe.com/news-and-advice/24-highest-paying-trade-jobs-no-bachelors-degree-required.

[274] The Indeed Editorial Team, "What Is the Average Salary for Bachelor Degree Graduates?" Indeed, February 22, 2021, https://www.indeed.com/career-advice/pay-salary/average-salary-for-college-graduates.

[275] Melanie Hanson, "Average Student Loan Debt," EducationData.org, updated July 10, 2021, https://educationdata.org/average-student-loan-debt/.

Chapter 10

[276] Rebecca Pifer, "Medicare insolvency still expected by 2026, unchanged by COVID-19, trustees say," Healthcare Dive, September 1, 2021, https://www.healthcaredive.com/news/medicare-insolvency-still-expected-by-2026-unchanged-by-covid-19-trustees/605877/ (accessed March 2, 2022).

[277] United Kingdom, House of Commons, Hansard Parliamentary Record (1947). Speech by W. Churchill. HC Deb, vol. 444 cc203–321. 3.33 pm, November, 11, 1947, https://api.parliament.uk/historic-hansard/commons/1947/nov/11/parliament-bill.

[278] "U.S. Senate: Filibuster," United States Senate, https://www.senate.gov/reference/Index/Filibuster.htm.

[279] Jason Lemon, "Joe Manchin's Approval Nearly Double Biden's in West Virginia as He Opposes Dem Priorities," Newsweek, January 14, 2022, https://www.newsweek.com/joe-manchins-approval-nearly-double-bidens-west-virginia-he-opposes-dem-priorities-1669664.

[280] Roe v. Wade, 410 U.S. 113, 164 (1973).

[281] James S. Witherspoon, "Reexamining Roe: Nineteenth-Century Abortion Statutes and the Fourteenth Amendment," St. Mary's Law J., 29, 33-34 & nn. 15, 18 (1985).

[282] Lochner v. New York, 198 U.S. 45, 54 (1905).

[283] Id. at 65.

[284] Adkins v. Children's Hospital, 261 U.S. 525, 561-62 (1923).

[285] West Coast Hotel Co. v. Parrish, 300 U.S. 379, 398 (1937).

[286] Washington v. Glucksberg, 521 U.S. 702, 721 (1997).

[287] Id. at 728.

[288] Thomas Sowell, A Conflict of Visions (New York: W. Morrow, 1987).

[289] Ibid.

290 Richard H. Thaler and Cass R. Sunstein, *Nudge* (Penguin Books, 2009).

Appendices

291 "The Declaration of Independence, July 4, 1776." George
Washington's Mount Vernon. Accessed March 21, 2022.
https://www.mountvernon.org/education/primary-sources-2/
article/the-declaration-of-independence-july-4-1776/.
292 "The U.S. Constitution." The Constitution – Full Text | The
National Constitution Center. Accessed March 21, 2022. https://
constitutioncenter.org/interactive-constitution/full-text.
293 The Gettysburg Address by Abraham Lincoln. Accessed March 21, 2022.
http://www.abrahamlincolnonline.org/lincoln/speeches/gettysburg.htm.
294 "Read Martin Luther King Jr.'s 'I Have a Dream' Speech
in Its Entirety." NPR, January 14, 2022. https://www.npr.
org/2010/01/18/122701268/i-have-a-dream-speech-in-its-entirety.

ACKNOWLEDGMENTS

We would like to acknowledge David's assistant, Susan Twomey, for her dedication to completing this project. Additionally, thank you to the entire FreedomWorks Foundation team, especially Matt Carnovale, Spencer Chretien, Melanie Aycock, and Alex Deise, each of whom helped tremendously in the editing and production of this book; and thank you to Coleman Hopkins, who conducted extensive research and provided ample support.

ABOUT THE AUTHORS

David Sokol was born in Omaha, Nebraska. He worked as a paperboy, a caddie, and a grocery clerk before graduating from the University of Nebraska. He then embarked upon a business career, working as a structural engineer for one of the top five engineering firms in America. In 1984, David was selected to run a start-up waste energy subsidiary called Ogden Products, Inc., which by 1990 had grown from four to 1,200 employees. In 1991, David was named CEO of CalEnergy, which was renamed MidAmerican Energy Holdings Company in 1999. He went on to serve as chairman and CEO of MidAmerican, which was acquired by Berkshire Hathaway in 2000. In addition, he served as the chairman and CEO of NetJets as well as several additional Berkshire Hathaway companies. In 2011, David founded his own private equity firm, Teton Capital, LLC.

Adam Brandon is the president of FreedomWorks, a grassroots service center with millions of activists across the United States dedicated to the ideas of limited government, free enterprise, personal liberty, and the rule of law. Before joining FreedomWorks, Adam worked as a political campaign manager, high school teacher, and press secretary. He is a graduate of George Washington University (BA, MA),

Georgetown University (MA), and Jagiellonian University (MA).Adam and his wife Jaqueline live with their son Pierce in Alexandria, Virginia.

Made in the USA
Monee, IL
19 October 2022

412aa163-1d65-4e1b-aaf5-5edfcb91b938R01